Map **Guide**

Barcelona

The city, map by map

◆◆◆
Barcelona
Turisme

visit
Barcelona

TRIANGLE ▼ BOOKS

Contents

Hello! Welcome to Barcelona

Basic information about visiting the city and finding out about key aspects of life in Barcelona.

Barcelona, map by map

These handy maps are the best way to find your way around Barcelona's colourful and cosmopolitan neighbourhoods; Gaudí's landmarks and Picasso's work; its fantastic beaches, gardens and museums, and its restaurants, bars and shops. And, of course, Barcelona is much more! Near the city you'll discover a whole world of possibilities for enjoying leisure, culture and nature.

Barcelona icons

Information about must-see museums, landmarks and tourist attractions expanded from the previous section and including a description, brief history, opening times and prices.

Barcelona, capital of Catalonia

Discover a land with a rich and diverse landscape and culture.

Practical guide

Shopping, festivals and traditions, nightlife and entertainments, sporting events and much more.

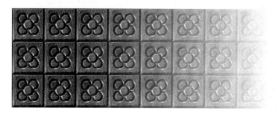

→ Barcelona, map by map

Welcome to Barcelona

Hello!

Getting there

Barcelona has excellent transport links with the rest of Spain and Europe and operates intercontinental flights with America and Asia.

By plane

Most flights arrive at **Barcelona Airport (Aeroport de Barcelona-El Prat** T 93 298 38 38; www.aena. es), 12 km from the city centre. **Connections by metro** (www.tmb.cat): Terminals T1 and T2 - Zona Universitària, 32 min on line L9Sud (every 7 min, 5am-midnight; price: 4.50 €) **Connections by bus**: (www.aerobusbcn. com): Terminal T1 - Pl. Catalunya, 35 min by Aerobús A1 (every 5 min, 5.30am-1.05am; price: 5.90 €); and Terminal T2 - Pl. Catalunya, 30 min by Aerobus A2 (every 10 min, 5.30am-1am; price: 5.90 €). **Connections by train** (T 902 240 202): Terminal T2 (free shuttle bus – journey time 10 min – to Terminal T1) - Passeig de Gràcia 27 min on line R2 (every 30 min, 5.21am-11.38pm; price: 4.10 €). By taxi (journey time 30 min). Some low-cost airlines use **Girona Airport** (T 972 186 600; www.aena.es), 80 km away. Connections: buses timed to tie in with flight arrivals and departures (T 902 361 550; www. sagales.com / journey time 70 min); and **Reus Airport** (T 977 779 800; www.aena.es), 80 km away. Connections: Bus Hispano Igualadina (T 93 804 44 51).

By train

Rail links with most cities in the rest of Spain and Europe depart from and arrive at Barcelona-Sants Station. The rail operator is the state-owned company RENFE (T 902 240 202; www.renfe.es) and many connections are by high-speed train.

By bus

The main intercity bus station is the **Estació del Nord** (T 902 260 606; www.barcelonanord.com), although many international services depart from Sants Station. The companies include Eurolines (T 902 405 040; www. eurolines.es), Alsa Internacional (T 902 422 242; www.alsa.es) and Linebús (T 93 265 07 00).

By boat

In addition to the regular ferry services with the Balearic Islands (Mallorca, Menorca, Ibiza), Italy (Genoa, Livorno, Rome, Sardinia), France (Sète), Morocco (Tangiers) and Tunisia (Radès), Barcelona has become Europe's leading cruise harbour with annual passenger figures of two and a half million.

Language

Barcelona is a bilingual city where Catalan and Spanish are spoken.

Catalan

Catalan is the language of Barcelona, the rest of Catalonia, the Balearic Islands, Valencia (where it is called *valencià*) and Andorra. It is spoken by eight million people. Its use is widespread in such areas of public life

Barcelona - El Prat Airport

More than 100 domestic and international airlines operate almost 900 daily flights to more than 150 destinations throughout the world. Barcelona Airport's T1 terminal opened in June 2009 and can handle 55 million passengers a year and 90 flights an hour, making it the leading airport in the Aena network in terms of traffic. Its facilities include one of the most advanced retail spaces in Europe which offers an innovative range of exclusive services, a wide range of shops selling prestigious brands and a wide variety of bars and restaurants, one of them run by a Michelin-starred chef.

as street and road signs, signage systems, maps, restaurant menus, etc.

Spanish
Spanish, or Castilian, is also an official language and is spoken by all Catalan speakers.

Other languages
Quite a few people in Barcelona understand English and French. A lot of restaurants have menus in other languages and public transport signs are also in English.

Banks and money
As in 19 other European Union countries, the official currency is the euro (€).

Banks and saving banks
Banking hours are 8.30am-2pm, Monday to Friday. There are banks at the airport and at Barcelona-Sants Station, which open daily from 8am to 10pm. The city also has one of the most extensive networks of ATM machines in the world, and Visa, MasterCard and American Express can be used to make cash withdrawals.

Changing money
Currency can be exchanged at banks, savings banks and bureaux de change. Commission rates vary.

Credit cards and travellers' cheques
Visa and MasterCard are accepted everywhere, with the exception of some small shops and restaurants; most hotels take American Express; and 50% of restaurants take Diner's Card. Travellers' cheques can be changed at all banks or bureaux de change.

Food and drink
Mealtimes in Barcelona (and the rest of Catalonia and Spain) are a little later than the rest of Europe. Lunchtime is between 2pm and 3pm and dinner from 9pm onwards.

Restaurants
Most restaurants open from 1pm to 4pm and from 8pm to 11pm, but many remain open all day, and some serve dinner until 2am. They usually close on one day a week.

Cafés and bars
They usually open at about 7.30am and many bars

close at 2am. You can also have a drink at nightclubs and discotheques after this time. Some of them also serve food.

Shopping
Over the past decade, Barcelona has become a European haven for shoppers. Most shops open from 10am to 2pm and 4pm to 9pm, Monday to Friday, although few shops in the city centre close for lunch. Department stores and shopping centres open from 10am to 10pm, Monday to Saturday.

Sales
There are two sales periods: in summer, from 1st July to the end of August, and in winter, from 7th January to the end of February.

Encants Barcelona Fira de Bellcaire
Barcelona also has a flea market with a long-standing tradition, known locally as Els Encants Vells. Its origins can be traced back to the 14th century, and, until recently, it stood on a site in the centre of the Plaça de les Glòries. In 2013, it moved to new, purpose-built, state-of-the-art premises designed

Cruise liner in the harbour

Having lunch on the Passeig Marítim

Welcome to Barcelona

by the architect Fermín Vázquez. It now covers a surface area of more than 10,000 m². Its most eye-catching feature is the large mirrored roof suspended like a canopy some 25 metres above the ground, protecting the site from the rain and the sun's rays. (p. 71).

Public holidays

Shops and banks are closed on Sundays, 1st and 6th January, Good Friday, Easter Monday, 1st May, 24th June, 15th August, 11th and 24th September, 12th October, 1st November and 6th, 8th, 25th and 26th December. (www.gencat.cat/especial/comerc/eng/index.htm)

Climate

Barcelona enjoys a privileged Mediterranean climate with mild winters and warm, occasionally wet summers. The average winter temperature is 54°F and it seldom rains. Summer temperatures usually reach 86°F, and are often higher. There are occasional storms. Spring and autumn (average temperatures of 70°F) are the best times to visit the city, although it does rain more often.

Safety and healthcare

As in every major city, there are places (public transport, etc.) where you should keep an eye on your belongings.
The emergency telephone number is 112, as in the rest of the European Union. In Barcelona, calls are dealt with in Catalan, Spanish, English and French and there is a translation service in other languages. The number is used to contact the police, fire brigade and ambulance service.

Police

Other emergency numbers include 112, the Catalan Police (Mossos d'Esquadra); 091, Spanish Police (Policía Nacional); and 092, local police (Guàrdia Urbana). There is a help centre for tourists at 43, La Rambla which opens 24 hours a day (T 93 256 24 30) to help visitors who have been victims of crime or have had an accident.

Hospitals

There are many hospitals in Barcelona, some of them renowned throughout the world. These are some of the most important. They all have an A & E department: Hospital de Sant Pau (Sant Quintí, 89. T 93 291 90 00), Hospital Clínic (Villarroel, 170. T 93 227 54 00), Hospital Dos de Maig (Dos de Maig, 301. T 93 507 27 00), Hospital de la Vall d'Hebron (Passeig de la Vall d'Hebron, 119-129. T 93 489 30 00) and Hospital del Mar (Passeig Marítim, 25-29. T 93 248 30 00).

Ambulances

The 061 number deals with all ambulance calls.

Chemists

These are the only places in BCN where you can buy medicinal drugs dispensed by qualified pharmacists. They also stock homoeopathic medicines and have an illuminated green cross outside. They open 9am to 2pm and 4pm to 8pm. All neighbourhoods have duty chemists that are open all night (the rota is displayed on the door of every chemists). There are increasing numbers of 24-hour chemists, particularly in the city centre.

Encants Barcelona

LGBTI tourism

LGBTI tourism

The city offers a whole host of possibilities so that its LGBTI visitors can enjoy their stay in Barcelona in a welcoming atmosphere that is open to everyone. The annual calendar of LGBTI events combines fun with activities defending gay rights as well as cultural and sporting events. Highlights include Pride Barcelona in July (www.pridebarcelona.org) and, during the first fortnight in August, the Circuit Festival (www.circuitfestival.net), Europe's biggest gay and lesbian festival.

Accessible tourism

Barcelona is a pioneering city in accessibility issues for different types of disability: visual, hearing, motor and cognitive. The TMB (Barcelona Metropolitan Transport) bus network has been fully adapted for passengers with reduced mobility since 2007 and more than 80% of the metro network is now barrier free.
The Turisme de Barcelona website for disabled people (**www.barcelona-access.com**) features information in English,
Catalan, Spanish and French about museums adapted for blind and visually impaired visitors, barrier-free hotels, accessible beaches, sign-language tours and all the information they'll need to enjoy an unforgettable holiday to the full, and independently. Its programme, Barcelona Sustainable Tourism, is also running a new guided tour:

Easy Walking Tour ✦✦✦ Gòtic

A one-hour, barrier-free tour led by professional guides specially designed for people with reduced mobility who want to discover the "heart" of Barcelona: the Gothic Quarter, which brings together past and present in its streets, squares and hidden corners. Price: 13.50 € (includes loan of transportable chairs for those who need them). Times: first and third Friday of the month at 10am (English) and 12 noon (Catalan and Spanish). Tour departs from the Turisme de Barcelona Information Office (C/Ciutat, 2).

Sustainable tourism

Barcelona is the first city in the world to be awarded Biosphere World Class Destination certification by the Responsible Tourism Institute (RTI), an organisation created under the auspices of UNESCO. The distinction was awarded in June 2011, when the RTI recognised the city as a sustainable tourism destination in the economic, socio-cultural and environmental spheres. This is the result of the endeavours of the City Council and Turisme de Barcelona.

Passeig de les Aigües

Barcelona by bike

Discover the city along more than 100 km of cycle lanes with this sustainable and environmentally friendly means of transport. The section "Getting around the city" on the **visitbarcelona.com** website features more than 30 options for hiring bikes or signing up for guided tours to suit all tastes.

Barceloneta

Welcome to Barcelona

History

Before the Romans

Although the oldest surviving remains of human settlements on the Barcelona plain date from Neolithic times (5000 BC), the city has its origins in the Laietan tribe of the Iberians (6th century BC), who founded a settlement called Barkeno.

Barcino

The *Colonia Iulia Augusta Paterna Faventia Barcino* was founded circa 10 BC under the protection of Emperor Augustus. The colony is described in documents dating from the 2nd century (Pliny and Ptolemy) as a pleasant place, with fertile land and a small harbour. The city has a classic colonial walled layout, with four gateways which marked the entrance to the *decumanus* (now Carrer del Bisbe and Carrer de la Ciutat) and the *cardo* (Carrer del Call and Carrer de la Llibreteria), which converged in the centre, or forum (Plaça de Sant Jaume).

Early Roman era

Between the 2nd and 4th centuries, the city enjoyed a major period of prosperity and its products (wine and *garum* – a fish-based sauce) were sold throughout the empire. The second wall (the one we can see today) dates from the end of this period and saw the arrival of an important Christian community, whose bishops were the true defenders of the Roman civilisation.

Visigothic rule

In 415, the Visigothic king Ataülf established his court in the city, and, with the fall of the Roman Empire (476), Barcino came under the rule of the Visigothic kingdom of Toulouse and was then governed by the Peninsular kingdoms.

From Islamic to Carolingian rule

In 717, the city came under Islamic rule, although it retained its civic and religious authorities. It became part of Emperor Charlemagne's empire in 797 and his son Louis the Pious conquered the city in 801, establishing the county of Barcelona as part of the Hispanic Marches.

The city of the counts

The counts of Barcelona gradually distanced themselves from Frankish rule. In 985, the city was attacked by a Muslim army led by Al-Mansur, and when the Frankish king declined to intervene, Count Borrell II refused to recognise the king's sovereignty, an action that marked the beginning of independence for the region that would later be called Catalonia. In 1137, Ramon Berenguer IV married Petronella of Aragon and their son, Alfons II, became the first king of Aragon and count of Barcelona. Both territories kept their courts, languages and laws.

Museu d'Arqueologia de Catalunya

El Call

Barcino, Joan Brossa

The medieval golden age

Jaume I, the Conqueror (1208-1276) took Mallorca, Menorca, Valencia and Murcia from the Muslims, marking the start of a phase during which Barcelona became the hub of maritime trade in Europe in the Middle Ages. The Gothic Quarter bears witness to this period.

Consell de Cent

Jaume I founded a municipal government in Barcelona, which first sat in 1265: three councillors elected by a council of 100 eminent people (noblemen, merchants, artists and craftsmen). It is considered to be the first European parliament.

Generalitat

The origins of the Catalan government, the Generalitat de Catalunya, can be traced back to the Catalan Parliament, or Corts, which was made up of representatives of different social groups.

1714

The War of the Spanish Succession divided Europe between the supporters of the Bourbon, Philippe of Anjou (France and Castile) and those of Archduke Charles of Austria (England, Austria, the Netherlands and the territories of the Crown of Aragon). The Bourbon victory led to the abolition of self-government in Catalonia and Barcelona.

Renaixença

In the mid-19th century, following a long period of decline, the industrial revolution triggered great economic prosperity (culminating in the 1888 Universal Exhibition) and Barcelona spearheaded a powerful cultural movement which revived the Catalan language and the notion of a Catalan nation. This had major political repercussions resulting in movements that reinforced the Catalan identity.

Modernisme

Catalonia's home-grown art nouveau, *modernisme*, was adopted as something of a national style in Barcelona and Catalonia after the *Renaixença*. The movement produced architectural landmarks of great artistic value.

20th century

Barcelona experienced many changes in fortune throughout this century.

The Republic

The first 30 years of the century were a period of turmoil and political revolution cut short by the start of the Civil War in 1936.

Dictatorship

After the victory of the fascists (1939), Barcelona, which had remained loyal to the Republic until the bitter end, endured great hardship. However, slow economic and cultural recovery began towards the end of the 1950s, as a result of which the city led the fight for democracy in the 1970s.

Democracy

With the reinstatement of civil liberties and autonomy, the city embarked on a period of urban renewal and social cohesion which has created a model that is universal in scope.

Olympic Barcelona

The 1992 Olympics were a milestone in the aforementioned process of renewal which has continued into the 21st century with the hosting of the Forum of Cultures and the city's confirmation as the headquarters of the Union for the Mediterranean. www.bcn.cat/historia

Museu d'Història de Barcelona

Welcome to Barcelona

Art

Barcelona has had an intense and fruitful relationship with art throughout its history and has bequeathed a legacy of major figures of worldwide renown, particularly in the field of fine art and architecture, such as Gaudí, Domènech i Montaner, Sert, Picasso, Miró, Dalí and Tàpies.

Architecture

With a history dating back more than 2,000 years, Barcelona offers visitors examples of architecture spanning classical antiquity and the era of the Roman Empire to contemporary, state-of-the-art, sustainable buildings. The Middle Ages saw Barcelona reach a creative pinnacle. Indeed, in the 13th, 14th and 15th centuries, many religious and civil buildings were constructed in its home-grown Gothic style, known as Catalan Gothic. The style is characterised by its sober decorative elements and the choice

of the hall-style layout in its cathedrals, where the side naves and central nave are of equal or similar height, letting in more light and creating a wide distance between the columns (in Santa Maria del Mar there is a 13-metre span between the columns: the broadest in a Gothic building). This gives a feeling of height which uplifts the spirits. When Le Corbusier visited Barcelona in 1928, he remarked on the excellence of some of these buildings, such as Santa Maria del Mar and Pedralbes Monastery, exclaiming: "What modern simplicity!" The distinguishing feature of this formal simplicity certainly stemmed from the European Gothic style. In addition to the basilica of Santa Maria del Mar and Pedralbes Monastery, the basilicas of Santa Maria del Pi and Sants Just i Pastor and, particularly, the cathedral are other extraordinary examples

of Barcelona's religious gothic architecture. Barcelona has also brought us some of the finest examples of Civil Gothic architecture in Europe: the great hall, the Saló del Tinell, inside the medieval royal palace, the Palau Reial Major; the old commodities exchange, the Llotja; the great chamber, the Saló de Cent, inside City Hall; the medieval shipyards, the Reials Drassanes; and the old Hospital de Sant Pau bear this out.

However, if there is one movement that stands head and shoulders above the rest it is undoubtedly Catalonia's home-grown art nouveau, *modernisme*, one of the artistic trends that spanned the 19th and 20th centuries. The rise of a new Barcelona moneyed class and the existence of a new generation of artists who had made *modernisme* the flagship of Catalan identity, turned Barcelona into Europe's art-nouveau

Gothic hall inside the Llotja de Mar

Casa Comalat

capital. Out of the dozens of outstanding *modernista* landmarks in the city, eight have been designated UNESCO World Heritage Sites. They are the Park Güell, the Palau Güell, the Casa Milà "La Pedrera", the Casa Vicens, the Sagrada Família and the Casa Batlló, all designed by the architect Antoni Gaudí, and the Palau de la Música Catalana and Hospital de Sant Pau, by Lluís Domènech i Montaner.

As far as contemporary architecture is concerned, in Barcelona you'll find some of the buildings that were the cornerstones of the avant-garde architectural trends of the early 20th century, such as Mies van der Rohe's German Pavilion which dates from 1929, Josep Lluís Sert's Casa Bloc housing development and the Tuberculosis Central Dispensary which date from the 1930s, as well as works by some of today's best-known architects, including Jean Nouvel, Norman Foster, Enric Miralles, Richard Meier, Rafael Moneo, Santiago Calatrava, Toyo Ito and Arata Isozaki.

Fine art

Barcelona is not only a showcase for medieval painting and sculpture. The city has also made a major contribution to leading 20th century avant-garde movements such as cubism, surrealism and abstraction. Pablo Picasso, Joan Miró, Salvador Dalí and Antoni Tàpies are just some of the artists who lived and worked in the city.

The city's museums contain many examples of their works. The MNAC (Museu Nacional d'Art de Catalunya) showcases Europe's most important collection of Romanesque frescoes as well as outstanding examples of Gothic painting and sculpture from Catalonia, and Catalan art to the early 20th century. The MACBA (Museu d'Art Contemporani de Barcelona) and CaixaForum feature the finest collections of avant-garde art from the mid-20th century to the present day. Other essential museums are the Museu Picasso, the Fundació Joan Miró and the Fundació Antoni Tàpies, which devote their permanent collections to their namesakes.

Barcelona is a veritable open-air sculpture museum with extraordinary works by some of the finest sculptors of the last 100 years: Arnau, Llimona, Clarà, Gargallo, Picasso, Tàpies, Miró, Alfaro, Plensa, Brossa, Botero, Horn, Pepper, Oldenburg and Lichtenstein.

Sgraffito frieze by Picasso in the Pl. Nova

Cloud and Chair, Antoni Tàpies

Gastronomy

There's no denying that gastronomy is one of the cornerstones of Catalan culture. Barcelona's famous chefs have cemented its reputation as a culinary treasure trove offering top-quality food with 20 Michelin-starred restaurants.

A bit of history

The first mention of Barcelona's culinary prowess dates back to the 1st century AD, when the Greek historian, Strabo, praised the quality of the oysters from the then Roman colony of Barcino. Later, in the 2nd century AD, praise was lavished on the excellent qualities of the city's *garum* (a sauce made from fermented oily fish in brine), which was exported to Rome.

As you would expect of the capital of the greatest seafaring empire in the Mediterranean, during the Middle Ages, Barcelona's cuisine was one of the most solid and prestigious. Rupert de Nola's recipe book, the *Llibre de Coch* (1520), is an example of refined, flavoursome and aristocratic cuisine, which was highly reputed and influential in its time. The fruit and vegetables that came from America changed the repertoire of recipes of all the cuisines on the continent forever and left a deep imprint on local gastronomy.

Barcelona has absorbed – and continues to absorb – the influences of all the cuisines it has come into contact with throughout its history. This is, without doubt, one of the signs of its identity. Barcelona will go down in the history of haute-cuisine thanks to a world-famous chef: Ferran Adrià. He has been named chef of the year five times and spearheaded a gastronomic revolution which has had a worldwide impact.

Some dishes you have to know about

Although it would be impossible to list all the dishes, if you get the chance, you must try some of the following dishes: white beans with pancetta and *botifarra* sausage, spinach with raisins and pine nuts, Barcelona-style cannelloni, *escudella barrejada* (meat and vegetable stew), cod fritters, chickpeas with cod and spinach, *esqueixada* (shredded salt cod salad), fricandeau, Catalan style broad beans, *capipota amb samfaina* (a type of brawn served with stewed aubergines and peppers) and, of course, *pa amb tomàquet* (bread rubbed with tomato and drizzled with olive oil) topped with anchovies (or Catalan cured meats or sausage), seafood rice dishes, fish and shellfish from the Barceloneta, and some of the classic or avant-garde tapas served at the city's bars and pavement cafés.

El Vermut and tapas

The time-honoured Barcelona custom *Anar a fer el vermut* – which literally translates as "to do the

Aperitif-time in the Plaça Reial

Pa amb tomàquet (bread rubbed with tomato)

vermouth" – involves the ritual of sitting at a pleasant pavement café or at the bar of a bustling café and ordering some tapas (olives, cockles, anchovies, spicy potatoes...) washed down with a glass of vermouth, a small draught beer or soft drink to whet your appetite before lunch. Tapas have also been influenced by haute-cuisine, giving rise to a phenomenon some people have dubbed "miniature haute-cuisine". Now, in Barcelona, classic tapas coexist with state-of-the-art varieties.

The world of cakes and pastries

Barcelona's cakes and pastries are renowned as the best in the country. At Barcelona's patisseries, visitors will find respect for tradition as well as technical refinement that makes the good simply sublime. They'll be amazed at the array of specialities displayed in the cake-shop windows throughout the year, tying in with the calendar of local festivals. For instance, during the Feast of All Saints, you'll find *panellets*, sweet mor-

Colour, flavour, aroma

sels made from marzipan. At Christmas, many cake shops make their own types of nougat, *torró*, including the almond and egg *torró de crema*, crumbly *xixona* and marzipan. On 6th January, Epiphany, the traditional dessert is the *tortell de Reis*, a ring cake filled with marzipan. In March, you have to try the Catalan equivalent of crème brûlée, *crema catalana* or *crema de Sant Josep*; for Lent, special fritters, *bunyols de vent*, and in June, for the Midsummer's Eve celebrations, we mark the occasion with flatbreads, known as *coques*, topped with candied fruit, confectioner's custard, or made with lardons.

The chocolate capital

The people of Barcelona couldn't live without chocolate. Not for nothing was the city's port one of the main European trade routes bringing cacao from America. Cafés specialising in cakes and dairy produce, known as *granges*, are a Barcelona institution. Although they originally sold dairy produce, they became renowned for a speciality drink of thick hot chocolate topped with whipped cream, known as *suís*. The best time to see the Barcelona locals' fascination with chocolate is probably at Easter when the cake shop windows are transformed into veritable galleries of chocolate sculptures, known as *mones*, which godparents give to their godchildren.

Michelin-starred restaurants

Near Barcelona

Less than an hour away from the city, you can also enjoy a wealth of aromas, colours and flavours that will captivate the most demanding palates:

SANT PAU ***
Sant Pol de Mar
www.ruscalleda.com

CAN JUBANY *
Calldetenes
www.canjubany.com

CAPRITX *
Terrassa
www.capritx.com

ELS CASALS *
Sagàs
www.elscasals.cat

ELS TRES MACARRONS *
El Masnou
www.tresmacarrons.com

ESTANY CLAR *
Cercs
www.estanyclar.com

FONDA SALA *
Olost
www.fondasala.com

L'Ó *
Sant Fruitós de Bages
www.monstbenet.com

LLUERNA *
Santa Coloma de Gramanet
www.lluernarestaurant.com

For further information
www.barcelonaesmoltmes.cat/web/descobreix/gastronomia

BCN discounts

Barcelona Turisme
visitbarcelona.com

visit **Barcelona**

BARCELONA CARD EXPRESS

2 days experiences!
Discounts guide

Barcelona Card Express

Enjoy two days' **unlimited and free travel on public transport** (metro, bus and tram network and airport train) and more than **100 discounts** at city sights and museums, on visits and tours, leisure and entertainments, nightlife, at restaurants, shops, on unique means of transport and other services. Includes a city map showing the location of the places offering discounts and metro map.
Price: €20.
To buy your card and for further details:
www.barcelonacard.com

Barcelona Card

The best option if you're visiting the city for three, four or five consecutive days. **Free admission to more than 25 museums and visitor attractions, unlimited and free travel on public transport** (metro, bus and tram network and airport train) and more than **70 discounts** at city sights, on visits and tours, leisure and entertainments, nightlife, at restaurants, shops, on unique means of transport and other services. Includes a map and guide showing the participating attractions.
Price:
3 days, €45 (children, €21)
4 days, €55 (children, €27)
5 days, €60 (children, €32)

To buy your card and for further details:
www.barcelonacard.com

Barcelona Bus Turístic

The most convenient way of discovering the city's most attractive sights and landmarks on three routes. Price: €27, 1 day (children, €16) and €38, 2 days (children, €20). The same ticket can be used on all three routes. Includes an informative guide describing each stop and a discount-voucher booklet to be used at the main landmarks and attractions. There is also the **night-time Barcelona Bus Turístic**, which runs in summer and reveals the beauty of Barcelona's landmark buildings floodlit at night, and the Magic Fountain on Montjuïc. Friday, Saturday and Sunday, May to September.
tickets.visitbarcelona.com

Barcelona Metro Walks

Seven routes combining travel on the metro, city walks and bus or tram rides, to discover Barcelona from an insider's point of view, as well as its history, neighbourhoods, urban development... as if you were one of the locals, at your own pace. Includes a guide featuring the routes, maps and public transport.
tickets.visitbarcelona.com

Museums

There are two tickets featuring discounts. You can buy them at museums, tourist information offices and at tickets.visitbarcelona.com

ArtTicket

Single ticket providing admission to six BCN museums and art centres: Centre de Cultura Contemporània de Barcelona (CCCB); Fundació Antoni Tàpies; Fundació Joan Miró; Museu Nacional d'Art de Catalunya; Museu d'Art Contemporani de Barcelona (MACBA) and Museu Picasso. Valid for 3 months from purchase date.
Price: €30.

ArqueoTicket

Multi-ticket providing admission to four Barcelona museums with archaeological collections: Museu d'Arqueologia de Catalunya, Museu Egipci de Barcelona, Museu d'Història de Barcelona and El Born Centre de Cultura i Memòria. Valid for one year from purchase date.
Price: €13.50.

Others

Hola Barcelona!

Hola Barcelona! 2 (€14)
Hola Barcelona! 3 (€20.50)
Hola Barcelona! 4 (€26.50)
& Hola Barcelona! 5 (€32) offer unlimited travel on the days indicated.
They allow you to travel throughout the entire public transport network and can be purchased at metro stations, tourist offices and on-line:
www.tmb.net
www.fgc.cat

Youth and student discount cards

Holders of the International Student Card (ISIC: www.isic.org) and the Euro26 card (www.euro26. org) can obtain discounts at the main landmarks and attractions.

Senior citizens

People aged over 65 are entitled to discounts on a wide range of services.

For more offers, go to visitbarcelona.com

The city, map by map

Key to the maps

- Museum
- Tourist information
- Metro
- FGC
- Train
- Bus station
- Transport to the airport
- Ferry / Cruise terminal
- Cable car
- Funicular
- Left-luggage
- Hospital
- Police
- Panoramic view

Ciutat Vella

Ciutat Vella is the historic quarter of Barcelona, a major city which was hemmed in by its boundary walls until the middle of the 19th century. The irregular, haphazard layout of the district bears the traces of the last 2,000 years: from the Roman settlement of Barcino to the Barcelona of the 21st century, which is part of a globalised world. The 450 hectares of the city are divided into four zones. The central one being the Gothic Quarter, the oldest part of the city. On its left, on the other side of La Rambla, is El Raval. On the right, is the area comprising Sant Pere, Santa Caterina and La Ribera, where you'll find El Born. And, below it, Barceloneta, the maritime district built in the 18th century.

Must-sees
✳

BARCELONA CATHEDRAL
Pla de la Seu | www.catedralbcn.org
→(C2)

Barcelona's Gothic cathedral is the result of the tenacious endeavour of the local community: it took 600 years to build, from the 13th to 19th centuries. Today it stands gracefully on the former boundary of the Roman city. The cathedral has three naves, with cross-vaulted ceilings and its façade is flanked by two octagonal towers. Highlights include the shady cloisters, where fruit trees, bubbling waters and a flock of geese create a special romantic atmosphere. +INFO: p.100

MUSEU PICASSO
Carrer Montcada, 15-23 | T 93 256 30 00 | www.museupicasso.bcn.cat
→(D2)

Pablo Picasso trained in Barcelona and the city is home to one of the finest collections of paintings and drawings from his youth, as well as important later works. These are on display at the Museu Picasso, which is housed in five medieval palazzos on Carrer Montcada. These refurbished buildings retain their original external appearance and their spacious interior contains a unique pictorial treasure trove, which makes this museum one of Barcelona's biggest tourist attractions. +INFO: p.101

PALAU DE LA MÚSICA CATALANA

Palau de la Música, 4-6 | T 93 295 72 00 | www.palaumusica.cat
→(C2)

Domènech i Montaner made the Palau de la Música his greatest *modernista* jewel: a dazzling, lavishly decorated, multicoloured concert hall, which was the result of his architectural talents and local craftsmanship. Built between 1905 and 1908, the Palau is Barcelona's music venue par excellence. It hosts hundreds of concerts every year and a recent extension has added a chamber-music hall and improved facilities. The Palau also runs guided tours. +INFO: p.102

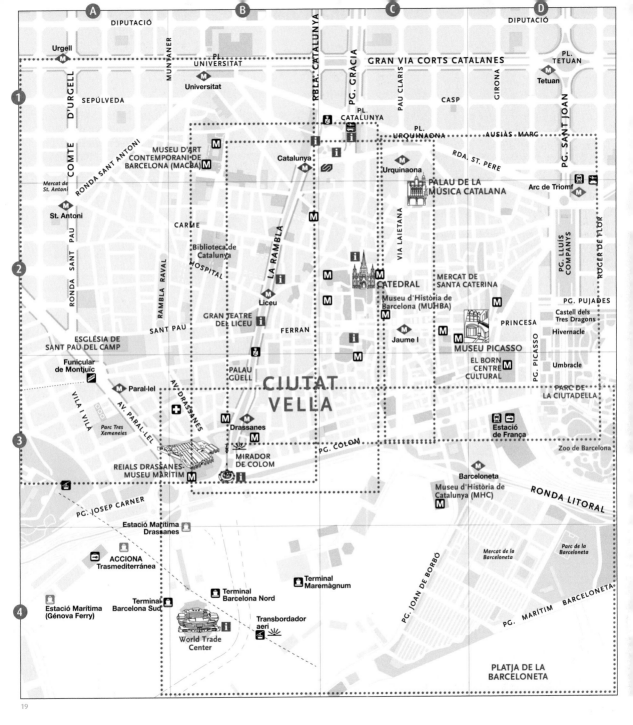

Barri Gòtic

✳ **Must-sees:** BARCELONA CATHEDRAL → p. 18

The heartbeat of ancient Barcelona can still be felt in the Gothic Quarter. Built over the Roman settlement of Barcino, which stood on Mount Taber, its narrow, cobbled streets preserve the traces of the medieval city and the Jewish Quarter. Centuries-old churches and a variety of museums coexist with modern shops in this neighbourhood, where sightseeing trails alternate with havens of tranquillity.

Barcelona Cathedral → (C2)

Museu Picasso → (D2)

Palau de la Música Catalana → (C2)

BARCELONA WALKING TOURS
Gòtic

Two-hour walking tour led by professional guides. The streets, squares and secluded corners of Barcelona's Gothic Quarter bring together past and present. Landmarks on the tour include the cathedral cloisters and the gardens in the Palau Reial Major, as well as the Plaça del Rei, Plaça de Sant Felip Neri and Plaça de Sant Jaume. Price: adults, €16; under 12s, free. Times: Monday to Sunday, 9.30am (English); Saturday, 11.30am (Catalan and Spanish). Departs from the Turisme de Barcelona Information Office (Ciutat, 2).

Roman Trail

Barcelona was founded by the Romans (15-10 BC) at the time of Emperor Augustus. Many architectural remains can still be seen as you walk through its streets (the Temple of Augustus, the aqueduct, the city walls, the necropolis...).
A route taking in the most interesting points begins at the Museu d'Història de Barcelona (Plaça del Rei). Each of the 12 points on the trail have a sign with information in English, Catalan and Spanish.

Jewish Quarter Trail

Although small, Barcelona's medieval Jewish Quarter (el Call, in Catalan) was a major cultural hub in the Mediterranean between the 11th and 14th centuries. 2008 saw the opening of the Centre d'Interpretació del Call (Placeta Manuel Ribé s/n) housed in the former house of the "Rabbi" or "Alchemist" (14th century) which marks the departure point of a trail visiting the most interesting Sephardic heritage landmarks. Each of the points features a sign with information in English, Catalan and Spanish.

Museums

MUSEU D'HISTÒRIA DE BARCELONA
→ (G3) + INFO: p. 104

MUSEU D'IDEES I INVENTS DE BARCELONA
Ciutat, 7 → (F3)
www.mibamuseum.com
The city's first permanent museum showcasing a wide variety of exhibits that put the world of invention and creativity in the spotlight.

MUSEU DE LA CATEDRAL
Pla de la Seu, s/n → (F2)
www.catedralbcn.org
Collection of religious art belonging to the guilds and monarchs who governed the city for centuries.

MUSEU DE LA MOTO
De la Palla, 10 → (F2)
www.museumoto.com
Dedicated exclusively to the world and history of the motorcycle.

MUSEU DIOCESÀ - THE GAUDÍ EXHIBITION CENTER
Av. de la Catedral, 4 → (G2)
Permanent exhibition Walking with Gaudí divided into four sections: Influences, The Worlds of Gaudí, The Masterpieces and His Legacy.

MUSEU FREDERIC MARÈS
Pl. de Sant Iu, 5-6 → (G2)
www.museumares.bcn.cat
Showcases sculptures from the pre-Roman era to the 20th century and a collection of thousands of everyday objects from the 19th century.

Restaurants

Michelin-starred
KOY SHUNKA ✳
Copons, 7 → 1(G2)
T 93 412 79 39
(> €60)
Born in Toyota and trained in Tokyo, chef Hideki Matsuhisa serves Japanese haute cuisine with a Catalan twist in Barcelona.

CAFÈ DE L'ACADÈMIA
Pl. de Sant Just, s/n → 3(G3)
T 93 319 82 53
(€20-40) + SET LUNCH MENU

A charming eatery. Summer terrace. Market-fresh Catalan cuisine.

EL GRAN CAFÈ
Avinyó, 9 →4(F3)
T 93 318 79 86
(€20-40) + SET LUNCH MENU
A selection of traditional Catalan dishes served in a beautiful *modernista* setting.

ELS QUATRE GATS
Montsió, 3 →5(F1)
T 93 302 41 40
(€20-40) + SET LUNCH MENU
The legendary focus of artistic life in the early 20th century with Rusiñol, Picasso, etc. Catalan cuisine.

IRATI TAVERNA BASCA
Cardenal Casañas, 17
→6(E2)
T 93 302 30 84
(€30-50)
One of BCN's first Basque restaurants. Tapas.

SELF NATURISTA
Santa Anna, 11 →7(F1)
T 93 318 26 84
(€10-20) + SET LUNCH MENU
One of Barcelona's first vegetarian restaurants. Self-service, 11am-8pm.

Cafés and bars

BAR DEL PI
Pl. de Sant Josep Oriol, 1
→8(F2)
Café and tapas bar with a wonderful terrace where you can savour the atmosphere of the neighbourhood.

CAELUM
Carrer de la Palla, 8
→9(F2)
Shop selling products from different convents. Café on the premises where you can sample them.

GRANJA LA PALLARESA
Petritxol, 11 →10(E2)
Serving one of the best thick hot chocolates in the city since 1947.

EL MESÓN DEL CAFÉ
Llibreteria, 16
→11(G3)
Since 1909. The current décor dates from 1929. Tiny bar serving great coffee.

EL PARAIGUA
Pas de l'Ensenyança, 2
→12(F3)
Historic cocktail bar and café. *Modernista* décor. Live music. Exhibitions.

L'ASCENSOR
Bellafila, 3 →13(F3)
An elegant bar with old-style, *modernista* décor, which serves excellent cocktails.

LA CERERÍA
Baixada de Sant Miquel, 3
→14(F3)
Organic vegetarian cuisine. Highlights include its pizzas, pastries and cakes made with a variety of flours to suit the customer's taste.

LA GRANJA
Banys nous, 4 →15(F3)
A café since 1872, it retains all its charm. The interior houses a section of the Roman wall.

ZIM
Dagueria, 20 →16(G3)
Tiny bar where you can sample fine wines and pair them with an excellent selection of artisan cheeses.

Shopping

ART MONTFALCON
Boters, 4 →17(F2)
Gift shop selling an endless array of items. There is also an art gallery on the premises.

ARTUR RAMON
De la Palla, 25 →18(F2)
One of Barcelona's finest antique shops, now run by the fourth generation of the same family.

BARRETS OBACH
Call, 2 →19(F3)
Legendary shop selling hats, caps and berets since 1924.

BCN ORIGINAL SHOPS
Ciutat, 2 →20(F3)
Pl. de Catalunya, 7
A wide range of gift items inspired by Barcelona.

CERERIA SUBIRÀ
Llibreteria, 7 →21(G3)
The finest candles since 1761. Baroque décor.

Plaça Ramon Berenguer →(G3)

Carrer del Bisbe →(F3)

Plaça del Rei →(G3)

Temple of Augustus →(G3)

FARGAS
Pi, 16 →**22(F2)**
A long tradition of chocolates, truffles and chocolate on premises that still retain their *modernista* décor.

FORMATGERIA LA SEU
Daqueria, 16 →**23(G3)**
Delightful shop specialising in local artisan cheeses.

GUANTERIA I COMPLEMENTS ALONSO
Santa Anna, 27
→**24(F1)**
Modernista-style shop founded over 100 years ago specialising in gloves, fans and accessories.

JOANA M. PRAT 1850
Pi, 4 →**25(F2)**
A century-old emporium which has been located in the same neighbourhood since 1850. It offers quality, contemporary fashions for men and women.

LA BASÍLICA GALERIA
Sant Sever, 7 →**26(F2)**
Jewellers showcasing the work of more than 100 contemporary jewellers from around the world.

LA COLMENA
Pl. de l'Àngel, 12
→**27(G3)**
A classic BCN patisserie (1928) renowned for its cakes and nougats. Spain's oldest hand-made sweet manufacturer.

LA MANUAL ALPARGATERA
Avinyó, 7 →**28(F3)**
70 years selling espadrilles and natural footwear.

ÓPTICA COTTET
Portal de l'Àngel, 40
→**29(F1)**
This opticians is now run by the fourth generation of the family and specialises in all kinds of eyewear. Iconic thermometer on the façade.

PAPABUBBLE
Ample, 28 →**30(F4)**
Authentic handmade, inventive and custom-made sweets created in front of the customers.

PAPIRUM
Baixada de la Llibreteria, 2
→**31(F3)**
A unique place for lovers of select stationery and writing implements.

PLANELLES DONAT
Portal de l'Àngel, 7 and 27
→**32(F1)**
Long tradition of producing artisan *torró* nougats, ice cream and *orxata*.

RAIMA
Comtal, 27 →**33(G1)**
Exquisite selection of writing implements and gifts.

SOMBRERERÍA MIL
Fontanella, 20 →**34(G1)**
For more than a century this emporium has been catering to hat lovers with a wide variety of models.

TOMÀS COLOMER
Portal de l'Àngel, 7
→**35(F2)**
150 years in the world of jewellery and watches.

TORRONS VICENS
Petritxol, 15 →**36(E2)**
The Barcelona shop run by master *torró*-makers from Agramunt. Purveyors of hand-made *torrons* and chocolates since 1775.

UTERQÜE
Portal de l'Àngel, 15
→**37(F1)**
Fashion accessories and a carefully chosen selection of top-quality textile and leather clothing.

ZARA
Portal de l'Àngel, 32
→**38(F1)**
World-renowned Spanish clothing and accessories brand for men, women and children.

And also

CASA DE L'ARDIACA
Santa Llúcia, 1 →**(F2)**
15th-century Gothic palazzo with a Renaissance façade attached to the Roman wall with a beautiful interior courtyard.

CHURCH OF SANTA ANNA
Santa Anna, 29 →**(F1)**
A hidden treasure and a haven of peace right in the city centre. The church was founded by the Order of the Holy Sepulchre and is mainly Gothic in style. It was built between the 12th and 13th centuries.

Church of Santa Anna →**(F1)**

Fira de Santa Llúcia →**39(F2)**

Portal de l'Àngel →**(F1)**

Guanteria Alonso →**24(F1)**

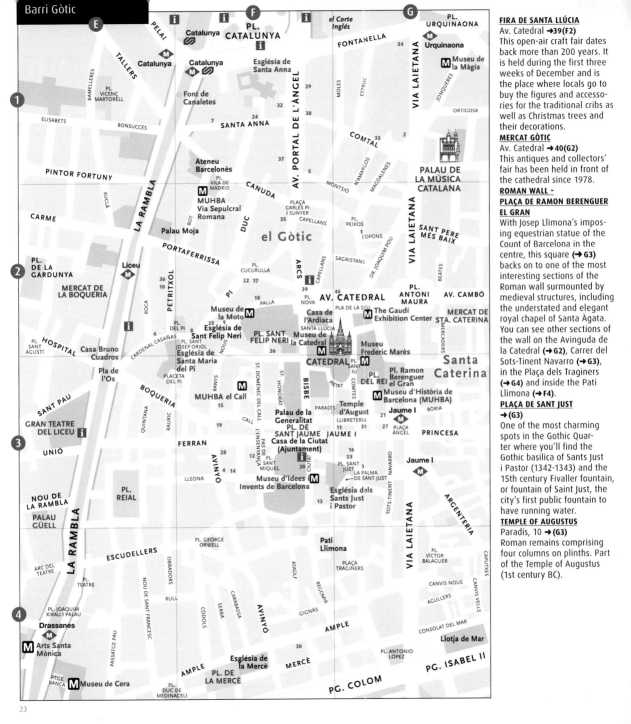

FIRA DE SANTA LLÚCIA

Av. Catedral →39(F2)

This open-air craft fair dates back more than 200 years. It is held during the first three weeks of December and is the place where locals go to buy the figures and accessories for the traditional cribs as well as Christmas trees and their decorations.

MERCAT GÒTIC

Av. Catedral →40(G2)

This antiques and collectors' fair has been held in front of the cathedral since 1978.

ROMAN WALL - PLAÇA DE RAMON BERENGUER EL GRAN

With Josep Llimona's imposing equestrian statue of the Count of Barcelona in the centre, this square (→G3) backs on to one of the most interesting sections of the Roman wall surmounted by medieval structures, including the understated and elegant royal chapel of Santa Àgata. You can see other sections of the wall on the Avinguda de la Catedral (→G2), Carrer del Sots-Tinent Navarro (→G3), in the Plaça dels Traginers (→G4) and inside the Pati Llimona (→F4).

PLAÇA DE SANT JUST

→(G3)

One of the most charming spots in the Gothic Quarter where you'll find the Gothic basilica of Sants Just i Pastor (1342-1343) and the 15th century Fivaller fountain, or fountain of Saint Just, the city's first public fountain to have running water.

TEMPLE OF AUGUSTUS

Paradís, 10 →(G3)

Roman remains comprising four columns on plinths. Part of the Temple of Augustus (1st century BC).

Highlights

CONJUNT MONUMENTAL DE LA PLAÇA DEL REI
Plaça del Rei, s/n → (G3)
T 93 256 21 22
www.museuhistoria.bcn.cat
The splendour of medieval Catalonia can still be seen in the Plaça del Rei, one of the best-preserved squares in the Gothic Quarter. It is overlooked by the Palau Reial Major, the former residence of the kings of Catalonia and Aragon, with its Great Hall, the Saló del Tinell, and arches which merge with the Watchtower of King Martí. The Lieutenant's Palace, the Palau del Lloctinent, and the chapel of Santa Àgata complete this monumental ensemble. On one side of the square, the Casa Padellàs houses the Museu d'Història de Barcelona which provides access to the Roman and early-Christian archaeological remains below the Plaça del Rei.
+ INFO: p. 104

MUHBA Roman remains → (G3)

MUHBA Saló del Tinell → (G3)

PLAÇA DE SANT JAUME
→ (F3)
The Plaça Sant Jaume is the city's power base. On one side, the seat of Catalan government, the Palau de la Generalitat, with its Renaissance façade. On the other, City Hall, whose Great Hall, the Saló de Cent, has been a meeting point for the community since the 14th century. www.gencat.cat www.bcn.cat

Plaça de Sant Jaume → (F3)

EL CALL AND PLAÇA DE SANT FELIP NERI
→ (F2, F3)
El Call (BCN's Jewish Quarter) was the main cultural hub in Catalonia from the 11th to 14th centuries. It was here that doctors, philosophers, mathematicians and astronomers disseminated their knowledge. Time seems to have stood still in its secluded corners such as Plaça de Sant Felip Neri, with its bomb-scarred buildings.

Plaça de Sant Felip Neri → (F2)

El Born & La Ribera

❋ **Must-sees:** MUSEU PICASSO + PALAU DE LA MÚSICA CATALANA → p. 18

La Ribera – meaning shore – bears witness to the city's former relationship with the sea. La Ribera was built in the 13th century outside the city walls and partially demolished to make way for a military citadel which was later turned into a park. It still retains its higgledy-piggledy medieval layout where Santa Maria del Mar, El Born, and the Santa Caterina Market stand out like clearings in a dense forest.

BARCELONA WALKING TOURS
Picasso
Two-hour walking tour led by professional guides exploring the life and work of the painter during the time he spent in Barcelona. The tour includes Els Quatre Gats, the Col·legi d'Arquitectes, Carrer Avinyó, the Porxos d'En Xifré, Llotja de Mar, La Ribera district and ends at the Museu Picasso. Price: adults, €22; children, €8 (includes guided tour of Museu Picasso). Times: Tuesday to Saturday at 3pm (English); Wednesday and Saturday at 3.30pm (French). Departs from the Turisme de Barcelona Information Office (Plaça de Catalunya, 17-S).

Museums

MUSEU PICASSO → (I3)
+ INFO p. 101

MUSEU DE CULTURES DEL MÓN
Montcada, 12 → (H3)
www.museuculturesmon.bcn.cat
Housed in two medieval palaces, the museum showcases the artistic heritage of a number of African, Asian, American and Oceanic cultures.

MUSEU DE LA XOCOLATA
Comerç, 36 → (I3)
www.pastisseria.cat

A journey tracing the origins of chocolate, its arrival in Europe and widespread use.

MUSEU EUROPEU D'ART MODERN
Barra de Ferro, 5
→ (H3)
www.meam.es
Dedicated solely to the best figurative art of the 20th and 21st centuries.

Restaurants

BAR MUNDIAL
Plaça de Sant Agustí Vell, 1
→ 1(I2)
T 93 319 90 56
(€20-30)
A neighbourhood classic that opened in 1925. A wide variety of tapas and fish and seafood dishes.

CAL PEP
Plaça de les Olles, 8
→ 2(I4)
T 93 310 79 61
(€50-60)
Very popular. Home cooking with a Basque flavour and excellent tapas.

ESPAI SUCRE
Princesa, 53 →3(I3)
T 93 268 16 30
(€30-45)
The pastry chef Jordi Butrón presents a creative dessert menu in the first restaurant of its kind in the world.

CUINES DE SANTA CATERINA
Av. de Francesc Cambó, 16
→ 4(H2)
T 93 268 99 18
(€20-30)
Modern and spacious.

Inside the Santa Caterina Market. Mediterranean, oriental and vegetarian cuisine.

EL 300 DEL BORN
Plaça Comercial, 12
→ 5(I4)
T 93 310 24 28
(€20-30)
Gastro bar and restaurant run by the Moritz brewery inside the city's new cultural centre, the refurbished Born Market.

EL PASSADÍS D'EN PEP
Pla de Palau, 2 → 6(H4)
T 93 310 10 21
(> €60)
Seafood cuisine at one of the city's finest shellfish restaurants. It is supplied by six fishing harbours.

LA BÀSCULA
Flassaders, 30 →7(I3)
T 93 319 98 66
(< €20)
Housed in a former chocolate factory, La Bàscula offers a wide variety of vegetarian pasta dishes.

MERCAT PRINCESA
Flassaders, 21 →8(I3)
T 93 268 15 18
(€20-30)
Housed in a medieval palace, this gourmet food hall has 17 different stands where you can sample dishes from around the world.

SENYOR PARELLADA
Argenteria, 37 →9(H3)
T 93 310 50 94
(€25-40)
Charming restaurant.

Generous servings of traditional Catalan cuisine.

TEN'S
Rec, 79 → 10(I4)
T 93 319 22 22
(€20-40)
Haute-cuisine tasting platters and tapas by the chef Jordi Cruz on the ground floor of the Park Hotel.

Cafés and bars

BOCAMEL
Comerç, 8 → 11(J2)
Creative, artisan patisserie and tea room serving products made from natural ingredients.

COCKTAIL BAR JUANRA FALCES
Rec, 24 → 12(I3)
One of Barcelona's oldest and finest cocktail bars.

LA VINYA DEL SENYOR
Pl. de Santa Maria, 5 → 13(H4)
A wide selection of wines to accompany tasting dishes of Catalan cured sausage, ham, cheese...

EL XAMPANYET
Montcada, 22 → 14(H3)
Since 1929, the best anchovies in Barcelona and its signature fizz: *xampanyet*.

Shopping

ALMACÉN MARABI
Cirera, 6 → 15(I3)
Dolls, marionettes, sculptures and hand-made soft toys by the artist Mariela Marabi.

BUBÓ
Caputxes, 10 → 16(H4)
Carles Mampel, the world's top chocolatier in 2005, offers us his modern creations.

CAFÉS EL MAGNÍFICO
Argenteria, 64 → 17(H4)
A wide selection of quality teas and coffees from around the world.

CASA CALICÓ
Plaça de les Olles, 9 → 18(I4)
Emporium founded over 100 years ago for lovers of fishing and the sea.

DAVID VALLS & INGRID VALLS
Vidrieria, 3 → 19(I4)

Unique knitwear made from exclusive and natural materials.

DEMASIÉ
Princesa, 28 → 20(I3)
Delicious, hand-made biscuits in designer wrappings.

DESIGUAL
Argenteria, 65 → 21(H4)
Barcelona streetwear full of colour and imagination.

E&A GISPERT
Sombrerers, 23 → 22(H4)
At Gispert they have been roasting nuts in their wood-fired oven since 1851. Deli.

LA CAMPANA
Princesa, 36 → 23(I3)
Long tradition of artisan ice creams, *torró* nougats and crumbly almond biscuits, *polvorones*.

LA COMERCIAL
Rec, 52 → 24(I4)
Created for the enjoyment of fashion. A carefully chosen selection of accessories.

LES LUNETTES
Rec, 56 → 25(I4)
Eyewear by emerging designers and independent brands. Top-quality, hand-crafted materials.

LOISAIDA
Flassaders, 42 → 26(I3)
Quirky shop combining vintage items and contemporary fashions.

MUNICH SPORTS
Rec, 22 → 27(I3)
Sports shoes that have set the benchmark for streetwear in Spain.

ON LAND
Princesa, 25 → 28(I3)
Very special, different and colourful designs for men and women.

PASTISSERIA HOFMANN
Flassaders, 44 → 29(I4)
Following the success of her Michelin-starred restaurant, the chef Mey Hofmann opened this superb gourmet deli and patisserie.

PAULA WATERS JOIES
Espaseria, 18 → 30(H4)
Hand-crafted signature jewellery.

El Born CCM → (I4)

Born, Jaume Plensa → 38(I4)

Plaça de Santa Maria → (H4)

Museu de la Xocolata → (I3)

SANS & SANS
Argenteria, 64 ➜ **31(H4)**
A wide selection of spiced teas. The shop which sells and roasts coffees is directly opposite and opened in 1919.

STUDIOSTORE
Comerç, 17 ➜ **32(I3)**
Gallery, design studio and concept store with unique, original pieces.

SYNGMAN CUCALA & LURDES BERGADA
Pl. Santa Maria, 2 ➜ **33(H4)**
Men's and women's fashion. Functional and minimalist clothes in sober colours.

VILA VINITECA
Agullers, 7 ➜ **34(H4)**
Since 1932. The world's finest wines. Club for wine lovers and tasting courses.

VITRA
Plaça Comercial, 5 ➜ **35(I3)**
Well-known contemporary furniture brand that reissues design classics and produces projects by young designers.

And also

ARC DE TRIOMF
Pg. de Lluís Companys ➜ **(J2)**
Designed by Josep Vilaseca, this triumphal arch was the gateway to the 1888 Universal Exhibition.

CARRER DE MONTCADA ➜ **(H3)**
This was the main area where Barcelona's nobility lived from the 13th to the 18th centuries. The street is lined with Gothic palaces and mansions of great architectural value to which Renaissance and baroque elements have been added. Over the years, these buildings have been converted into museums and other cultural facilities. Highlights are the Palau Aguilar, Palau Baró de Castellet, Palau Meca, Palau Finestres and the Casa Mauri (which house the Museu Picasso), the Palau Cervelló and the Palau Dalmases.

CONVENT OF SANT AGUSTÍ
Comerç, 36 ➜ **(I3)**
The old convent of Sant Agustí dates from the mid-14th century, and although it was destroyed in 1714, some original parts such as the west wing of the Gothic cloister are still preserved. The cloister and bar inside are reached through a light installation called *Deuce Coop* (1992) by the Californian James Turrel.

EL REI DE LA MÀGIA
Princesa, 11 ➜ **36(H3)**
www.elreydelamagia.com
This unique shop has been dedicated to magic since 1881. Beautiful magic boxes and all kinds of accessories. Nearby, at 15 Carrer de Jonqueres, you'll find the Theatre-Museum which hosts magic shows. ➜ **37(H1)**

FUNDACIÓ GASPAR
Montcada, 25 ➜ **40(H3)**
www.fundaciogaspar.com
Housed in a 15th-century Gothic building (the Palau Cervelló), the foundation holds contemporary art exhibitions featuring some of the world's leading artists.

PLAÇA DEL FOSSAR DE LES MORERES ➜ **(H4)**
The burial site of the fallen during the Siege of Barcelona, which ended on 11th September 1714 when the city surrendered to the Bourbon troops. In 2001, the monument surmounted by a cauldron, designed by Alfons Viaplana, was placed on the site. An eternal flame burns at the top, a symbol of permanent tribute.

BARCELONA ZOO ➜ **(J4)**
Opened in 1902 in the grounds of the Parc de la Ciutadella, Barcelona Zoo covers an area of 13 hectares. It is home to more than 400 species of animals from all around the world and adheres to the World Zoo Conservation Strategy.

Carrer de Montcada ➜ **(H3)**

Palau Dalmases ➜ **39(H3)**

Fossar de les Moreres ➜ **(H4)**

El Rei de la Màgia ➜ **36(H3)**

Map labels:

H / **I** / **J**

1
- Urquinaona (M)
- JONQUERES 37
- TRAFALGAR
- Urquinaona
- BRUC
- GIRONA
- BAILÉN
- Urquinaona (M)
- RDA. ST. PERE
- PG. SANT JOAN
- ALÍ BEI
- ORTIGOSA
- TRAFALGAR
- MENDEZ NUÑEZ
- Arc de Triomf (M)
- AV. VILANOVA

2
- PALAU DE LA MÚSICA CATALANA
- SANT PERE MÉS ALT
- St. Pere de les Puelles
- PL. ST. PERE
- Arc de Triomf
- Sant Pere
- VERDAGUER I CALLÍS
- MARE DE DÉU DEL PILAR
- PL. DE L CALLÍS
- SANT PERE
- PERE
- MITJÀ
- REC COMTAL
- ALMOGÀVERS
- DR. JOAQUIM POU
- VIA LAIETANA
- SANT PERE MÉS BAIX
- JAUME GIRALT
- BASSES SANT PERE
- CORTINES
- PORTAL NOU
- PG. LLUÍS COMPANYS
- BEATES
- FREIXURES
- PL. MARQUILLES
- 11
- PL. ANTONI MAURA
- AV. FRANCESC CAMBÓ 4
- MERCADERS
- AVELLÀ
- FREIXURES
- MERCAT DE STA. CATERINA
- C. TARROS
- PL. SANT AGUSTÍ VELL 1
- PL. ACADÈMIA
- COMERÇ

3
- Santa Caterina
- Pl. Ramon Berenguer el Gran
- PL. STA. CATERINA
- SANT JACINT
- CORDERS
- PL. LLANA
- PLACETA D'EN MARCÚS
- CARDERS
- PL. SANT CUGAT
- BLANQUERIA
- ASSAONADORS
- TANTARANTANA
- Convent de Sant Agustí
- Museu de la Xocolata 32
- PL. LA PUNTUAL 3
- PG. PUJADES
- BÒRIA
- Jaume I (M)
- PL. ÀNGEL
- PRINCESA 36
- Museu Europeu d'Art Modern 28
- 20
- 23
- PRINCESA
- Castell dels Tres Dragons
- Hivernacle
- BARRA DE FERRO
- VIGATANS
- Museu de Cultures del Món (M)
- MUSEU PICASSO (M) 8
- 7
- FUSINA
- Jaume I (M)
- 9
- MIRALLERS
- BANYS VELLS
- MONTCADA
- CIRERA
- FLASSADERS
- REC
- 39 40
- 14
- 12
- 35
- COMERÇ
- Umbracle
- PG. PICASSO

4
- SOTS-TINENT NAVARRO
- 17
- 31
- 21
- SOMBRERERS
- 29
- 26
- EL BORN CENTRE DE CULTURA I MEMÒRIA (M) 5
- PARC DE LA CIUTADELLA
- ARGENTERIA
- STA. MARIA DEL MAR
- PG. BORN 38
- la Ribera
- 19
- ESPARTERIA
- ANTIC DE SANT JOAN
- RIBERA
- PL. VÍCTOR BALAGUER
- CAPUTXES
- PL. SANTA MARIA
- 16 13
- CANVIS NOUS
- CANVIS VELLS
- 33
- 30
- Pl. Fossar de les Moreres
- 24 25
- REC 10
- 34
- AGULLERS
- 6
- PL. OLLES 18
- Correus
- CONSOLAT DEL MAR
- PLA DEL PALAU
- AV. MARQUÈS DE L'ARGENTERA
- PL. ANTONIO LÓPEZ
- Llotja de Mar
- OCATA
- VIA LAIETANA
- PG. ISABEL II
- GRAL. CASTAÑOS
- Estació de França
- Zoo de Barcelona

Convent of Sant Agustí ➜ (I3)

Arc de Triomf ➜ (J2)

Castle of the Three Dragons ➜ (J3)

Barcelona Zoo ➜ (J4)

Highlights

SANTA MARIA DEL MAR
Pl. de Santa Maria, 1
→ (H4)
The façade of the 14th century Gothic church of Santa Maria del Mar features two octagonal towers and a beautiful rose window. Its stunning, high-ceilinged interior is elegant and spacious, with slender, sober columns underpinning the vaulted roof.
+INFO: p. 105

Santa Maria del Mar → (H4)

EL BORN CENTRE DE CULTURA I MEMÒRIA
Pl. Comercial, s/n
→ (I4)
T 93 256 68 51
http://elborncultura
imemoria.barcelona.cat
From 1876, throughout a century, the metal structure of El Born housed Barcelona's main food market. Now a cultural centre which houses magnificent archaeological remains.
+INFO: p. 107

El Born CCM → (I4)

PARC DE LA CIUTADELLA
→ (J4)
Designed in 1872, the park was altered in 1888 for the Universal Exhibition. It is home to the Catalan Parliament, the Castle of the Three Dragons, the Plant House, the Glasshouse, the Zoo, the monumental waterfall with its boating lake and sculptures by Josep Llimona, Frederic Marès and Pau Gargallo.

MERCAT DE SANTA CATERINA
Av. de Francesc Cambó, 16
→ (H2)
www.mercatsantacaterina.net
The dynamic, curving roof of the Santa Caterina Market, underpinned by an expressive structure, reproduces the colours of fruit and vegetables, and spreads its infectious and youthful spirit to a historic market (1848). It was designed by Miralles and Tagliabue.

Parc de la Ciutadella → (J4)

Mercat de Santa Caterina → (H2)

Ciutat Vella

La Rambla

There's no street in Barcelona like La Rambla: an explosion of life and colour which attracts people of all countries and backgrounds. La Rambla is the dividing line between the Gothic Quarter and El Raval: a broad pedestrian walkway, bustling with people night and day, which links the Mediterranean with the Eixample. It is lined with news-stands and flower stalls.

BARCELONA WALKING TOURS
Gourmet
Two-hour walking tour led by professional guides exploring Barcelona's culinary culture. Places on the tour include Casa Gispert, Jamón Experience, Escribà and Xocolateria Fargas. Price: adults, 22 €; children, 7 € (includes tastings). Departs from the Turisme de Barcelona Information Office (Plaça de Catalunya, 17-S).

Museums
ARTS SANTA MÒNICA
Rambla Santa Mònica, 7
→ (K4)
www.artsantamonica.cat
A space of convergence and crossover between the different disciplines of contemporary artistic creation and science, thought and communication.
LA VIRREINA CENTRE DE LA IMATGE
La Rambla, 99 → (K2)
www.bcn.cat/virreinacen
tredelaimatge
Two gallery spaces devoted to pioneering visual arts.
MUSEU DE CERA
Passatge de la Banca, 7
→ (K4)
www.museocerabcn.com
Some of the most eminent figures in history come to life inside this Renaissance-style building.
MUSEU DE L'ERÒTICA
La Rambla, 96 bis
→ (K2)
www.erotica-museum.com
More than 800 pieces of great historical value from Greece, Rome and the Far East to the early 1900s trace the history of eroticism.

Restaurants
AGUT
Gignàs, 16 → 1(L4)
T 93 315 17 09
(€20-45) + SET LUNCH MENU
A former inn (1924) with a bohemian atmosphere. Excellent traditional Catalan cuisine.
BAR LOBO
Pintor Fortuny, 3 → 3(K2)
T 93 481 53 46
(€20-30) + SET LUNCH MENU
Tapas and quick bites with a bold touch.
BIOCENTER
Pintor Fortuny, 25
→ 4(K2)
T 93 301 45 83
(< €20)
Pioneers in vegetarian cuisine made from organic produce and wholefoods.
CAN CULLERETES
Quintana, 5 → 5(L3)
T 93 317 30 22
(€20-30) + GROUP MENU
Barcelona's oldest restaurant (1786). Traditional Catalan fare.
CENT ONZE
La Rambla, 111 → 6(K1)
T 93 318 62 00
(€20-40) + SET LUNCH MENU
The chef Eugeni Cortés serves contemporary Mediterranean cuisine

with traditional culinary roots.
EGIPTE
La Rambla, 79 → 7(K2)
T 93 317 95 45
(€15-20) + SET LUNCH MENU
Traditional Catalan cuisine offering good value for money.
L'HORTET
Pintor Fortuny, 32 → 8(K1)
T 93 317 61 89
(< €20)
A family-friendly, welcoming restaurant offering a wide variety of vegetarian dishes.
LA CUINA DEL DO
Plaça Reial, 1 → 9(K3)
T 93 481 36 66 (€40-60)
Carefully prepared Mediterranean-inspired dishes in a unique historic setting.
LOS CARACOLES
Escudellers, 14 → 10(K3)
T 93 302 31 85
(€30-45) + TAPAS MENU
Historic restaurant (1835). Simple, traditional Catalan cuisine.
PINOTXO
Mercat de la Boqueria
→ 11(K2)
T 93 317 17 31
(€15-25)
Small, famous bar inside the Boqueria Market. Dishes of the day and sandwiches.
TERESA CARLES
Jovellanos, 2 → 12(K1)
T 93 317 18 29
(€20-30)
One of the city's iconic vegetarian restaurants

(they make their own fresh pasta). You can also buy food to take away.

VIENA
La Rambla, 115 → **13(K1)**
T 93 317 14 92
(< €20)
Beer served in ceramic tankards. Top-quality sandwiches. Fast food Catalan style.

Cafés and bars

BAR KASPARO
Pl. de Vicenç Martorell, 4 → **14(K1)**
A classic pavement café. Breakfasts, snacks, tapas...

BAR PASTIS
Santa Mònica, 4 → **15(K4)**
Since 1947, it has remained true to French chanson, live music and, of course, the drink it is named after.

BOADAS
Tallers, 1 → **16(L1)**
The Barcelona cocktail bar (1933). Classic décor and excellent cocktails.

CAFÈ DE L'ÒPERA
La Rambla, 74 → **17(K3)**
Legendary city café. It still has its mid-19th-century décor.

CÈNTRIC CANALLA
Ramalleres, 27 → **18(K1)**
A classic neighbourhood bar which has been restored where you can sample tapas and tasting platters.

ESCRIBÀ
La Rambla, 83 → **19(K2)**
Café located in a patisserie founded over 100 years ago. You simply have to try its cakes and pastries.

GRANJA VIADER
Xuclà, 6 → **20(K2)**
Opened as a dairy in 1904. Delicious thick hot chocolate, topped with whipped cream, and honeys, curd cheese, etc.

OCAÑA
Plaça Reial, 13 → **21(K3)**
T 93 676 48 14
Multispace (café, bar, restaurant, club) with splendid Belle Époque decoration.

SCHILLING
Ferran, 23 → **22(L3)**
Minimalist but cosy café. Open until 3am.

ZURICH
Pl. de Catalunya, 1 → **23(L1)**
A meeting place for locals for 80 years.

Shopping

CASA GIMENO
La Rambla, 100 → **24(K2)**
The world's finest tobacco since 1920.

CASAS INTERNACIONAL
La Rambla, 125 → **25(L1)**
Shoe retailers since 1923. The top footwear collections and latest trends.

CUSTO BARCELONA
Ferran, 36 → **26(L3)**
Everything in men's and women's fashion by BCN's top international designer.

GANIVETERIA ROCA
Pl. del Pi, 3 → **28(L2)**
Cutler's founded almost 100 years ago selling leading European brands of knives and razors.

HERBORISTERIA DEL REI
Vidre, 1 → **29(K3)**
Since 1823. Décor dating from 1860. The oldest herbalist's in Catalonia.

PALAU MOJA - THE CATALAN HERITAGE HOUSE
Portaferrissa, 1 → **2(L2)**
You can find a wide range of products of all kinds related to crafts, history, food and wine, books, etc. related to Catalan culture.

VIALIS
Elisabets, 20 → **30(K1)**
Unmistakeable, comfortable designer shoes made from the finest materials.

XOCOA
Petritxol, 11 → **31(L2)**
Barcelona-based chocolatier combining interior design with quality cacao.

And also

CASA BRUNO CUADROS
La Rambla, 82 → **(K2)**
A building pre-dating the Catalan art-nouveau, or *modernista*, period which was completely remodelled in 1883 by Josep Vilaseca. It features eye-catching decorative elements, which reveal strong

La Rambla

Cafè de l'Òpera → **17(K3)**

Escribà → **19(K2)**

Granja Viader → **20(K2)**

Oriental influences, such as the cast-iron umbrellas and fans and the cast-iron Chinese dragon which holds up an iron street lamp. An umbrella is suspended from the base of the lamp.

CARRER DE PETRITXOL
→ (L2)

With its busy *granjes*, which specialise in dairy products and cakes, and chocolate houses, the street opened in 1465, although the current buildings date from the 18th and 19th centuries (highlights include number 5, the Sala Parés, an art gallery since 1840). The street begins in the Plaça del Pi, with its Gothic church and 10-metre-diameter rose window.

CANALETES FOUNTAIN
La Rambla, 133
→ (L1)

This 19th century cast-iron fountain with its four drinking spouts, surmounted by a four-armed street lamp is one of the symbols of Barcelona and a favourite meeting point for locals and visitors alike. Since the 1950s, FC Barcelona fans have met here to celebrate their sporting victories. Legend says that anyone who drinks from the fountain will return to the city.

ROMAN NECROPOLIS
Plaça de la Vila de Madrid
→ (L2)

This Roman cemetery was in use in the 1st and 3rd centuries AD. A walkway above the site provides views of the different funerary monuments: altar stones, stelae and cupae which are particularly numerous. An interpretation centre displays the objects found on the site and explains the complex funerary world of Roman times.

PLA DE L'OS
→ (K2)

Also known as the Pla de la Boqueria, this section of La Rambla where it widens has a large pavement mosaic designed by Joan Miró in 1976.

PLAÇA DE LA MERCÈ
→ (L4)

This square with its neo-classical appearance, takes its name from the baroque-style basilica of La Mercè, with its dome surmounted by a statue of Our Lady of Mercy. The basilica was built in the 18th century although the original church, which once stood on this site, dated back to 1267. The Neptune fountain, which dates from 1826, stands in the middle of the square.

SANTA MARIA DEL PI AND PLAÇA DEL PI
→ (L2)

The Plaça del Pi which is presided over by the pine tree from which it takes its name ("pi" is the Catalan word for "pine"), together with the adjacent Plaça de Sant Josep Oriol, are two of the Gothic Quarter's most typical and lively places at any time of the day. The centrepiece of the square is the basilica of Santa Maria del Pi, one of the most representative examples of the Catalan Gothic style. Built between 1319 and 1391, it has a square façade flanked by two prismatic towers, with a giant rose window measuring 10 metres in diameter, which is big enough to rival the largest one in Europe at Notre-Dame in Paris.

Casa Bruno Cuadros **→ (K2)**

Carrer de Petritxol **→ (L2)**

Roman necropolis **→ (L2)**

Basilica of La Mercè **→ (L4)**

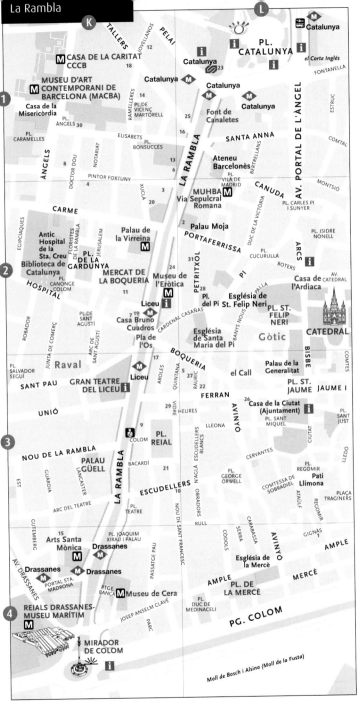

La Rambla (map)

K L

TALLERS PELAI
JOVELLANOS 12

M CASA DE LA CARITAT
CCCB 18

M MUSEU D'ART
CONTEMPORANI DE
BARCELONA (MACBA)

Casa de la
Misericòrdia

PL.
CARAMELLES

ÀNGELS

8

DOCTOR DOU

4

PINTOR FORTUNY

NOTARIAT

XUCLA

RAMELLERES 14
PL. DE
VICENÇ
MARTORELL

ELISABETS
PL.
BONSUCCÉS
13
6

PL.
ÀNGELS 30

3
20

M Catalunya

i Catalunya

PL.
CATALUNYA

i

M Catalunya

Font de
Canaletes

SANTA ANNA

Ateneu
Barcelonès

PL.
VILA DE
MADRID

MUHBA **M**
Via Sepulcral
Romana

CARME

EGIPCÍAQUES

Antic
Hospital
de la
Sta. Creu

Biblioteca de
Catalunya

HOSPITAL

PL.
CANONGE
COLOM

11

PL.
FLORISTES
DE LA RAMBLA

JERUSALEM

Palau de
la Virreina
M

PL.
DE LA
GARDUNYA

MERCAT DE
LA BOQUERIA

2 Palau Moja

PORTAFERRISSA

PETRITXOL

PI

PL.
CUCURULLA

BOTERS

24
310

28

M Catalunya

ARCS

i

el Corte Inglés

FONTANELLA

AV. PORTAL DE L'ÀNGEL

ESTRUC

COMTAL

MONTSIÓ

CANUDA

DUC DE LA VICTÒRIA

PL. CARLES PI
I SUNYER

PL. ISIDRE
NONELL

PALLA

Casa de
l'Ardiaca

AV.
CATEDRAL

Museu de
l'Eròtica
i

Liceu **M**

Casa Bruno
Cuadros

Pla de
l'Os

7 19

Església
de Santa
Maria del Pi

CARDENAL CASAÑAS

BANYS NOUS

Pl.
del Pi

Església de
St. Felip Neri

Gòtic

PL. ST.
FELIP
NERI

CATEDRAL

BISBE

COMTES

Raval

17

ROBADOR

JUNTA DE COMERÇ

ARC DE
SANT AGUSTÍ

PL. DE
SANT
AGUSTÍ

Liceu **M**

GRAN TEATRE
DEL LICEU **i**

BOQUERIA

AROLES

QUINTANA

27
22

RAURIC

el Call

VIDRE

FERRAN

26

HEURES

Casa de la Ciutat
(Ajuntament) **i**

PL. SANT
MIQUEL

Palau de la
Generalitat

PL. ST.
JAUME

JAUME I

SANT PAU

UNIÓ

GUARDIA

LANCASTER

NOU DE LA RAMBLA

PALAU
GÜELL

9

i
COLOM

PL.
REIAL

BACARDÍ

21

ESCUDELLERS

10

AVINYÓ

ESCUDELLERS
BLANCS

NAGLA

LLEONA

CERVANTES

PL.
GEORGE
ORWELL

OBRADORS

COMTESSA DE
SOBRADIEL

CIUTAT

PL.
SANT
JUST

LLEDÓ

PL.
REGOMIR

Pati
Llimona

ATAÜLF

PLAÇA
TRAGINERS

REGOMIR

EST

ARC DEL TEATRE

PL.
TEATRE

RULL

SERRA

CODOLS

CARABASSA

AVINYÓ

GIGNÀS

AMPLE

15
Arts Santa
Mònica
M

Drassanes

GUTEMBERG

AV DRASSANES

Drassanes **M**

Drassanes **M**

PORTAL STA.
MADRONA

PTGE
BANCA

M Museu de Cera

PL. JOAQUIM
XIRAU I PALAU

PASSATGE PAU

PL. DE SANT FRANCESC

Església de
la Mercè

AMPLE

PL. DE
LA MERCÈ

MERCÈ

REIALS DRASSANES-
MUSEU MARÍTIM
M

MIRADOR
DE COLOM

i

JOSEP ANSELM CLAVÉ

PL.
DUC DE
MEDINACELI

PG. COLOM

PARC

Moll de Bosch i Alsina (Moll de la Fusta)

Canaletes Fountain → **(L1)**

Santa Maria del Pi → **(L2)**

Pla de l'Os → **(K2)**

La Rambla

Highlights

GRAN TEATRE DEL LICEU
La Rambla, 51-59
➔ (K3)
T 93 485 99 00
www.liceubarcelona.cat
Barcelona's opera house has experienced many changes in fortune: memorable performances (featuring Montserrat Caballé, Josep Carreras and Jaume Aragall, to name just three), fights between Verdi supporters and Wagnerians, and two major fires. It was renovated and extended following the fire in 1994.

MERCAT DE SANT JOSEP "LA BOQUERIA"
Plaça de la Boqueria, s/n
➔ (K2)
T 93 318 25 84
www.boqueria.info
La Boqueria is Barcelona's best-stocked and most colourful food market. Under its shady metal structure, the stallholders sell an exquisite selection of fresh produce – meat, fish, fruit, vegetables – in a bustling, vibrant setting. +INFO: p. 108

PLAÇA REIAL
➔ (K3)
Barcelona's great porticoed square is made particularly outstanding by its rectilinear layout, tall palm trees, Gaudiesque street lamps and sunny terraces. It brings together bars, restaurants and music venues, hosting flamenco and jazz performances.

PALAU GÜELL
Nou de la Rambla, 3-5
➔ (K3)
T 93 472 57 75
www.palauguell.cat
This Gaudí landmark is defined by its majestic air which is expressed in its façade and large drawing room with its domed roof which lets in natural light. The rooftop contains 20 chimneys with cowls covered in multicoloured ceramics. +INFO: p. 108

Gran Teatre del Liceu ➔ (K3)

Mercat de "la Boqueria" ➔ (K2)

Plaça Reial ➔ (K3)

Palau Güell ➔ (K3)

El Raval

El Raval is a laboratory for the Barcelona of the future. For years, it was marked by neglect and the shabby Barrio Chino, but today it is a constantly evolving gateway to the city, the home to communities of different nationalities, and a place where culture, retail and leisure activities converge. The splendid Rambla del Raval now presides over the traditional heart of the neighbourhood.

Museums

MUSEU D'ART CONTEMPORANI DE BARCELONA (MACBA)
➔ (N2) +INFO: p. 110

CENTRE DE CULTURA CONTEMPORÀNIA DE BARCELONA (CCCB)
➔ (O1) +INFO: p. 36

Art galleries
Since the MACBA and the CCCB opened in this neighbourhood, countless galleries and designer shops have enriched a range of cultural attractions that barely existed a decade ago. Most of them are dedicated to new artistic trends and showcase avant-garde artists from around the world. Below is a short list of shops and galleries but we recommend you explore this vibrant Barcelona neighbourhood at a leisurely pace to soak up its unique atmosphere. La Capella [Hospital, 56 ➔ 1(N3)]; Àngels Barcelona [Pintor Fortuny, 27 ➔2(O2)]; Tinta Invisible [Lleó, 6 ➔3(N2)]; Antídoto 28 [Ferlandina, 53 ➔4(N2)]; EtHall [Joaquín Costa, 30 ➔5(N2)].

Restaurants

BAR CAÑETE
Unió, 17 ➔6(O3)
T 93 270 34 58
(€20-30) + SET LUNCH MENU
An informal eaterie, steeped in the Andalusian spirit and style, serving classic tapas and tasting platters with a contemporary twist.

BUTIPÀ
Ramelleres, 16 ➔7(O2)
T 93 205 30 01 (< €20)
The "fast food premium" Catalan sandwich is based on the classic combination of bread with botifarra sausage.

CA L'ISIDRE
Les Flors, 12 ➔8(M3)
T 93 441 11 39
(> €60)
A classic which is still up there with the greats. Market-fresh Catalan cuisine.

CAN LLUÍS
Cera, 49 ➔9(M2)
T 93 441 11 87
(€20-30) + SET LUNCH MENU
A Raval classic. Family atmosphere. Catalan home cooking.

CARMELITAS
Carme, 42 ➔10(O2)
T 93 461 59 11
(€20-30)
Chefs Xavier Pellicer and Rafael Vertamatti bring you their timeless bistrot where you can sample tapas, small tasting platters and typical Catalan dishes.

DOS PALILLOS
Elisabets, 9 ➔11(O2)
T 93 304 05 13
(€45-60) + TASTING MENU
Asian haute-cuisine tapas and excellent sakes, wines, beers and teas.

FLAX & KALE
Tallers, 74 ➔12(O1)
T 93 317 56 64 (€20-40)
Healthy flexitarian restaurant where gastronomic pleasure and nutritional value take pride of place.

FONDA ESPAÑA
Sant Pau, 9-11 ➔13(O3)
T 93 318 17 58
(€30-45) + SET LUNCH MENU
Catalan cuisine in a *modernista* dining room by Domènech i Montaner.

LA MONROE
Pl. Salvador Seguí, 1-9
➔ 14(N3)
T 93 441 94 61
(< €20) + SET LUNCH MENU
The Filmoteca bar is a true all-rounder: breakfasts, tapas, sandwiches, set menu, drinks at night.

LA TAVERNA DEL SUCULENT
Rambla del Raval, 39
➔ 15(N3)
T 93 329 97 07
(< €20)
Small old-style tavern where you can sit at the bar and sample tapas and tasting platters from the south of Spain.

ÒSTIES PEDRÍN
Jerusalem, 30
➔ 16(O2)
T 93 277 82 08
(€20-30) + SET LUNCH MENU
Traditional cuisine focusing on Barcelona's most typical dishes. Locally sourced, seasonal produce.

PAELLA BAR BOQUERIA
Mercat de la Boqueria
→ 17(O3)
T 93 348 77 83
(€30-40)
Located under the arcades inside the market, this restaurant specialises in rice dishes, fish and seafood.

SUCULENT
Rambla del Raval, 43
→18(N3)
T 93 443 65 79 (€20-40)
Tapas and signature tasting platters made with top-quality, market-fresh produce. Outdoor terrace.

YANGO URBAN FOOD
Mercat de la Boqueria
→ 19(O3)
(< €20) + SET LUNCH MENU
Chef Carles Abellán presents his urban food sandwich bar: Catalan sausage sandwiches seasoned with exotic ingredients.

Cafés and bars
ALMIRALL
Joaquín Costa, 33 **→20(N2)**
A bar founded more than 150 years ago and with *modernista*-style décor.

BAR MARSELLA
Sant Pau, 65 **→21(N3)**
Since the late 19th century this bar has been a refuge for artists and bohemians. In addition to its interior décor, the Marsella is also renowned for serving absinthe.

LA CONFITERIA
Sant Pau, 128 **→ 22(M3)**
Former confectioner's shop with *modernista* décor dating back to 1912. A fine selection of cheeses and cured meats to accompany beer, wine, coffee or tea.

LONDON BAR
Nou de la Rambla, 34
→23(N3)
A Barcelona classic which has been a favourite haunt of artists since it opened in 1910. Picasso and Dalí once frequented its tables. It retains its *modernista* décor and hosts live music events.

Fonda España **→13(O3)**

Antic Hospital de la Santa Creu **→(N2)**

Museu d'Art Contemporani de Barcelona **→(N2)**

London Bar **→23(N3)**

Shopping

B.HUNO
Elisabets, 18 ➜ **25(02)**
Original, exclusive clothes by cutting-edge Spanish designers.

BARCELONAREYKJAVÍK
Doctor Dou, 12 ➜ **26(02)**
Catalan-Icelandic bakery which is a pioneer in making bread with 100% natural ingredients. You'll also find buns, *coca* flatbreads and other delicacies.

CASA PARRAMON
Carme, 8 ➜ **27(02)**
Luthiers since 1897. Stringed instruments, accessories and repairs.

FUTBOLMANIA
Ronda de Sant Pau, 25 ➜ **28(M3)**
Merchandising from all the Spanish and European squads.

HOLALA!
Valldonzella, 4 ➜ **29(01)**
Vintage and second-hand clothes, furniture, accessories, books and magazines.

HOME ON EARTH
Hospital, 76 ➜ **30(N2)**
Scandinavian-designed homeware. One-off signature pieces with multi-ethnic influences made from natural and recycled materials.

LA CENTRAL DEL RAVAL
Elisabets, 6 ➜ **31(02)**
Bookshop housed in a former church.

LA PORTORRIQUEÑA
Xuclà, 25 ➜ **32(02)**
Emporium founded over a hundred years ago that roasts and sells coffee from every corner of the world. It also has a wide variety of teas.

LA VARIÉTÉ
Pintor Fortuny, 30 ➜ **33(02)**
Decorative objects and accessories by local designers.

PMED WINDS
Elisabeths, 7 ➜ **34(02)**
Clothing and accessory brand born in the Raval which stays true to a Mediterranean style made with natural fabrics.

OLEOTECA GOURMET LA CHINATA BCN
Àngels, 20 ➜ **35(02)**
Extra-virgin olive oil and related products, gourmet produce and cosmetics.

ASTISSERIA LIS
Riera Alta, 19 ➜ **36(N2)**
High-quality traditional cakes and confectionery. The sugar-coated, custard-filled doughnuts, known as *xuixos*, are excellent.

SASTRERIA EL TRANSWAAL
Hospital, 67 ➜ **37(N3)**
El Transwaal has been selling workwear and uniforms for every sector since 1888.

And also

ANTIC HOSPITAL DE LA SANTA CREU
Hospital, 56 ➜ **(N2)**
Founded in 1401, it is a superb example of civic Gothic and baroque architecture. Originally a poor hospital, today its different rooms are home to the library, the Biblioteca Nacional de Catalunya, the Escola Massana, and the Institut d'Estudis Catalans. Don't miss out on its gardens which will take you back to medieval times.

TEATRE LLANTIOL
Riereta, 7 ➜ **38(N2)**
T 93 329 90 09
www.llantiol.com
Charming café-theatre with old-fashioned décor and unmistakeable character.

Rambla del Raval ➜ **(N3)**

Cat. Rambla del Raval ➜ **(N3)**

La Confitería ➜ **22(M3)**

Bar Cañete ➜ **6(03)**

Plaça Vicenç Martorell →(02)

Casa Almirall → 20(N2)

La Central del Raval →31(02)

Dos Palillos →11(02)

Highlights

MACBA
Plaça dels Àngels, 1
→ (N2)
T 93 412 08 10
www.macba.cat
The Museu d'Art Contemporani de Barcelona, one of the world's foremost art museums, is housed in a light, airy building designed by Richard Meier, and hosts a wide variety of exhibitions and artistic, academic and recreational events.
+INFO: p. 110

MACBA → (N2)

CCCB
Montalegre, 5
→ (01)
T 93 306 41 00
www.cccb.org
The Centre de Cultura Contemporània de Barcelona is an innovative cultural attraction which organises and produces exhibitions, debates, festivals, concerts, and film seasons on urban themes and public space. It is housed in the former workhouse, the Casa de la Caritat, and following its refurbishment won a much-deserved FAD architecture prize.

CCCB → (01)

BIBLIOTECA DE CATALUNYA
Hospital, 56
→ (N2)
T 93 270 23 00
www.bnc.cat
Founded at the beginning of the 20th century and housed in the imposing Gothic building of the old Hospital de la Santa Creu since 1940. The Biblioteca de Catalunya contains over three million documents and in 1998 underwent a major extension during which new buildings were added.

Biblioteca de Catalunya → (N2)

SANT PAU DEL CAMP
Sant Pau, 101-103
→ (N3)
The earliest records of this Romanesque monastery date from the 10th century. The church, cloister, chapterhouse and abbot's residence were built between the 12th and 14th centuries, and painstakingly restored in the 20th century.

Sant Pau del Camp → (N3)

Ciutat Vella

Port Vell and Barceloneta

Barcelona's old harbour, the Port Vell, has berths for yachts, areas with shops, offices and leisure amenities, services for boats, and quays used by the fishing fleet. Barceloneta was built in the 18th century between the harbour and the beach and consists of rectangular blocks. You can still feel the Mediterranean atmosphere you would expect to find in a fishing community.

Maremagnum
→ (Q2)
www.maremagnum.es
A shopping complex which boasts a superb seafront setting. Open seven days a week and on public holidays, except 25th December and 1st January. A one-stop destination for fashion boutiques and shoe shops; bars and restaurants; leisure attractions; perfumeries and hairdressers; jewellery and accessories; shops selling coffee, sweets, and chocolates; ice cream parlours; phone, photography and computer shops; toys; homewares and souvenirs. Opening times: shops, 10am-10pm; restaurants, until 1am.

ELX RESTAURANT
Moll d'Espanya, s/n, local 9
→ 1(Q2)
T 93 225 81 17
(€20-40)
Specialises in rice dishes from Alicante, such as rice with a crunchy topping, black rice, rice broth and the paella with ready-peeled seafood.

TAPA TAPA
Moll d'Espanya, s/n, local 10 → 2(Q2)
T 93 225 86 97
(< €20)
Traditional tapas and salads, including pasta and king prawn.

Museums
MUSEU D'HISTÒRIA DE CATALUNYA - MHC
Plaça de Pau Vila, 3 → (R2)
T 93 225 47 00
www.mhcat.cat
Since 1996, the former harbour warehouses have been home to the Museu d'Història de Catalunya, which aims to bring Catalan history to a wider audience, placing special emphasis on national identity. It spans the Palaeolithic period almost to the present day. +INFO: p. 111

L'AQUÀRIUM
Moll d'Espanya, s/n → (Q2)
www.aquariumbcn.com
This is the foremost leisure and educational marine centre in the world with a Mediterranean theme. It has 35 aquariums with 11,000 examples of 450 different species and a huge Oceanarium with an 80-metre-long underwater tunnel. +INFO: p. 111

Restaurants
In this area you'll find typical seafood cuisine featuring a wide variety of rice, fish and shellfish dishes.

7 PORTES
Pg. Isabel II, 14 → 3(R1)
T 93 319 30 33
(€30-50) + GROUP MENU
Since 1836. It is more than a BCN legend. Specialises in paellas and other typical dishes. From 1pm to 1am.

AGUA
Passeig Marítim de la Barceloneta, 30 → 4(S2)
T 93 225 12 72
(€30-40)
Mediterranean cuisine right on the beach. Good value for money.

MARÍTIM
Moll d'Espanya, 4 → 5(Q2)
T 93 221 17 75
(€30-40)
Superb seafood cuisine at this time-honoured club.

PEZ VELA
Pg. del Mare Nostrum, 19-21 → 6(P4)
T 93 221 63 17
(€30-40)
A new concept of *chiringuito* snack bar right on the seafront specialising in salads and rice dishes.

RESTAURANTE GALLITO
Pg. del Mare Nostrum, 19-21 → 7(P4)
T 93 312 35 85
(€30-40)
Home cooking with influences from around the world.

SAGÀS PAGESOS, CUINERS & CO
Pla de Palau, 13 → 8(R1)
T 93 330 03 03
(€20-30)
Catalan and international cuisine with the focus on gourmet sandwiches and salads made from locally

sourced, artisan produce.

SAL CAFÉ
Passeig Marítim de la
Barceloneta, 23 → 9(S2)
T 93 224 07 07
(€20-30) + SET LUNCH MENU
Modern beachfront restaurant. Contemporary fusion
dishes.

TORRE D'ALTA MAR
Passeig Joan de Borbó, 88
→ 10(Q3)
T 93 221 00 07
(> €60)
Located at the top of the
cross-harbour cable car
tower, the Torre de Sant
Sebastià (1931), 75 metres
above the city, and with a
cutting-edge interior.

Palau de Mar Area:
This 19th century former
harbour warehouse was
refurbished in 1992 and is
home to restaurants specialising in rice and fish dishes.

CAL PINXO
Pl. de Pau Vila, 1 → 11(R1)
T 93 221 22 11
(€40-60)
Seafood cuisine based on
rice and fish dishes.

EL MAGATZEM DEL PORT
Pl. Pau Vila, 1 → 12(R1)
T 93 221 06 31
(€20-40)
Simple, quality cuisine made
with the finest produce from
the Boqueria Market.

LA GAVINA
Pl. Pau Vila, 1 → 13(R1)
T 93 221 05 95
(€40-60)
Seafood dishes and Mediterranean cuisine. Large
terrace overlooking the sea.

MERENDERO DE LA MARI
Pl. Pau Vila, 1 → 14(R1)
T 93 221 31 41
(€20-40)
A classic in the old harbour
with wonderful views.
Specialises in fish, shellfish
and rice dishes.

Barceloneta Area:
Home to the city's classic
seafood restaurants, some
of them with a culinary
tradition dating back more
than 100 years.

CAN COSTA
Passeig Joan de Borbó, 70
→ 15(Q3)

T 93 221 59 03
(€20-40)
Authentic Catalan seafood
cuisine in one of the city's
historic restaurants.

CAN MAJÓ
Almirall Aixada, 23
→ 16(R3)
T 93 221 54 55
(€20-40)
Market-fresh cuisine. Specialises in seafood and rice
dishes.

CAN RAMONET
Maquinista, 17 → 17(R2)
T 93 319 30 64
(€40-60)
One of the best paellas in
the city. A Barcelona classic
of many years' standing.

CAN SOLÉ
Sant Carles, 4 → 18(R2)
T 93 221 50 12
(€20-40)
A century-old classic
specialising in seafood,
Catalan and market-fresh
cuisine.

CHERIFF
Ginebra, 15 → 19(R2)
T 93 319 69 84
(€30-50)
Typical Spanish shellfish
restaurant. Excellent rice
dishes and paellas.

KAIKU
Plaça del Mar, 1 → 20(Q3)
T 93 221 90 82
(< €20) + SET LUNCH MENU
Seafood and Mediterranean cuisine right by the
sea. It has its own eco-
allotment.

L'ARRÒS
Passeig Joan de Borbó, 12
→ 21(R2)
T 93 221 26 46
(€40-60)
Wide selection of rice dishes. Home-made desserts.

LA BARRACA
Passeig Marítim de la
Barceloneta, 1 → 22(R3)
T 93 330 36 62
(€20-40)
Chef Xavier Pellicer's
latest culinary project
specialising in rice dishes
and Mediterranean tapas.

SUQUET DE L'ALMIRALL
Passeig Joan de Borbó, 65
→ 23(R3)
T 93 221 62 33

L'Aquàrium → (Q2)

Wounded Star. R. Horn → (R3)

Las Golondrinas → (P2)

Clock Tower → (Q2)

(€40-60)
Seafood recipes made with the freshest, organic produce of the finest quality.

SOMORROSTRO
Sant Carles, 11 →**24(R2)**
T 93 225 00 10
(< €20)
Signature Mediterranean cuisine from chef Andrés Gaspar.

Cafés and bars

EL VASO DE ORO
Balboa, 6 →**25(R1)**
Historic beer house. Small bar serving excellent tapas.

JAI-CA
Ginebra, 13 →**26(R2)**
T 93 319 50 02
Another classic. Typical, tasty tapas.

LA BOMBETA
La Maquinista, 3 →**27(R2)**
Tapas bar which is a neighbourhood classic. Delicious, spicy *bombes* (mince and potato balls in breadcrumbs with hot sauce).

LA COVA FUMADA
Baluard, 56 →**28(R2)**
A neighbourhood classic. They invented the *bomba* (a large meat and potato croquette served with a spicy sauce), and serve up the freshest prawns and other mouthwatering tapas.

MUSEU D'HISTÒRIA DE CATALUNYA TERRACE
Pl. de Pau Vila, 3 →**29(R1)**
Bar and café with splendid panoramic views of the harbour.

Shopping

ANTONY MORATO
Moll d'Espanya, (Maremagnum) →**30(Q2)**
Italian menswear and accessories brand for the young, urban male.

FORN BALUARD
Baluard, 38-40 →**31(R2)**
An artisan baker's producing bread that tastes like it did in the old days.

ROXY
Plaça del Mar 1-4 →**33(Q3)**
Sportswear for men, women and children plus surfing and snowboarding accessories.

TUSET & RIERA
Moll d'Espanya, (Maremagnum) →**34(Q2)**
Bags and accessories. Contemporary urban designs and a range of sports bags.

VINOTECA VORAMAR
La Maquinista, 14 →**35(R2)**
Shop selling wines and cavas. The best brands.

And also

BARCELONA HEAD
Moll de la Fusta →**(Q1)**
Large sculpture by Roy Lichtenstein that pays homage to Barcelona.

THE WOUNDED SHOOTING STAR
Platja de la Barceloneta →**(R3)**
Four iron and glass cubes stacked on top of each other to form this sculpture by Rebecca Horn.

LAS GOLONDRINAS
Portal de la Pau, s/n →**(P2)**
T 93 442 31 06
www.lasgolondrinas.com
Las Golondrinas, the pleasure boats that have been in service since 1888, berth at the foot of the Columbus Monument. They offer harbour rides and cruises along the coastline as far as the Fòrum.

CLOCK TOWER
Moll de Pescadors →**(Q2)**
BCN's old lighthouse. It takes its name from the four-faced clock that was fitted in the 18th century.

WORLD TRADE CENTER BARCELONA
Moll de Barcelona →**(P3)**
Business centre next to the Mediterranean and a member of the WTCA. Convention centre (430-seater auditorium), offices, retail area and 5-star hotel.

RAMBLA DE MAR
Porta de la Pau, s/n →**(P2)**
This wavy walkway stretches from the end of La Rambla over the waters of the harbour as far as the leisure and shopping complex, Maremagnum, with its shops, bars and restaurants, and L'Aquàrium.

Rambla de Mar →**(P2)**

World Trade Center →**(P3)**

Marenostrum Tower →**(S2)**

Torre de Jaume I →**(P2)**

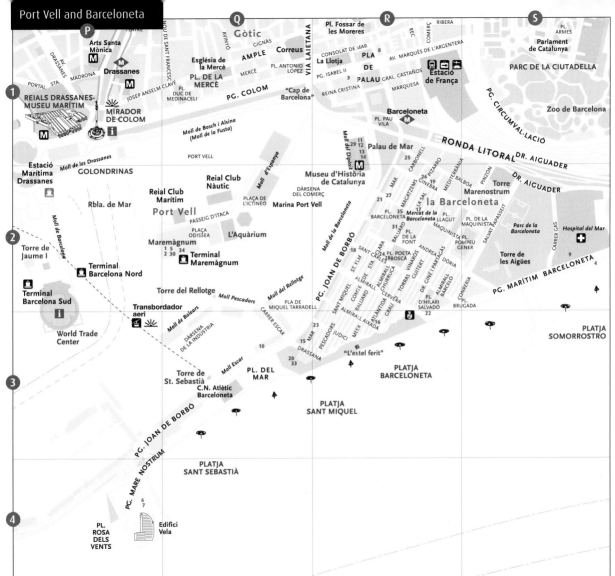

Q Gòtic

R

S

Pl. Fossar de les Moreres

Pl. ARMES

Parlament de Catalunya

PARC DE LA CIUTADELLA

P

Arts Santa Mònica **M**

Església de la Mercè

AMPLE Correus

GIGNAS

CONSOLAT DE MAR

La Llotja

RIBERA

COMERÇ

Av. MARQUÉS DE L'ARGENTERA

Drassanes **M**

JOSEP ANSELM CLAVÉ

PL. DE LA MERCÈ

MERCÈ

PL. ANTONIO LÓPEZ

PG. ISABEL II

PLA DE PALAU

GRAL. CASTAÑOS

MARQUESA

Estació de França

1

REIALS DRASSANES-MUSEU MARÍTIM **M**

PL. DUC DE MEDINACELI

PG. COLOM

"Cap de Barcelona"

REINA CRISTINA

Zoo de Barcelona

PG. CIRCUMVAL·LACIÓ

MIRADOR DE COLOM

Moll de Bosch i Alsina (Moll de la Fusta)

Barceloneta

PL. PAU VILA **M**

RONDA LITORAL

DR. AIGUADER

Estació Marítima Drassanes

Moll de les Drassanes

GOLONDRINAS

PORT VELL

Moll d'Espanya

11
29
13
14

Palau de Mar

Museu d'Història de Catalunya

Moll del Dipòsit

CARBONELL

PIZARRO

25

MAR

CARBONELL

MEDITERRANIA

BALBOA

PINZON

DR. AIGUADER

Torre Marenostrum

Rbla. de Mar

Reial Club Marítim

Reial Club Nàutic

PLAÇA DE L'ICTINEO

DÀRSENA DEL COMERÇ

Marina Port Vell

26

19

la Barceloneta

31

35

17

Mercat de la Barceloneta

PL. DE LA MAQUINISTA

Parc de la Barceloneta

Hospital del Mar

Torre de Jaume I

Port Vell

PASSEIG D'ITACA

PLAÇA ODISSEA

L'Aquàrium

27

21

GINEBRA

MAGATZEMS

SAL

VINAROS

BARCELONETA

PL. DE LA FONT

LLAGUT

MAQUINISTA

PL. POMPEU GENER

Torre de les Aigües

2

Terminal Barcelona Nord

Maremàgnum

1 5
2 30
34

Terminal Maremàgnum

18

PL. POETA BOSCA

CONRERIA

PG. MARÍTIM BARCELONETA

Terminal Barcelona Sud

Moll de Barcelona

Torre del Rellotge

Moll Pescadors

PLA DE MIQUEL TARRADELL

ST. ELM

STA. CLARA

STA. CARLES

ANDREA DÒRIA

28

TORRAS

GUITERT

DR. GINÉ I PARTAGÀS

SALVADO

BRUGADA

World Trade Center

Transbordador aeri

Moll de Balears

DÀRSENA DE LA INDÚSTRIA

Moll del Rellotge

CARRER ESCAR

PESCADORS

JUDICI

SANT MIQUEL

COMTE

BALUARD

ALMIRALL

CERVERA

ATLÀNTIDA

GRAU

D'HILARI

ALMIRALL BARCELÓ

22

PLATJA SOMORROSTRO

Moll Escar

23

DRASSANA

MAR

Torre de St. Sebastià

PL. DEL MAR

10

15
33

20
33

"L'estel ferit"

"L'estel ferit"

PLATJA BARCELONETA

3

C.N. Atlètic Barceloneta

PLATJA SANT MIQUEL

PG. JOAN DE BORBÓ

PLATJA SANT SEBASTIÀ

PG. MARE NOSTRUM

6
7

4

PL. ROSA DELS VENTS

Edifici Vela

JAUME I TOWER
Moll de Barcelona, s/n
→ (P2)
Designed by Carles Buïgas and built in 1931, the Jaume I Tower is the second highest cable-car tower in the world, standing a good 100 metres above the ground. It boasts breathtaking views of the waters in the harbour below.

MARENOSTRUM TOWER
Passeig Marítim de la Barceloneta, 15
→ (S2)
The surprising volumes of the Marenostrum Tower, the headquarters of the gas company, Gas Natural, combine the vertical lines of a skyscraper with an imposing horizontal canopy. The glass-clad building, which reflects the sky and cityscape, was designed by Miralles/Tagliabue.

La Barceloneta

Highlights

MIRADOR DE COLOM
Pl. del Portal de la Pau → **(P1)**
T 93 302 52 24
visitbarcelona.com
The statue of Christopher Columbus presides over Barcelona harbour from the top of his column, 60 metres above the ground. At the same time, he encapsulates the city's seafaring tradition and the debt of gratitude it owes the sea, which witnessed the arrival of some of its founders and saw its explorers depart in search of new lands. A viewing gallery at the top of the tower boasts spectacular views of this meeting point. It also has a wine tourism centre.

REIALS DRASSANES - MUSEU MARÍTIM
Av. Drassanes, s/n → **(P1)**
T 93 342 99 20
www.mmb.cat
Barcelona's medieval shipyards (Reials Drassanes), which date from the 14th century, are worth visiting for two reasons. The first is the building, comprising a series of stone naves which are one of the finest and best-preserved examples of civic Gothic architecture. The second is the Museu Marítim, which brings together a wonderful collection of nautical equipment and ships. These include a replica of the galley used by Juan of Austria. +INFO: P. 112

BARCELONETA BEACHES
→ **(R3)**
www.bcn.cat/platges
Barceloneta is Barcelona's old fishing quarter. A popular place with a warren of narrow streets around its main food market, which has undergone a state-of-the-art refit, and large central square. Barceloneta's four beaches are its main attraction. They occupy a strip of sand stretching from the breakwater to the Olympic Village. They are packed with bathers in summer but remain popular all year round.

Mirador de Colom → **(P1)**

Museu Marítim → **(P1)**

Barceloneta beach → **(R3)**

The "Quadrat d'Or"

L'Eixample
+ Gaudí Trail (1)

The Eixample is Barcelona's central area. With its rationalist grid layout, designed by Ildefons Cerdà in the middle of the 19th century, and leafy, light-dappled avenues, which abound in *modernista* architectural gems, the Eixample defines Barcelona's personality: an enterprising, cultural, trading city which is now one of the world's benchmark destinations. A large area of the district is known as *El Quadrat d'Or* – The Golden Square – because of its dazzling array of *modernista* architecture. This is where Gaudí, Domènech i Montaner, Puig i Cadafalch and the other greats of Catalonia's home-grown art nouveau left their legacy in the form of buildings that retain their original splendour although they are now used for different purposes.

Must-sees
✳

BASILICA OF THE SAGRADA FAMÍLIA

Mallorca, 401 | T 93 207 30 31 | www.sagradafamilia.cat
→ **(D1)**
Gaudí devoted the last 40 years of his life to this immense, cathedral-like building. It is characterised by its eight tapering towers, surmounted by vividly coloured ceramic pinnacles. Each tower is 100 metres high but will be dwarfed by the future dome, which will stand 170 metres when completed. The church, which was begun in 1882 and is scheduled for completion in 2025, is one of Barcelona's most visited landmarks. +INFO: p. 113

LA PEDRERA (CASA MILÀ)

Passeig de Gràcia, 92 | T 902 202 138 | www.lapedrera.com
→ **(A1)**
La Casa Milà – dubbed by locals as La Pedrera, Catalan for stone quarry – has an outstanding undulating façade which evokes incredible stone waves. Originally designed as a residential block, today part of the building is a cultural centre. The Espai Gaudí, in the attic space, traces the architect's research and secrets. The restored flats display the wide range of plaster mouldings, carpentry and ironwork. But the main surprise awaits on the roof: a forest of sculptural chimneys. +INFO: p. 115

CASA BATLLÓ
Passeig de Gràcia, 43 | T 93 216 03 06 | www.casabatllo.cat
→ **(A2)**
Gaudí carried out a brilliant exercise in restyling in the Casa Batlló in 1904. He added an extra storey and an attic space to the existing building and radically changed its inner and outer appearance. This change in direction means that the Casa Batlló and Park Güell are considered his first works to throw off completely the influences of historic styles – Gothic, Mudejar, Baroque... – and where he began to apply his own artistic convictions, based on the shapes he observed in nature, in all their purity. +INFO: p. 117

Basílica of the Sagrada Família ➜ **(D1)**

La Pedrera ➜ **(A1)**

Casa Batlló ➜ **(A2)**

Dreta de l'Eixample
Sagrada Família and Fort Pienc

The Dreta de l'Eixample (the right side of the Eixample) stretches from Carrer Balmes to Passeig de Sant Joan and was the favourite place for Barcelona's bourgeoisie to build their homes in the late 19th century and show off their growing economic power. They made this district an open-air museum showcasing the finest art-nouveau architecture in Europe. Beyond Passeig de Sant Joan, two neighbourhoods have grown up around iconic buildings: the Sagrada Família, around Gaudí's basilica, and Fort Pienc, around the former railway station, the Estació del Nord (1861-1910).

BARCELONA WALKING TOURS
Modernisme
Two-hour walking tour led by professional guides exploring the *Quadrat d'Or*, the centre of *modernista* Barcelona: a true open-air museum. Landmarks include works by **Gaudí** (Casa Milà, Casa Batlló), **Domènech i Montaner** (Palau de la Música Catalana, Casa Lleó Morera, Fundació Tàpies) and **Puig i Cadafalch** (Casa Amatller). Price: adults, €16; children aged 0 to 12, free. Times: 1st April to 31st October, Wednesday, 10.30am (French), Friday, 6pm (English) and Sunday at noon (Catalan and Spanish); 1st November to 31st March, Wednesday and Friday, 3.30pm (English). Departs from the Turisme de Barcelona Information Office (Pl. de Catalunya, 17-S).

Gaudí Trail (1)
Includes tours of three major landmarks by this architectural genius, all of them World Heritage Sites. They are icons of art rather than buildings and they are all open to visitors.

They include Casa Batlló (Passeig de Gràcia, 43; www.casabatllo.cat), the Casa Milà "La Pedrera" (Passeig de Gràcia, 92; www.lapedrera.com) and Sagrada Família (Mallorca, 401; www.sagradafamilia.cat). Download the audio guide Gaudí's Barcelona onto your MP3 player (tickets.visitbarcelona.com) and from the Apple Store (http://apps.barcelonaturisme.com).

Art galleries
The Eixample is home to most of the city's art galleries. For full details visit www.circuitartcontemporani.cat and www.galeriescatalunya.com

Museums

FUNDACIÓ ANTONI TÀPIES
→(A2)
+INFO: p. 119

FUNDACIÓN ALORDA-DERKSEN
Aragó, 314 →(B2)
www.fundacionad.com
Private collection of the latest in contemporary art.

Visits by prior arrangement only.

FUNDACIÓN MAPFRE CASA GARRIGA NOGUÉS
Diputació, 250
→(A2)
www.fundacionmapfre.org
Housed in the Casa Garriga Nogués (1902-1904), a building designed by Enric Sagnier, it hosts world-class exhibitions devoted to the start of the modern movement in the world of the visual arts.

MUSEU DEL MODERNISME DE BARCELONA
Balmes, 48
→(A2)
www.mmbcn.cat
Modernista objects, paintings and sculptures.

MUSEU EGIPCI
València, 284
→(A1)
T 93 488 01 88
www.museuegipci.com
The Fundació Arqueològica Clos showcases one of Europe's most important private collections of Ancient Egyptian antiquities. The collection comprises more than one thousand exhibits, including sarcophagi, mummies and jewellery.

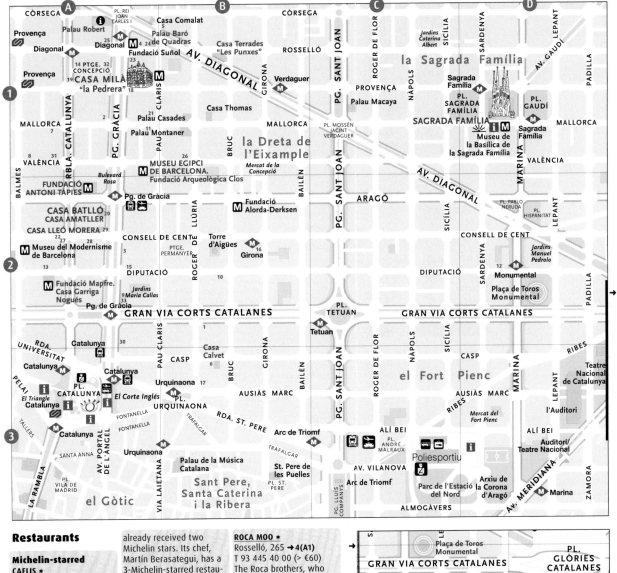

Restaurants

Michelin-starred

CAELIS ∗
Gran Via, 668 →1(B2)
T 93 510 12 05 (> €60)
At the Hotel El Palace, the chef Romain Fornell serves his innovative and delicious Mediterranean cuisine at this luxury restaurant.

LASARTE ∗∗
Mallorca, 259 →2(A1)
T 93 445 32 42 (> €60)
Open since 2006, it has already received two Michelin stars. Its chef, Martín Berasategui, has a 3-Michelin-starred restaurant in Guipúzkoa (Basque Country).

MOMENTS ∗∗
Passeig de Gràcia, 38 →3(A2)
T 93 151 87 81 (> €60)
Traditional yet modern Catalan cuisine by Carme Ruscalleda (7 Michelin stars) and her son Raül Balam.

ROCA MOO ∗
Rosselló, 265 →4(A1)
T 93 445 40 00 (> €60)
The Roca brothers, who have a 3-starred Michelin restaurant in Girona, develop their vision of Catalan haute cuisine.

BAR MUT
Pau Claris, 192 →5(B1)
T 93 217 43 38 (€20-40)
Bar specialising in gourmet tinned conserves and warm tapas.

→ +INFO: p. 70 (Plaça de les Glòries Catalanes)

Highlights

CASA AMATLLER
Passeig de Gràcia, 41
→ (A2)
T 93 487 72 17
www.amatller.org
The Casa Amatller, designed by Puig i Cadafalch, dates from the late 19th century. Its façade is a combination of Gothic-inspired windows with a profusion of ceramic details and a stepped cornice reminiscent of Dutch architecture.

Casa Amatller → (A2)

CASA LLEÓ I MORERA
Passeig de Gràcia, 35
→ (A2)
T 93 676 27 33
www.casalleomorera.com
Designed by Lluís Domènech i Montaner and built between 1902 and 1906. This is one of the key Catalan art nouveau landmarks with magnificent works by sculptors, mosaicists, stained-glass artists and other craftsmen.
+INFO: p. 118

Casa Lleó i Morera → (A2)

CASA TERRADES - CASA DE LES PUNXES
Avinguda Diagonal, 416
→ (B1)
Designed by Josep Puig i Cadafalch and dating from 1905. It has a peculiar structure resembling a castle as a result of the four rounded turrets with their pointed, conical roofs, from which it takes its nickname "les punxes" ("spikes" in Catalan). It has been home to the Museu Puig i Cadafalch since 2016.

Casa de les Punxes → (B1)

FUNDACIÓ ANTONI TÀPIES
Aragó, 255 → (A2)
T 93 487 03 15
www.fundaciotapies.org
Housed in a brick and metal *modernista* building, the Fundació Antoni Tàpies showcases the finest collection of works produced by the Barcelona-born artist, including paintings, sculptures, drawings and prints. The building is surmounted by his sculpture *Cloud and Chair*.
+INFO: p. 119

Fundació Antoni Tàpies → (A2)

CASA CALVET
Casp, 48 → 6(B3)
T 93 412 40 12
(> €50) + SET LUNCH MENU
In a house by Gaudí, exquisite Catalan cuisine.

CERVECERÍA CATALANA
Mallorca, 236 → 7(A1)
T 93 216 03 68
(< €20)
Long bars serving hot and cold tapas and canapés all day.

CORNELIA & CO
València, 225 → 8(A1)
T 93 330 03 03
(€30-50)
Delicious Mediterranean cuisine made with market-fresh ingredients.

EL NACIONAL
Pg. de Gràcia, 24 → 9(A2)
T 93 518 50 53
(€20-60) + SET LUNCH MENU
Multi-zone gastronomic space where you can enjoy traditional recipes from across the Iberian Peninsula.

LOIDI
Mallorca, 248 → 11(A1)
T 93 492 92 92
(€40-50) + TASTING MENU
Traditional Basque cuisine reinvented with the flavours of Martín Berasategui.

MANAIRÓ
Diputació, 424 → 12(D2)
T 93 231 00 57
(> €60)
Creative Catalan cuisine with signature dishes by chef Jordi Herrera.

MONVÍNIC
Diputació, 249 → 13(A2)
T 93 272 61 87
(> €60)
Perhaps the best wine bar in the world with a dining area run by the chef Guillem Oliva.

PETIT COMITÈ
DE NANDU JUBANY
Passatge de la Concepció, 13
→ 14(A1)
T 93 550 06 20
(> €60)
With one Michelin star under his belt, Nandu Jubany serves up the finest traditional Catalan cuisine.

TAPAS 24
Diputació, 269 → 15(A2)
T 93 488 09 77
(€20-30)

Small servings and traditional tapas from Carles Abellán, who earned a Michelin star at his restaurant Comerç 24.

Cafés and bars
CAFÉ DEL CENTRE 1873
Girona, 69 → 16(B2)
Café dating back more than 100 years which continues to serve breakfast, lunch and dinner with that time-honoured flavour.

CASA ALFONSO
Roger de Llúria, 6 → 17(B3)
Since 1934, an iconic tapas and sandwich bar.

EL CAFÉ DE LA PEDRERA
Pg. de Gràcia, 92 → 18(A1)
There's nowhere like it to have a coffee, lunch or dinner.

MAURI
Rambla de Catalunya, 102
→ 19(A1)
Excellent cake shop with a popular tea room.

Shopping
Passeig de Gràcia and its neighbouring streets are a showcase for Barcelona's top fashion brands (Furest, Antonio Miró, Loewe, Camper, Mango, Bel, Sita Murt...) and the world's leading designers (Chanel, Louis Vuitton, Liu Jo, Valentino, Dolce & Gabbana, Miu Miu, Stella McCartney, Furla, Michael Kors...).

Shopping centres
BULEVARD ROSA → (A2)
EL CORTE INGLÉS → (A3)
EL TRIANGLE → (A3)
+INFO: p. 148

Passeig de Gràcia

BAGUÉS-MASRIERA
Pg. de Gràcia, 41
→ 20(A2)
Founded in 1839. Exclusive art-nouveau and art-deco jewellery.

BERIESTAIN INTERIORES
Pau Claris, 159
→ 21(A1)
Vintage furniture, books, textiles, fragrances, objets d'art and a pleasant café.

CACAO SAMPAKA
Consell de Cent, 292
→ 22(A2)
Chocolate made using artisan methods from specially selected cocoa. There is a small area at the back where you can sample the produce and have something to drink.

CAMPER
Passeig de Gràcia, 100
→ 23(A2)
The most functional, comfortable and colourful shoe designs, made in Mallorca.

DOS I UNA
Rosselló, 275 → 24(A1)
For more than 40 years, designer gifts Made in Barcelona for adults and kids.

IMAGINARIUM
Pg. de Gràcia, 103
→ 25(A1)
Beautiful toys designed to foster children's development and social values.

J. MÚRRIA
Roger de Llúria,85 → 26(B1)
A *modernista* delicatessen (1898). Purveyors of fine foods and wines.

KONEMA
Rambla de Catalunya, 43
→ 27(A2)
Cutting-edge shop with a

wide range of gifts and fine stationery.

LA CUINA D'EN GARRIGA
Consell de Cent, 308
→ 28(A2)
Exquisite gourmet grocery with a small area for sampling the produce.

LOEWE
Pg. de Gràcia, 35
→ 29(A2)
Synonymous with classic elegance. Their handbags and briefcases are iconic items.

MANGO
Pg. de Gràcia, 8
→ 30(A2)
Latest trends in fashion for the urban woman.

NICE THINGS
València, 235 → 31(A1)
Comfortable, original and colourful retro fashion for women of all ages.

SANTA EULALIA
Pg. de Gràcia, 93 → 32(A1)
Since 1843. An exquisite selection of luxury fashions for men and women.

TOUS
Pg. de Gràcia, 18
→ 33(A2)
Family-run jewellers. Internationally renowned since 1985 when it launched its famous teddy bear.

And also

CASA CALVET
Carrer de Casp, 48 → (B3)
Gaudí's first residential building (1898-1900) in which he recreated the Catalan baroque style, particularly on the balcony. There is a restaurant on the ground floor which preserves much of the original furniture designed by the architect.

PALAU BARÓ DE QUADRAS
Avinguda Diagonal, 373
→ (B1)
This *modernista* mansion with its two distinct façades was designed by the architect Puig i Cadafalch and built between 1904 and 1906. It is currently the headquarters of the Institut Ramon Llull and runs guided tours.

PALAU ROBERT
Passeig de Gràcia, 107
→ (A1)
T 93 238 80 91
http://palaurobert.gencat.cat
Designed by the French architect Henry Granpierre, it was built between 1898 and 1903 in the neoclassical style. It is currently home to the Catalan Government's Tourist Information Centre and its garden has been turned into a public park.

PASSEIG DE SANT JOAN
→ (C1, C2, C3)
This elegant thoroughfare was laid out in the late 19th century and runs from the Arc de Triomf to the district of Gràcia. Although less well known than the Passeig de Gràcia, this peaceful boulevard is a pleasure to walk along while you discover its gardens and sculptures, such as the extraordinary monument to Doctor Robert (1910), a *modernista* sculpture by Josep Llimona; the Fountain of Hercules, Barcelona's oldest monumental fountain (1802), by Salvador Gurri; or its *modernista* buildings, such as the Casa Macaya (1901), designed by Josep Puig i Cadafalch.

PARC DE L'ESTACIÓ DEL NORD
Nàpols, 70 → (C3)
A small, delightful park which is simple yet complex. It is one of the few places in the city to feature land art. Here it takes the form of two ceramic interventions by Beverly Pepper: *Cel Caigut* (*Fallen Sky*) and *Espiral arbolada* (*Spiral of Trees*). Both works are clearly inspired by Gaudí's aesthetic and determine the layout of the park, combining green and wooded areas.

Casa Calvet → (B3)

Palau Baró de Quadras → (B1)

Casa Garriga Nogués → (A2)

J. Múrria → 26(B1)

Sant Antoni
and Esquerra de l'Eixample

The Esquerra de l'Eixample (the left side of the Eixample) runs from Carrer de Balmes to the Plaça d'Espanya above Gran Via, and the Sant Antoni district covers the area below Gran Via to the Paral·lel. They were both built at a later date than the Dreta de l'Eixample and took several decades to complete. However, they contain landmarks that define their history and urban development. Sant Antoni grew around the iconic market from which it takes its name and the Esquerra de l'Eixample developed around Barcelona University, the Hospital Clínic and the city's first technical college, the Escola Industrial de Barcelona.

Restaurants

Michelin-starred
ANGLE *
Aribau, 54 ➔1(G2)
T 672 208 691
(> €60)
The young Catalan chef Jordi Cruz, who garnered two Michelin stars at Àbac, blends tradition and modernity in a great gastronomic experience.

CINC SENTITS *
Aribau, 58 ➔2(G2)
T 93 323 94 90
(> €60)
A unique take on contemporary Catalan cuisine with creative touches from around the world.

DISFRUTAR *
Villarroel, 163 ➔3(F1)
T 93 348 68 96
(> €60)
Three experienced chefs from elBulli, Mateu Casañas, Oriol Castro and Eduard Xatruch express themselves in total freedom while investigating flavours using the latest techniques.

GAIG *
Còrsega, 200 ➔4(G1)
T 93 453 20 20
(> €60)
Originally housed in an inn founded in Horta in 1869. Carles Gaig has brought his traditional dishes to the centre of Barcelona.

HOJA SANTA *
Av. Mistral, 54 ➔5(E3)
T 93 348 21 92
(€40-60)
Albert Adrià and Paco Méndez present tapas and tasting platters in this free and contemporary take on ancestral Mexican cuisine.

NECTARI *
València, 28 ➔6(F2)
T 93 226 87 18
(> €60)
Jordi Esteve proposes a balance between creative and traditional cooking with locally grown products.

TICKETS *
Av. Paral·lel, 164 ➔7(E3)
T 93 292 42 50
(> €60)
Albert Adrià's tribute to traditional tapas and tasting platters that reinvents the concept of going out for tapas.

ALVART
Aribau, 141 ➔8(G1)
T 93 430 57 58
(€30-50)
Small restaurant run by the skilful young chef Alvar Ayuso Thorell who uses carefully picked seasonal produce.

ARTTE
Muntaner, 83 ➔9(G2)
T 93 454 90 48
(< €20)
Bistrot and tea room with live music in spacious, welcoming premises. 9am-11.30pm.

BAR CALDERS
Parlament, 25
➔10(F3)
T 93 329 93 49
(< €20)
Tasty yet simple and unpretentious dishes with a lovely, welcoming terrace that is always busy.

BITXARRACU
València, 212 ➔11(G2)
T 93 114 84 44
(< €20) + SET LUNCH MENU
Gastrobar serving fun, informal dishes. Top-quality tapas and tasting platters.

BODEGA 1900
Tamarit, 91
➔12(E3)
T 93 325 26 59
(€20-40)
Albert Adrià's new project: a select vermouth bar serving signature platters with the "Bulli" touch at aperitivo-time.

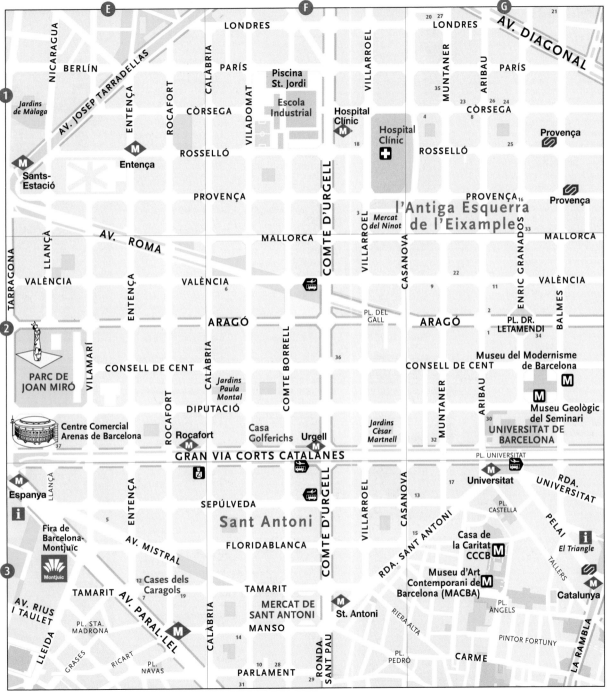

Highlights

PARC DE JOAN MIRÓ
Aragó, 2 → (E2)
Covering an area equivalent to four blocks in the Eixample, this park was one of the first projects to come out of Barcelona's new urban planning initiative in the 1980s and combines wooded and paved areas. Standing 22 metres high, Joan Miró's sculpture *Dona i Ocell* (Woman and Bird) towers over the large plaza. It is covered with pieces of broken tile, using the *trencadís* mosaic technique pioneered by Gaudí, and its title (and shape) evoke masculine and feminine forms. The sculpture was donated to Barcelona by the artist.

UNIVERSITAT DE BARCELONA
Gran Via, 585 → (G2)
Barcelona University was founded in 1450. The current building was constructed between 1863 and 1882 and marked the return of the university to the city (it had been closed more than a hundred years earlier and transferred to the town of Cervera in retaliation against the city for having opposed the Bourbon claimant to the throne, Philip V). Elies Rogent designed an imposing, neo-medieval structure with two large symmetrical cloisters on either side of the central building and two towers, resembling belfries, at both ends of the main façade.

MERCAT DE SANT ANTONI
Comte d'Urgell, 1 → (F3)
Opened in 1882, this was the first market built outside the medieval city walls and is one of the biggest in the city. It was designed by Antoni Rovira i Trias and, together with the Born, is one of the finest examples of cast-iron architecture in Barcelona. It has a cross-shaped floor plan with an octagonal section in the centre surmounted by a dome.

Parc de Joan Miró → (E2)

Universitat de Barcelona → (G2)

Mercat de Sant Antoni → (F3)

BODEGA SEPÚLVEDA
Sepúlveda, 173 → 13(G3)
T 93 454 70 94
(€20-40)
Traditional Barcelona cuisine with a modern twist. A wide range of tapas and more elaborate dishes.

BOHÈMIC
Manso, 42 → 14(F3)
T 93 424 06 28
(€20-40)
Tapas made from the finest produce with refined techniques that reinterpret traditional flavours.

FÀBRICA MORITZ
Ronda Sant Antoni, 41 → 15(G3)
T 93 423 54 34
(€20-40)
The oldest brewery in Spain (1856), redesigned by Jean Nouvel as a multipurpose space. 4,500 m² of beer-related culture with the Michelin-starred chef, Jordi Vilà, at the helm.

GRESCA
Provença, 230 → 16(G1)
T 93 451 61 93
(€40-50) + SET LUNCH MENU
Catalan cuisine by the chef Rafael Peña.

LA VOLÀTIL BAR DE VINS
Muntaner, 6 → 17(G3)
T 93 172 11 99
(€20-40)
Simple tapas and casseroles. More than 180 natural wines.

LA TAVERNA DEL CLÍNIC
Rosselló, 155 → 18(F1)
T 93 410 42 21
(€30-50)
Tapas and tasting platters made with painstaking care from quality produce.

LOLITA TAPERÍA
Tamarit, 104 → 19(E3)
T 93 424 52 31
(€20-30)
Serves some of the city's finest tapas in a relaxed and friendly atmosphere.

NONONO
Pge. Lluís Pellicer, 12 → 20(G1)
T 93 444 99 01
(< €20)
Biodynamic, organic cuisine with no carbon footprint.

RESTAURANT FERMÍ PUIG
Balmes, 175 → 21(G1)
T 93 624 18 35
(€40-50) + SET LUNCH MENU
The renowned chef's first signature restaurant.

TAKTIKA BERRI
València, 169 → 22(G2)
T 93 453 47 59 (€20-40)
Basque cuisine featuring high-quality tapas and canapés.

TANTA BARCELONA
Còrsega, 235 → 23(G1)
T 93 667 43 72 (€20-40)
The chef Gastón Acurio showcases Peru's culinary diversity with influences of Chinese and Japanese cuisine.

THE MIRROR
Còrsega, 255 → 24(G1)
T 93 202 86 86
(> €60)
21st-century seafood cuisine prepared by the chef Paco Pérez, who has already earned two Michelin stars at Enoteca.

Cafés and bars

AKASHI
Rosselló, 197 → 25(G1)
Small Japanese tea room where you can also have dinner and see art exhibitions.

DRY MARTINI
Aribau, 162 → 26(G1)
Classic cocktail bar with vintage bottles displayed on its shelves and an art collection on its walls.

EL VELÓDROMO
Muntaner, 213 → 27(G1)
A time-honoured classic (opens from 6am-3am) run by the Moritz brewery and with the chef Jordi Vilà at the helm.

FEDERAL
Parlament, 39 → 28(F3)
Specialises in breakfasts, brunches and hamburgers. Organic, natural produce. A relaxing spot with an open-fronted ground floor.

ORXATERIA SIRVENT
Parlament, 56 → 29(F3)
In summer, people from all over town make a pilgrimage to Sirvent for an *orxata*, a milky drink made from tiger nuts.

Casa de la Papallona → 37(E2)

Hospital Clínic → (F1)

Escola Industrial → (F1)

Lolita Taperia → 19(E3)

LA VALENCIANA
Aribau, 16 ➜**30(G2)**
Coffee shop and ice-cream parlour specialising in *orxata* and *torró* nougats.

Shopping
EL RECIBIDOR
Viladomat, 9 ➜**31(F3)**
Furniture showroom where you'll also find all kinds of perfectly restored vintage goods.

ESSÈNCIA
Gran Via, 569 ➜**32(G2)**
High-end perfumery and cosmetics outlet with a long-standing tradition and many years' experience. It stocks a wide range of leading brands from Spain and around the world.

L'APPARTEMENT
Enric Granados, 44 ➜**33(G1)**
Design, art and the latest in furniture, kitchenware and gifts for the home.

LA PASTISSERIA
Aragó, 228 ➜**34(G2)**
After winning the 2011 World Pastry Cup, the pastry chef Josep Maria Rodríguez opened this shop and tea room where you can sample his croissants, brioches and painstakingly crafted cakes.

OBBIO
Muntaner, 177 ➜**35(G1)**
Organic supermarket where you'll also find pre-cooked dishes to take away. It also has a lovely café.

TAKASHI OCHIAI
Comte d'Urgell, 110 ➜**36(F2)**
All kinds of traditional Catalan and European cakes and pastries, traditional Japanese sweets and tarts and innovative Japan-inspired creations.

And also
MERCAT DOMINICAL DE SANT ANTONI
Comte d'Urgell, 1 ➜**(F3)**
Every Sunday, the *modernista* Sant Antoni Market hosts a collectors' fair selling second-hand books, comics, films...

ESCOLA INDUSTRIAL
Comte d'Urgell, 173 ➜**(F1)**
The Fàbrica Batlló, a former factory, was refurbished and extended between 1908 and 1931 by several architects, including Gaudí's assistant Joan Rubió i Bellver. It became the city's first technical college. Highlights include the hall with its radial roof and small pavilion in the centre.

HOSPITAL CLÍNIC
Casanova, 141 ➜**(F1)**
One of Barcelona's world-class hospitals. Covering two blocks in the Eixample district, it was designed by Josep Domènech i Estapà and built between 1890 and 1906. The central section, which houses the Faculty of Medicine, is one of the most eye-catching features. It has a monumental façade which draws inspiration from classical architecture: a portico with six Corinthian columns and a semi-circular pediment bearing a relief which is an allegory of medicine.

CASA GOLFERICHS
Gran Via, 491 ➜**(F2)**
Joan Rubió i Bellver, one of Gaudí's most important assistants, built this Gothic-inspired *modernista* house in 1901. Highlights include the gallery on the corner and the combination of exposed brick, stone and ceramics.

CASES DELS CARGOLS
Tamarit, 89 ➜**(E3)**
Buildings dating from 1895 designed by Carles Bosch Negre. The name ("cargols" or "snails" in Catalan) comes from the painted, stone, metal and terracotta snails that decorate the façade, balconies, balustrades and other architectural elements.

Fàbrica Moritz ➜**15(G3)**

Mercat de Sant Antoni ➜**(F3)**

Cases dels Cargols ➜**(E3)**

Casa Golferichs ➜**(F2)**

Former village

Gràcia
+ Gaudí Trail (2)

With its curious, narrow streets and timeless charm, Gràcia – which is now one of the city's 10 districts – epitomises the old rural villages which were absorbed by Barcelona in the late 19th century during its urban development without losing any of their character. Visitors will find almost everything they need in this central area of the city, which has retained its human scale, making it the perfect place to have a relaxing stroll and where surprises await round every corner. The imprint of *modernista* architecture, particularly Gaudí's, can also be found in Gràcia: from the Casa Vicens to the magnificent Park Güell. They are all part of a neighbourhood with a strongly defined personality set around squares that reflect its vitality. A close-knit community with its neighbourhood associations that are still very much alive and organise a wide range of events, including the unique local festival, the *Festa Major*.

Must-sees
※

PARK GÜELL
Olot, s/n | T 902 200 302 | www.parkguell.cat
➔ **(B2, C2)**

Gaudí gave free rein to his fantastic imagination in this garden-city project. The gatehouses at the park entrance resemble the gingerbread house in Hansel and Gretel and once visitors have passed between them, a monumental staircase presided over by a large ceramic dragon awaits them. Above it are the columns of the hypostyle hall which underpins the plaza with its magnificent views of Barcelona, and a sinuous bench around it clad in shards of broken tile, crockery and bottles that anticipated the collage technique by several decades. At the top of the Park is Calvary, an ancestral structure with three unique crosses. All the spaces are linked by a network of winding paths: viaducts with colonnades that Gaudí made using stone from the site so that they would integrate perfectly into the surrounding natural landscape. +INFO: p.120

CASA VICENS
Carolines, 24 ➔ **(A3)**

This was Antoni Gaudí's first major project. It was designed as a detached residence and built between 1883 and 1888. Gaudí was commissioned by the tile manufacturer, Manuel Vicens Montaner, and recreated, and even improved on, the Mudéjar style – which was very widely used by Barcelona architects at the time – in the building, combining tiles and brick with sold masonry walls to create a work of extraordinary power. Highlights include the stunning railings at the entrance which represent the leaves of the fan palm that grew on the site – likewise, the tiles on the façade depict the humble French marigold that also grew naturally in the grounds of the building – and the overhanging balconies on the corners. It is said that, after they were completed, the master builder who worked with Gaudí kept watch all night outside the building because he was convinced that they would fall off into the street. The interior of the building will be open to visitors from March 2017 onwards. +INFO: p. 121

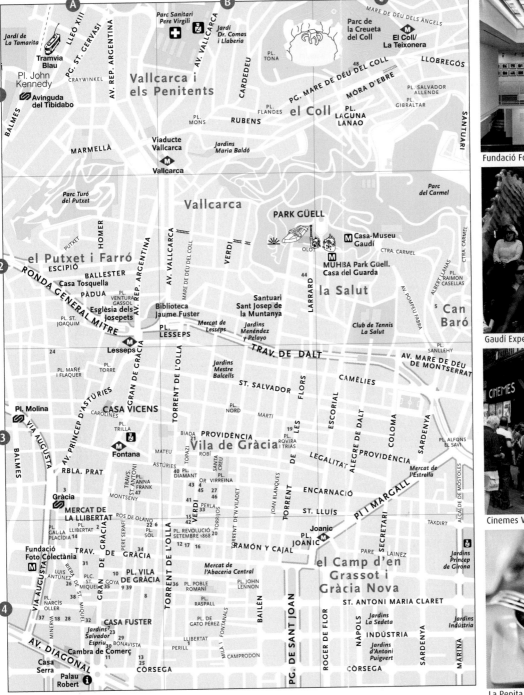

Fundació Foto Colectània →(A4)

Gaudí Experiència →44(B2)

Cinemes Verdi →45(B3)

La Pepita →13(A4)

Park Güell ➔ (B2, C2)

Casa Vicens ➔ (A3)

Gaudí Trail (2)

The old village of Gràcia is home to two major Gaudí landmarks: the **Casa Vicens**, his first major work, and the **Park Güell**, considered by many to be his greatest masterpiece. The park contains two interesting cultural facilities: the **MUHBA Park Güell** and the **Casa Museu Gaudí**, his former home which contains a major collection of objects associated with or designed by Gaudí. Download the audioguide Gaudí's Barcelona (tickets.visitbarcelona.com) and from the Apple Store (http://apps.barcelona turisme.com).

Museums

CASA MUSEU GAUDÍ
Park Güell ➔ (C2)
www.casamuseugaudi.org
The museum is located inside one of the two houses built in Park Güell (the original show house) where Gaudí lived from 1906 to 1925. The memory of the brilliant architect endures alongside an exhibition of the furniture and objects he designed.

FUNDACIÓ FOTO COLECTÀNIA
Julián Romea, 6 ➔ (A4)
www.colectania.es
More than 2,000 photos by more than 60 Spanish and Portuguese photographers from 1950 to the present day. Photography exhibitions and related activities.

MUHBA PARK GÜELL
Park Güell ➔ (C2)
www.museuhistoria.bcn.cat
The Casa del Guarda is the gatehouse and lodge designed by Gaudí as the park keeper's private residence. Over three floors inside the building, the Museu d'Història de Barcelona traces the history of the house, the park and the city at the time when Eusebi Güell and Antoni Gaudí were

planning their own private housing estate.

Restaurants

BILBAO
Perill, 33 ➔ 1(B4)
T 93 458 96 24
(€30-50) + SET LUNCH MENU
Traditional Basque cuisine with a Catalan twist.

BOTAFUMEIRO
Gran de Gràcia, 81 ➔ 2(A4)
T 93 218 42 30
(> €60) + GROUP MENU
The doyen of BCN's seafood restaurants. Galician cuisine.

CAPET
Benet Mercadé, 21-23 ➔ 3(A3)
T 93 115 53 66
(€20-40)
Small restaurant serving dishes made from rigorously selected seasonal produce by a young chef.

D.O.
Verdi, 36 ➔ 4(B3)
T 93 218 96 73
(€25-35) DINNER ONLY
Wines and creative tapas until 1am, in a contemporary setting.

EL JARDÍ DE L'ÀPAT
Albert Llanas, 2 ➔ 5(C2)
T 93 285 77 50
(€20-30) + SET LUNCH MENU
A villa with a garden, terrace and beautiful views. Chargrilled meat and vegetables.

ENVALIRA
Plaça del Sol, 13 ➔ 6(A4)
T 93 218 58 13
(€30-40)
A Gràcia classic. Market-fresh cuisine, rice and seafood dishes.

GALAXÓ
Pg. de Gràcia, 132 ➔ 7(A4)
T 93 255 30 00
(> €60)
Housed in the *modernista* hotel Casa Fuster, it offers an innovative Mediterranean menu of signature dishes.

IPAR-TXOCO
Mozart, 22 ➔ 8(A4)
T 93 218 19 54
(€40-60)
Classic Basque cuisine. Top-quality produce takes

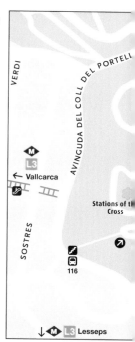

Park Güell ➔ (B2, C2)

Park Güell

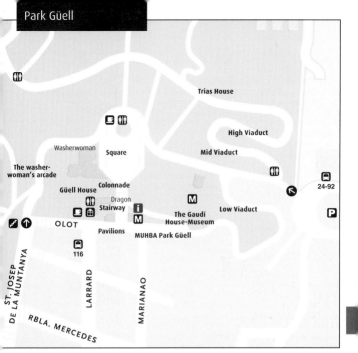

Trias House

High Viaduct

Mid Viaduct

Washerwoman

Square

The washer-woman's arcade

Colonnade

Güell House

Dragon

Stairway

OLOT

Pavilions

24-92

Low Viaduct

The Gaudí House-Museum

MUHBA Park Güell

116

ST. JOSEP DE LA MUNTANYA

LARRARD

MARIANAO

RBLA. MERCEDES

priority. Specialises in fish, meat and home-made desserts.

KIBUKA
Goya, 9 → **9(A4)**
T 93 237 89 44
(€20-40)
Excellent Japanese cuisine with a Mediterranean and Brazilian twist.

L'ANXOVETA
Sant Domènec, 14 → **10(A4)**
T 93 415 92 23
(€20-40)
Tapas and tasting platters made with the freshest and finest-quality ingredients.

L'EGGS
Pg. de Gràcia, 116 → **11(A4)**
T. 93 238 48 46
(€20-40)
Eggs are the stars at this restaurant run by chef Paco Pérez who earned two Michelin stars at the Enoteca.

LA LLAVOR DELS ORÍGENS
Ramón y Cajal, 12 → **12(B4)**
T 93 213 60 31
(€20-30) + SET LUNCH MENU
Catalan cuisine from 12.30pm to 1am.

LA PEPITA
Còrsega, 343 → **13(A4)**
T 93 238 48 93
(€20-40)
A small cosy restaurant specialising in classic tapas with an innovative twist.

LA PUBILLA
Plaça de la Llibertat, 23 → **14(A4)**
T 93 218 29 94
(< €20)
Traditional Catalan cuisine with a modern twist. Fresh daily produce.

LA VIBLIOTECA
Vallfogona, 12 → **15(B4)**
T 93 284 42 02
(€15-25)
More than 150 wines to accompany artisan cheeses and salads.

LA XULA TAPERIA
Mare de Déu dels D., 18 → **16(B4)**
T 93 165 01 01
(€15-25)
Creative tapas from the young chef David Guizy in an informal atmosphere.

PEPA TOMATE
Pl. de la Revolució, 17 → **17(B4)**
T 93 210 46 98
(€20-30)
Traditional tapas and tasting platters made with locally sourced produce.

ROIG ROBÍ
Sèneca, 20 → **18(A4)**
T 93 218 92 22
(> €60)
With a delightful terrace and garden. Mercè Navarro and her daughter Imma prepare family recipes with modern criteria.

Cafés and bars

BODEGA MANOLO
Torrent de les Flors, 101 → **19(B3)**
Genuine neighbourhood bodega with a unique atmosphere.

BODEVICI BIOCONCEPT
Torrijos, 21 → **20(B4)**
Home-made yogurts, ice creams and shakes guaranteed 100% organic.

CAFÈ CAMÈLIA
Verdi, 79 → **21(B3)**
Friendly, welcoming café featuring a selection of fair trade and organic products. Ideal for vegans and vegetarians.

CAFÈ DEL SOL
Plaça del Sol, 16 → **22(A4)**
A neighbourhood classic. The place for a pre-lunch drink and snack on the terrace beneath the magnolia trees.

CAFÈ VIENÈS
Passeig de Gràcia, 132 → **23(A4)**
In majestic surroundings with *modernista* décor, it serves teas, coffees, snacks and cocktails.

DALT DE TOT
Saragossa, 66 → **24(A3)**
Perfect hand-pulled draught beers, home-made vermouth and top-notch tapas.

LA CERVESERA ARTESANA
Sant Agustí, 14 → **25(A4)**
Barcelona's craft beer pioneers. They also run tastings and pairings of their exclusive beers with food.

Plaça de la Vila de Gràcia → (A4

Plaça Rovira i Trias → (B3)

Cafè Vienès → **23(A4)**

ROURE
Luis Antúnez, 7 →26(A4)
Since 1889. 7am-1am
Breakfast, aperitifs, tapas, lunch, dinner and drinks.

SALAMBÓ
Torrijos, 51 →27(B3)
Two levels: pool room and lounge bar. Drinks bar and restaurant.

Shopping

AOO
Sèneca, 8 →28(A4)
Selection of homewares by different brands and signature pieces by designers, craftsmen and women.

BE HOUSE
Bonavista, 7 →29(A4)
Original homeware and a wide variety of modern gift items.

BOO
Bonavista, 2 →30(A4)
Fashion and accessories by American, English and Swedish designers.

CASA ANITA
Vic, 14 →31(A4)
Delightful bookshop specialising in publications for children and young people.

CUERVO COBBLERBLACK BIRD
Sèneca, 2 →32(A4)
Classic bespoke hand-made shoes.

ELS BANDOLERS DE GRÀCIA
Verdi, 12 →33(B3)
Locally sourced Catalan products, most of them hand-made.

FLECA FORTINO
Travessera de Gràcia, 145 →34(A4)
All its breads are made using artisan methods in a wood-fired oven.

L'HORA EXACTA
Gran de Gràcia, 42 →35(A4)
Time-honoured watch and clockmakers. Cubist-, *modernista*- and medieval-inspired designs.

LA-A
Torrent de l'Olla, 86 →36(B4)
Hand-crafted subtle and timeless gift items. Concerts and workshops.

LYDIA DELGADO
Sèneca, 28 →37(A4)
One of Barcelona's great fashion designers for women.

MENCHÉN TOMÀS
Riera de Sant Miquel, 37 →38(A4)
Smart clothes for women and urban design.

NOSTÀLGIC
Goya, 18 →39(A4)
For lovers of analogue, lomographic and Polaroid photography.

OSLO
Torrent de l'Olla, 164 →40(B3)
Workshop and shop showcasing local artists: jewellery, accessories, clothing and other creative adventures.

PASTISSERIA PRÍNCIPE
Guilleries, 10 →41(B3)
The Príncipe has set the benchmark in Barcelona for Lebanese cakes and pastries and Arabic confectionery.

PIA ORGÀNIC JEWEL
Verdi, 3 →42(B4)
Jewellery with organic textures inspired by nature as well as ethnic and art-nouveau pieces. Fair-trade, semi-precious stones.

VIALIS
Verdi, 39 →43(B3)
Shoemakers of many years standing who take real pride in their work. The simplicity of the shapes, creativity and the quality of the materials make their footwear easily recognisable.

And also

GAUDÍ EXPERIÈNCIA
Larrard, 41 →44(B2)
www.gaudiexperiencia.com
Thanks to 4D technology you'll be able to experience first hand how nature inspired Antoni Gaudí's works: a forest that turns into imposing columns, a roof that conceals a dragon's skin.

CINEMES VERDI
Verdi, 32 →45(B3)

VERDI PARK
Torrijos, 49 →46(B3)
BCN's leading arthouse cinema for original-language-version films.

CENTRE ARTESÀ TRADICIONÀRIUS
Travessia de Sant Antoni, 6-8 →47(A3)
www.tradicionarius.com
Cultural centre devoted to traditional music. Organises the Tradicionarius Festival.

FINCA SANSALVADOR
Pg. de la Mare de Déu del Coll, 79 →48(C1)
Next to the Parc de la Creueta del Coll you'll find an interesting building by Gaudí's assistant Josep Maria Jujol. The project was never completed and all that remains is the caretaker's lodge and a series of magnificent underground tunnels leading to a well.

PARC DE LA CREUETA DEL COLL
Passeig de la Mare de Déu del Coll, 77 →(C1)
A former quarry transformed into a park with its own distinctive personality. It has a small lake that is used as a public swimming pool in summer. Here you'll also find Eduardo Chillida's sculpture *Elogi de l'aigua* (*In Praise of Water*). Made of concrete and weighing more than 50 tonnes, it is suspended over the water from four steel cables anchored to the rock, which imbues it with a surprising lightness despite its size.

JAUME FUSTER LIBRARY
Pl. Lesseps, 22 →(B2)
Designed by Josep Llinàs, who won the prestigious FAD Architecture Prize for the building in 2006. It is one of Barcelona's largest and most modern libraries.

Casa Museu Gaudí →(C2)

MUHBA Park Güell →(C2)

Parc de la Creueta del Coll →(C1)

Jaume Fuster Library →(B2)

Highlights

CASA FUSTER
Pg. de Gràcia, 132 →(A4)
www.hotelcasafuster.com
The *modernista*-style
Casa Fuster was designed
by Domènech i Montaner
and built between 1908
and 1911. It stands at the
top of Passeig de Gràcia
and boasts magnificent
views of this Barcelona
boulevard and the sea. Eye-
catching elements include
the turret and French-style
top floor, together with the
architect's trademark columns and floral motifs.

Casa Fuster →(A4)

SQUARES IN GRÀCIA
→(A4, B3, C4)
The squares are the focus
of recreational and social
life in this former village.
They include the Plaça de
la Vila de Gràcia – with the
local council building and its
33-metre-high clock tower
surmounted by a belfry –,
the Plaça del Diamant –
immortalised in Mercè
Rodoreda's novel –, the Plaça
del Sol, and the Plaça de la
Sedeta.

Plaça de la Vila de Gràcia →(A4)

GRÀCIA FESTIVALS
www.festamajordegracia.cat
The former village of Gràcia
still likes to be different from
the rest. And this difference
is expressed in its own festivals which endure today. This
is the case with the Festa
Major which has been held
in mid August every year
since 1817. The festival is
one of Barcelona's landmark
celebrations and the locals
compete with one another
for the best-decorated street.

Gràcia Festivals

MERCAT DE LA LLIBERTAT
Plaça de la Llibertat
→(A3)
This market was built
between 1888 and 1893. It
was designed by the architect Miquel Pasqual, but
its trademark *modernista*
decoration (in wrought iron
with interwoven, sinuous
elements) is by Gaudí's
friend and associate Francesc
Berenguer. The market was
refurbished in 2009.

Mercat de la Llibertat →(A3)

The biggest district

Sants-Montjuïc

Sants-Montjuïc is Barcelona's biggest district, covering a surface
area equivalent to a fifth of the municipal territory. It comprises
neighbourhoods with their own distinct personalities, such as the
former villages of Sants, Hostafrancs, Poble-sec and La Bordeta,
as well as the harbour and its free-trade area, the Zona Franca.
They are located in the environs of Montjuïc Hill, surmounted by
the castle that guarded its coastline. This "green lung", which
was built on for the 1929 Exhibition and the 1992 Olympics,
is home to the Olympic Ring, major museums, the Botanical
Gardens and other facilities for the entire community.

Must-sees
✳

MUSEU NACIONAL D'ART DE CATALUNYA
Parc de Montjuïc, s/n | T 93 622 03 76 | www.museunacional.cat
→(B3)
The Museu Nacional d'Art de Catalunya brings together the most important collections of Catalan art. Housed in the Palau Nacional, an iconic landmark which stands
out against the Barcelona skyline, the museum showcases 1,000 years of local
creativity. Its collection of Romanesque art from the Pyrenees is unique. It also has
noteworthy Gothic collections and a selection of art spanning the late 19th to the
mid 20th centuries. +INFO: p. 122

FUNDACIÓ JOAN MIRÓ
Parc de Montjuïc, s/n | T 93 443 94 70 | www.fundaciomiro-bcn.org
→(G1)
Joan Miró, the world-renowned Barcelona-born artist and one of the leading figures
of the surrealist movement, bequeathed this foundation and study centre to his
home town. It was designed by Josep Lluís Sert and showcases a large selection of
Miró's works, organises exhibitions by other major artists and fosters creativity by
young artists. The Fundació Miró boasts magnificent views of the city and is surrounded by trees and sculptures. +INFO: p. 123

MAGIC FOUNTAIN OF MONTJUÏC
Pl. de Carles Buïgas, 1
→(C3)
Water, light and colour. The engineer Carles Buïgas harnessed these three elements
to design his Magic Fountain at the foot of Montjuïc Hill. It consists of three con-
centric circles of water jets which create a water sculpture of constantly changing,
flowing forms: a poetic spectacle set to music, which Barcelona uses for its great city
festivals and celebrations.

Museu Nacional d'Art de Catalunya → **(B3)**

Fundació Joan Miró → **(G1)**

Magic Fountain of Montjuïc → **(C3)**

Sants, Plaça d'Espanya and trade fair site

✳ **Must-sees: MUSEU NACIONAL D'ART DE CATALUNYA**
+ MAGIC FOUNTAIN OF MONTJUÏC → p. 56

The Plaça d'Espanya is one of Barcelona's main traffic hubs. It connects the roads from the southern coast with the city's main arteries, including Gran Via, Paral·lel and Carrer Tarragona. It is also the gateway to Montjuïc and the trade fair site, Fira de Barcelona, with its halls set out at the foot of the hill.

Poble Espanyol de Barcelona
→ (B3)

www.poble-espanyol.com
This special complex was built for the 1929 International Exhibition. Designed like a village, with its own main square, it is an open-air museum showcasing all the Spanish architectural styles through replicas of famous landmark buildings. It is currently one of the city's most popular leisure attractions and is home to all kinds of craft workshops, shops, entertainment companies, art foundations, performing-arts and fine-art schools, restaurants, bars and discotheques. It is also home to the **Fundació Fran Daurel** and its contemporary art collection which encompasses informalism, expressionism, surrealism and hyperrealism. It also hosts activities for the whole family, particularly children. Every night in summer it provides a superb setting for concerts and other entertainments. Opening times: Monday, 9am-8pm; Tuesday to Thursday, 9am-2am; Friday and Saturday, 9am-5am; Sunday, 9am-11pm.

Museums

MUSEU NACIONAL D'ART DE CATALUNYA → (B3)
+ INFO: p. 122
CAIXAFORUM → (B3)
+ INFO: p. 125

Restaurants

Michelin-starred
PAKTA ✳
Lleida, 5 → 1(D3)
(> €60)
(Online bookings only). Albert Adrià presents his wonderful Nikkei (Japanese-Peruvian) cuisine project.

CASA DE TAPES CAÑOTA
Lleida, 7 → 2(D3)
T 93 325 91 71
(€20-40)
The Iglesias brothers serve great tapas in an informal atmosphere.

ESPAI KRU
Lleida, 7 → 3(D3)
T 93 300 47 97
(€40-60)
Dedicated to the very essence and diversity of raw produce.

LA LOLA DE LAS ARENAS
Gran Via, 373 → 4(C2)
T 93 425 57 14
(€20-30) + SET LUNCH MENU
From breakfasts to suppers, food with the full Spanish essence.

ÒLEUM
Parc de Montjuïc, → 5(B3)

T 93 289 06 79
(€30-50) + SET LUNCH MENU
Inside the MNAC. Creative Mediterranean cuisine.

RÍAS DE GALÍCIA
Lleida, 7 → 6(D3)
T 93 424 81 52
(> €60) + GROUP MENU
The finest seafood and fish from the Galician coast.

Cafés and bars

BAR BODEGA AMPOSTA
Amposta, 1 → 7(B2)
It still retains its original early 20th century decor. Tapas and vermouths in an authentic neighbourhood atmosphere.

BAR BODEGA SALVAT
Sagunt, 51 → 8(A1)
Amazing anchovies and dark beer on draught since 1880.

LA BODEGUETA DE CAL PEP
Canalejas, 12 → 9(A1)
Excellent aperitifs and tapas since 1920.

Shopping

The Sants-Creu Coberta shopping area → (B1-B2-C2) includes Europe's longest retail thoroughfare and has 500 shops and two municipal markets.

ARENAS DE BARCELONA
→ (C2)
This shopping centre is housed in a neo-Mudejar-style former bullring designed by August Font

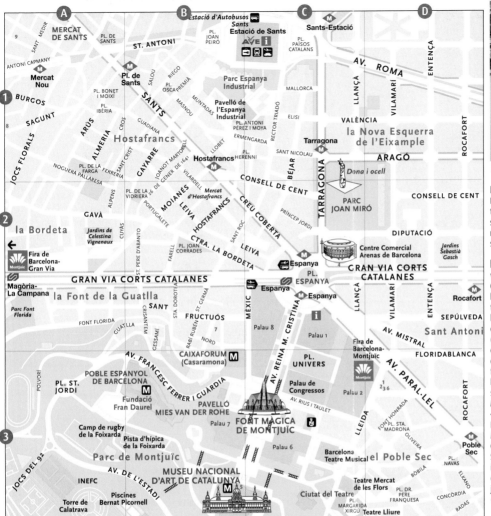

Map labels (Montjuïc / Sants area):

A · B · Estació d'Autobusos · C · D

MERCAT DE SANTS · PL. DE SANTS · ST. ANTONI · Sants · Estació de Sants · AVE · Sants-Estació

9 · SANT MEDIR · ANTONI CAPMANY · PL. JOAN PEIRÓ · PL. PAÏSOS CATALANS

Mercat Nou · PL. BONET I MOIXÍ · PL. de Sants · SALOU · RIEGO · PL. OSCA · PREMIÀ · MUNTADAS · MALLORCA · AV. ROMA · LLANÇA · VILAMARÍ · ENTENÇA

1 · BURGOS · SAGUNT · PL. IBÈRIA · SANTS · MASNOU · Parc Espanya Industrial · Pavelló de l'Espanya Industrial · SANT ANTONI PÉREZ I MOYA · ELISI · VALÈNCIA · ROCAFORT

8 · JOCS FLORALS · ARÚS · ALMERIA · CROS · GUADIANA · GAYARRE · SANT CRIST · SANT FERRERIA · JOANOT MARTORELL · 26 DE GENER DE 1641 · VILARDELL · ERMENGARDA · RECTOR TRIADÓ · la Nova Esquerra de l'Eixample · Tarragona · ARAGÓ

Hostafrancs · NOGUERA PALLARESA · PL. DE LA FARGA · MOIANÉS · LLORET · PL. HERENNI · SANT NICOLAU · BÉJAR · TARRAGONA · Dona i ocell · CONSELL DE CENT

2 · la Bordeta · Jardins de Celestina Vigneaux · GAVÀ · CUYÀS · ALPENS · PORTUGALETE · PL. DE LA VIDRIERA · Mercat d'Hostafrancs · HOSTAFRANCS · LEIVA · CREU COBERTA · CONSELL DE CENT · PRÍNCEP JORDI · PARC JOAN MIRÓ · DIPUTACIÓ · Jardins Sebastià Gasch

Fira de Barcelona-Gran Via · Magòria-La Campana · Parc Font Florida · la Font de la Guatlla · FARELL · ST. PERE D'ABANTO · PL. JOAN CORRADES · CTRA. LA BORDETA · SANT ROC · LEIVA · Espanya · PL. ESPANYA · Centre Comercial Arenas de Barcelona · GRAN VIA CORTS CATALANES

GRAN VIA CORTS CATALANES · SANT · STA. DOROTEA · STA. GERMANA · MÈXIC · Espanya · Espanya · LLANÇA · VILAMARÍ · ENTENÇA · Rocafort · SEPÚLVEDA

FONT FLORIDA · GUATLLA · CRISANTEM · CESSAMI · FRUCTUÓS · RABÍ RUBÈN · 7 · NORD · Palau 8 · Palau 1 · AV. MISTRAL · Sant Antoni · FLORIDABLANCA

Palau de Congressos · Fira de Barcelona-Montjuïc · AV. PARAL·LEL · ROCAFORT

POLVORÍ · AV. FRANCESC FERRER I GUÀRDIA · CAIXAFORUM (Casaramona) · PL. UNIVERS · Palau 2 · 1 2 3 6 · FONT HONRADA · Poble Sec

PL. ST. JORDI · POBLE ESPANYOL DE BARCELONA · Fundació Fran Daurel · PAVELLÓ MIES VAN DER ROHE · FONT MÀGICA DE MONTJUÏC · AV. RIUS I TAULET · LLEIDA · FONT PL. STA. MADRONA · OLIVERA

3 · Camp de rugby de la Foixarda · Pista d'hípica de la Foixarda · Palau 7 · Palau 6 · Barcelona Teatre Musical · el Poble Sec · BOBILA

Parc de Montjuïc · AV. DE L'ESTADI · MUSEU NACIONAL D'ART DE CATALUNYA · Ciutat del Teatre · Teatre Mercat de les Flors · PL. DR. PERE FRANQUESA · CONCÒRDIA · RADAS · ELKANO · PL. NAVAS

JOCS DEL 92 · INEFC · Piscines Bernat Picornell · Torre de Calatrava · PL. MARGARIDA XIRGU · Teatre Lliure

---

Poble Espanyol → (B3)

lake guarded by a statue of Neptune in which we can see the reflection of Venus, and shady areas dotted with trees make this park the perfect spot to relax.

Fira de Barcelona

www.firabarcelona.com
Opened in 1932 in the halls built for the 1929 International Exhibition. The Fira has the largest surface area of any trade fair in Spain (365,000 m² of dedicated exhibition space) and is one of Europe's leading exhibition facilities. A shuttle bus runs between the two trade fair sites when needed.

Montjuïc site
→ (C2-C3)
Eight halls at the foot of Montjuïc Hill.

Gran Via site
Six halls, some of them featuring interventions by architects of the stature of Toyo Ito, Alejandro Zaera and Arata Isozaki.

+INFO: p. 159

---

and built in 1900. The architect Richard Rogers kept the original façade and placed a dome over the top of the building. It has an observation deck that boasts some of the finest views of Barcelona.

And also

CIUTAT DEL TEATRE
Lleida, 59 → (C3)
A complex entirely devoted to the performing arts. Located in a 19th-century-

style building from the 1929 International Exhibition, it includes the **Mercat de les Flors** (dance), the **Teatre Lliure Montjuïc** (theatre) and the **Institut del Teatre** (school), with six theatre spaces seating more than 2,000 people.

PARC DE L'ESPANYA INDUSTRIAL
Muntadas, 1-37 → (B1-C1)
A giant iron dragon, which is used as a slide by children, a boating

Ciutat del Teatre → (C3)

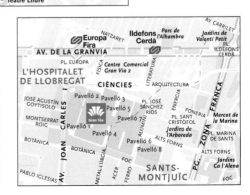

Map labels (L'Hospitalet / Gran Via area):

AV. CARRILET · Europa Fira · NATZARET · Ildefons Cerdà · Parc de l'Alhambra · Jardins de Valentí Petit · PL. ILDEFONS CERDÀ · AV. DE LA GRANVIA · PL. EUROPA · FÍSICA · Centre Comercial Gran Via 2 · LITERATURA · ARQUITECTURA · L'HOSPITALET DE LLOBREGAT · CIÈNCIES · ENERGIA · FRANÇA · JOSÉ AGUSTÍN GOYTISOLO · Pavelló 2 · Pavelló 3 · PL. JOSÉ SÁNCHEZ RÍOS · FONERIA · Mercat de la Marina · MONTSERRAT ROIG · Pavelló 5 · PL. SANT CRISTÒFOL · ALUMINI · PL. MARINA DE SANTS · JOAN CARLES I · Gran Via · Pavelló 1 · Pavelló 7 · Jardins de l'Arboreda · ALTS FORNS · ZONA FRANCA · BOTÀNICA · Pavelló 4 · Pavelló 6 · ALTS FORNS · Jardins Ca l'Alena · BOTÀNICA · Pavelló 8 · SANTS-MONTJUÏC · PABLO IGLESIAS · METAL·LÚRGIA · ACER · FOC · FERRO · PG. MARINA DE SANTS · FOC

Highlights

MIES VAN DER ROHE PAVILION
Francesc Ferrer i Guàrdia, 7 →(B3)
www.miesbcn.com
This modern masterpiece was designed by Mies van der Rohe as the German Pavilion for the 1929 International Exhibition. It was demolished after the event but faithfully rebuilt in 1986. It now houses an architectural foundation.
+INFO: p. 124

Mies van der Rohe Pavilion →(B3)

CAIXAFORUM
Francesc Ferrer i Guàrdia, 6 →(B3)
www.obrasocial.lacaixa.es
Puig i Cadafalch created a paradigm of industrial art nouveau in this factory. The "la Caixa" Foundation restored the building, preserving its original features, and today it hosts art exhibitions, concerts, literary and film events...
+INFO: p. 125

CaixaForum →(B3)

PLAÇA D'ESPANYA
→(C2)
Many of the city's main arteries, such as Gran Via and Paral·lel, radiate from this plaza. Iconic landmarks include the monumental central fountain by Gaudí's associate, Josep Maria Jujol; the former bullring, Las Arenas, with its rooftop observation deck which boasts breathtaking panoramic views; and the Venetian towers, which are the gateway to Montjuïc hill.

Plaça d'Espanya →(C2)

MERCAT DE SANTS
Sant Jordi, 6
→(A1)
This splendid example of *modernista* architecture at its most functional opened in 1913. It was designed by the architect Pere Falqués i Urpí, whose many works include the bench-streetlamps on the Passeig de Gràcia.

Mercat de Sants →(A1)

Sants-Montjuïc

Montjuïc
(Olympic Park + Castle) and Poble-sec

✱ **Must-sees:** FUNDACIÓ JOAN MIRÓ →p. 56

The Olympic Park on Montjuïc was the main site of the 1992 Games. It comprises the Olympic Stadium, the Palau Sant Jordi, the Picornell swimming pools, the Institut Nacional d'Educació Física and an eye-catching communications tower which are set out along a classically designed avenue. These facilities continue to host sporting events and musicals. Poble-sec was the first neighbourhood in Barcelona to be built outside the medieval city walls. It is a working-class district which has long-standing connections with the world of entertainment and theatre, due to its proximity to Barcelona's theatre strip, the Paral·lel.

Montjuïc Cemetery Trail
Dreams of Barcelona is the name of the free guided tour of 40 tombs, including mausoleums and sculptures of great artistic value made by architects and sculptors between 1888 and 1936 in a variety of artistic styles, including *modernista*, neo-Egyptian, neo-Gothic and realist.
Calendar: second and fourth Sunday in the month. Times: 11am.
www.cbsa.cat

Museums
MUSEU OLÍMPIC I DE L'ESPORT JOAN ANTONI SAMARANCH
Av. de l'Estadi, 60
→(F1)
www.museuolimpicbcn.cat
A pioneering museum in Europe and a showcase for sport with multimedia and interactive exhibits.
MUSEU D'ARQUEOLOGIA DE CATALUNYA
Pg. de Santa Madrona, 39
→(F1)
T 93 423 21 49

www.mac.cat
The Graphic Arts Pavilion built for the 1929 International Exhibition is home to the MAC's collections tracing the roots of Catalonia, from prehistoric times to the medieval era.
MUSEU ETNOLÒGIC
Pg. de Santa Madrona, 16
→(F1)
www.museuetnologic.bcn.cat
Collection of tangible and intangible heritage from Catalonia and all the world cultures present in Barcelona.
JARDÍ BOTÀNIC
Dr. Font i Quer, 2 →(F2)
www.jardibotanic.bcn.cat
Groundbreaking landscape design preserving Mediterranean plants from around the world.
MUHBA REFUGI 307
Nou de la Rambla, 169
→(H2)
www.museuhistoria.bcn.cat
This shelter was built by members of the local community in 1937 as protection from the bombing raids by fascist planes during the Spanish Civil War. You can visit more than 400 metres of tunnels. Sundays at 10.30am, 11.30am and 12.30pm.

Restaurants
EL SORTIDOR
Pl. del Sortidor, 5 →1(G1)
T 93 518 85 44
(€20-40)
Opened in 1908. El Sortidor retains its original *modernista* doors and marble tables. You can sample tapas, and have lunch or dinner in an intimate atmosphere.
ELCHE
Vila i Vilà, 71 →2(H1)
T 93 441 30 89
(€30-40) +GROUP MENU
Time-honoured restaurant. Seafood and Valencian cuisine. Excellent rice dishes.
LA BELLA NAPOLI
Margarit, 14 →3(H1)
T 93 442 50 56
(€15-30)
Wood-oven-baked pizzas and Neapolitan food prepared by the Naples-born owners.
LA TOMAQUERA
Margarit, 58 →4(G1)

(€20-30)
An informal, bustling restaurant with a youthful ambiance. Its specialities are chargrilled meat and snails, which have earned it a great reputation.

MONTJUÏC EL XALET
Av. de Miramar, 31
→5(G2)
T 93 324 92 70
(€50-60) + GROUP MENU
Mediterranean cuisine with a view: panoramic terrace and revolving restaurant.

QUIMET & QUIMET
Poeta Cabanyes, 25
→6(H1)
T 93 442 31 42
(€30-40)
Fourth generation serving delicious tapas in this tiny bar.

ROSAL 34
Roser, 34 →7(H1)
T 93 324 90 46
(€30-40)
Modern yet cosy bar serving signature tapas.

TAVERNA CAN MARGARIT
Concòrdia, 21
→8(G1)
T 93 441 67 23
(€20-40)
An old tavern which retains its authentic décor. The menu is short but features interesting, traditional Catalan, Valencian and Andalusian dishes.

Cafés and bars
GRAN BODEGA SALTÓ
Blesa, 36 →9(H1)
Century-old bar refurbished with exquisite taste. Wines, music, theatre...

SALA APOLO
Nou de la Rambla, 113
→10(H1)
Guest DJs from top nightclubs on the Paral·lel: **Nitsa** (Friday and Saturday); **Crappy Tuesdays** (Tuesday); **Canibal** (Wednesday) **Cupcake** (Thursday) and **Nasty Mondays** (Monday).

TINTA ROJA
Creu dels Molers, 17
→11(G1)
Drinks. Buenos Aires-style décor. Tango classes.

And also
ATHLETES' SHOE PRINTS
Av. de l'Estadi, 60
→16(F1)
Olympic champions and world-famous athletes have left the imprint of their sports shoes in circular paving stones.

CAMÍ DE MAR
→(F2)
A pleasant 20-minute walk from the Mirador de l'Alcalde to the Mirador del Migdia, which boasts magnificent views of the city, port and Llobregat Delta, with benches in the shade of the castle walls, monuments, including the sculpture dedicated to the metric system, and a picnic area when you reach the Mirador del Migdia.

EL PARAL·LEL
→(H1)
A legendary avenue dating from the early 20th century known for its slightly risqué popular entertainment (Barcelona's Montmartre). It is gradually regaining its former splendour with the restoration of its historic music halls such as **El Molino** (built in 1898 and refurbished in 2010) →12(H1), and theatres, including the **Victòria** →13(H1), **Apolo** →10(H1), **Condal** →14(H1) and **BARTS**-Barcelona Arts on Stage →15(H1).

GARDENS ON MONTJUÏC
Montjuïc hill is dotted with gardens from different periods and in different styles. Highlights include the historic **Jardins Laribal** →(F1), which were designed in the early 20th century by Forestier and Rubió i Tudurí and drew inspiration from ancient Arabic gardens; the **Jardins de Mossèn Cinto Verdaguer** →(G2), which specialise in bulbous, rhizome and aquatic plants; the **Jardins de Mossèn Costa i Llobera** →(H2), which showcase more than 800 cacti and succulent plant species; the **Jardí**

Montjuïc Cemetery →(E2)

Jardins Costa i Llobera →(H2)

Mirador del Migdia →(F2)

El Molino →12(H1)

Montjuïc cable car → (G2)

Jardins Laribal → (F1)

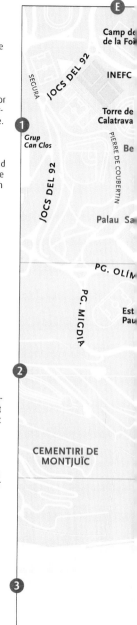

d'Aclimatació → (E1, F1), a peaceful place and a large-scale, open-air botany classroom; and the neo-classical **Jardins de Joan Maragall** → (F1).

MIRADOR DE L'ALCALDE
→ (G2)

The belvedere, the Mirador de l'Alcalde, is located further down from the castle. It is set among gardens and boasts wonderful views of the port and Mediterranean. The ground is decorated by a collage by J. J. Tharrats echoing an industrial theme.

SALA MONTJUÏC
→ (F2)

www.salamontjuic.org
Open-air cinema at the castle with recliners and picnics. In summer only.

SCULPTURE *CHANGE*
Pierre de Coubertin, s/n
→ (E1)

This sculpture by Aiko Miyawaki comprises 36 cement cylinders crowned by metal rings and steel cables which reflect back the light, especially at dusk.

TEATRE GREC
→ (G1)

In spite of its name, meaning "Greek theatre", it isn't actually Greek. It was built for the 1929 International Exhibition on the site of a disused quarry. It has become Barcelona's most iconic venue and the main stage for the Grec Summer Festival.

MONTJUÏC CABLE CAR
→ (G2)

T 93 430 47 16
www.tmb.net
The Montjuïc cable car offers aerial views of the hill and its modern cabins can seat eight people. There are three stations: Parc de Montjuïc (by the Plaça Dante), Mirador and Castell.

Jardí Botànic → (F2)

Mirador de l'Alcalde → (G2)

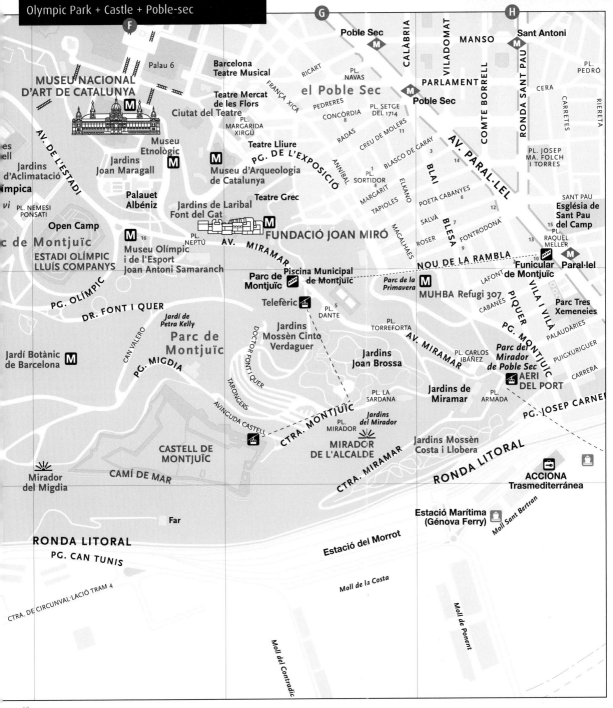

F

G

H

Poble Sec

CALÀBRIA

VILADOMAT

MANSO

Sant Antoni

Palau 6

MUSEU NACIONAL
D'ART DE CATALUNYA

Barcelona
Teatre Musical

RICART

PL.
NAVAS

PARLAMENT

PL.
PEDRÓ

Teatre Mercat
de les Flors

FRANÇA XICA

el Poble Sec

Poble Sec

COMTE BORRELL

RONDA SANT PAU

CERA

CARRETES

RIERETA

Ciutat del Teatre

PEDRERES

CONCÒRDIA

PL. SETGE
DEL 1714

AV. DE L'ESTADI

Museu
Etnològic

PL.
MARGARIDA
XIRGÚ

RADAS

CREU DE MOLERS

11

Jardins
d'Aclimatació
Olímpica

Jardins
Joan Maragall

Teatre Lliure

PG. DE L'EXPOSICIÓ

BLASCO DE GARAY

AV. PARAL·LEL

3

14

PL. JOSEP
MA. FOLCH
I TORRES

vi

PL. NEMESI
PONSATI

Palauet
Albéniz

Museu d'Arqueologia
de Catalunya

ANNIBAL

PL.
SORTIDOR

4

BLAI

Open Camp

Jardins de Laribal
Font del Gat

Teatre Grec

MARGARIT

ELKANO

POETA CABANYES

6

SANT PAU

Església de
Sant Pau
del Camp

c de Montjuïc

ESTADI OLÍMPIC
LLUÍS COMPANYS

Museu Olímpic
i de l'Esport
Joan Antoni Samaranch

16

PL.
NEPTÚ

AV. MIRAMAR

TAPIOLES

MACALHAES

SALVÀ

ROSER

BLESA

FONTRODONA

12

9

15

PL.
RAQUEL
MELLER

13

FUNDACIÓ JOAN MIRÓ

NOU DE LA RAMBLA

10

Funicular
de Montjuïc

Paral·lel

PG. OLÍMPIC

DR. FONT I QUER

Parc de
Montjuïc

Piscina Municipal
de Montjuïc

Parc de la
Primavera

MUHBA Refugi 307

LAFONT

CABANÉS

PIQUER

VILA I VILA

Parc Tres
Xemeneies

Jardí de
Petra Kelly

Telefèric

PL.
DANTE

5

PG. MONTJUÏC

PALAUDÀRIES

Jardí Botànic
de Barcelona

Parc de
Montjuïc

CAN VALERO

PG. MIGDIA

DOCTOR FONT I QUER

TARONGERS

Jardins
Mossèn Cinto
Verdaguer

PL.
TORREFORTA

Jardins
Joan Brossa

AV. MIRAMAR

PL. CARLOS
IBÁÑEZ

Parc del
Mirador
de Poble Sec

PUIGXURIGUER

CARRERA

AERI
DEL PORT

PG. JOSEP CARNER

AVINGUDA CASTELL

CTRA. MONTJUÏC

PL. LA
SARDANA

PL.
MIRADOR

Jardins
del Mirador

Jardins de
Miramar

PL.
ARMADA

Mirador
del Migdia

CASTELL DE
MONTJUÏC

MIRADOR
DE L'ALCALDE

Jardins Mossèn
Costa i Llobera

RONDA LITORAL

ACCIONA
Trasmediterránea

CAMÍ DE MAR

CTRA. MIRAMAR

Far

Estació Marítima
(Génova Ferry)

Moll Sant Bertran

RONDA LITORAL

PG. CAN TUNIS

Estació del Morrot

CTRA. DE CIRCUNVAL·LACIÓ TRAM 4

Moll de la Costa

Moll del Contradic

Moll de Ponent

Highlights

MONTJUÏC CASTLE
→ **(F2)**
T 93 329 86 13
www.barcelona.cat/
castelldemontjuic
Montjuïc Castle overlooks
Barcelona and its coastline.
A former watchtower, it
was added onto a 17th and
18th century fort. Highlights
include the parade ground
and bastions. It has an
exhibition about its future
uses as well as a perma-
nent exhibition, *Montjuïc:
the building of a castle*,
and temporary exhibitions
about the castle's and the
city's history.

Montjuïc Castle → **(F2)**

OLYMPIC STADIUM
LLUÍS COMPANYS
Pg. Olímpic, 17-19
→ **(F1)**
Barcelona built its stadium
in 1929. The city was due to
host the People's Olympiad
in 1936 but the event was
frustrated by the outbreak
of the Civil War. In 1992,
after a complete refurbishment, it hosted the Olympic
Games. The stadium seats
55,000.

Olympic Stadium → **(F1)**

PALAU SANT JORDI
Pierre de Coubertin, s/n
→ **(E1)**
This sports complex,
designed by Arata Isozaki,
is the major indoor venue
in the Olympic Ring. Its
roof evokes a turtle's shell.
It can hold 17,000 spectators, a number that can
be increased to 24,000 for
concerts and other cultural
events. +INFO: p. 126

Palau Sant Jordi → **(E1)**

AERI DEL PORT
→ **(H2)**
T 93 225 27 18
The cable car travels the
1,300 metres across the
harbour. It runs between
two tall towers – Sant
Sebastià, in Barceloneta,
and Jaume I, next to the
World Trade Center – and a
third station, at Miramar.

Aeri del Port → **(H2)**

The seafront

Sant Martí

The district of Sant Martí stretches from the edges of the old
town, Ciutat Vella, and the Eixample, to the Besòs river and
showcases the most recent transformation of the city and its
seafront. The regeneration of the former industrial area of
Poblenou as the new technology district, 22@, the reclaimed
city beaches, and the completion of the section of the Avinguda
Diagonal linking it to the sea, are just some of the town-planning
interventions that define modern Barcelona. The district of Sant
Martí summarises the past and the future of Barcelona: the city's
agricultural and industrial past and the future which looks to
modernity with the transformation of neighbourhoods, reclaimed
beaches and major contemporary architecture projects.

Must-sees
✳

AGBAR TOWER
Avinguda Diagonal, 209-211 | www.torreagbar.com → **(B2)**
The Agbar Tower is one of Barcelona's new architectural landmarks. Designed by
Jean Nouvel who drew inspiration from the mountains of Montserrat and the basilica
of the Sagrada Família, this tapering, cylindrical building stands 144 metres high.
It can be seen from all around the city, particularly at night, when it is transformed
into an enormous lamp of changing colours. +INFO: p. 127

PARC DEL FÒRUM
→ **(D4)**
The huge esplanade that hosted the Barcelona Universal Forum of Cultures in 2004
covers an area of 320,000 m², making it one of the largest recreational and cultural
public spaces on the planet. It also features some of the city's most iconic modern
buildings, such as the Barcelona International Convention Centre, designed by Josep
Lluís Mateo; the iconic triangular Forum Building, by the architects Jacques Herzog
and Pierre de Meuron; the Photovoltaic Pergola by Elies Torres and José Antonio
Martínez Lapeña; and the Telefónica Building by Enric Massip-Bosch. There is also
an innovative bathing area and a vast plaza (more than 100,000 m²) which hosts a
wide range of events such as the Primavera Sound Festival and the April Flamenco
Fair, the Feria de Abril de Catalunya.

BARCELONA'S NEW BEACHES
→ **(B4, B5)**
Barcelona reclaimed more than 2 km of its seafront for the 25th Olympic Games
which were hosted by the city in 1992. Until then it had been occupied by disused
industrial buildings and was cut off from the rest of the city by the insurmountable
barrier of the railway line that prevented access to the sea (which you could smell
but not see). At the present time, there are five city beaches set among parkland
and connected by a promenade. They have become some of the most popular places
for locals and visitors to spend their free time. The beaches are Nova Icària, Bogatell,
Mar Bella, Nova Mar Bella and Llevant.

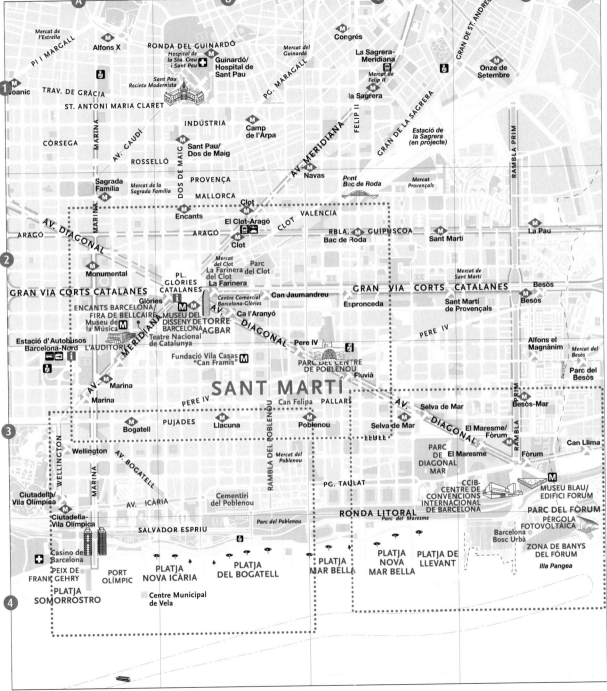

Agbar Tower → **(B2)**

Parc del Fòrum → **(D4)**

Barcelona's new beaches → **(B4, B5)**

Poblenou
and Vila Olímpica

Poblenou is one of Barcelona's districts with the most distinctive personality. By the end of the 19th century, Poblenou was the country's largest industrial area and it became known as the "Catalan Manchester ". Its industrial past has left a legacy of fine industrial buildings which have been put to new social and cultural uses, and a community network which still shows its vitality in its libraries and civic centres. Overlooking the sea, the Olympic Village was built to house the athletes taking part in the 1992 Games and laid the foundation stone for the transformation of the entire neighbourhood.

Restaurants

Michelin-starred
ENOTECA ✱✱
Marina, 19-21 → **1(E2)**
T 93 221 10 00
(> €60)
Signature cuisine by the chef Paco Pérez. "The freshness of the sea and the essence of the produce".

BESTIAL
Ramon Trias Fargas, 2-4 → **2(E2)**
T 93 224 04 07
(€30-50) + SET LUNCH MENU
Terrace and garden right on the beach. Mediterranean cuisine with an Italian twist.

ELS PESCADORS
Plaça Prim, 1 → **3(H2)**
T 93 225 20 18
(> €50)
Rafa Medrán and his team create freshly made dishes based on traditional and seafood recipes.

ELS "POLLOS" DE LLULL
Ramon Turró, 13 → **4(E1)**
T 93 221 32 06
(€10-20) + GROUP MENU
Specialists in spit-roast chickens. Inexpensive.

LA FONDA
DEL PORT OLÍMPIC
Moll de Gregal, 7 → **5(F3)**
T 93 221 22 10
(€30-50) + SET LUNCH MENU
Extensive à la carte menu. Mediterranean cuisine.

XIRINGUITO ESCRIBÀ
Av. Litoral, 42 → **6(F2)**
T 93 221 07 29
(€30-50)
Sea views combined with seafood cuisine. Make sure you try the desserts.

Cafés and bars
EL 58
Rambla del Poblenou, 58 → **7(H1)**
Laid-back bar serving quality tapas and small tasting platters.

EL TIO CHE
Rambla del Poblenou, 44 → **8(H1)**
Since 1912. Serves homemade *orxata*, a milky drink made from tiger nuts, and granitas.

Shopping
PATINALIA
Av. d'Icària, 180 → **10(F2)**
T 93 221 17 78
Shop specialising in in-line skates. They are also available for hire.

And also
CASINO DE BARCELONA
Marina, 19-21 → **(E2)**
www.casino-barcelona.com
A casino by the sea, with restaurants, bars and a discotheque.

POBLENOU CEMETERY
Taulat, 2 → **(G2)**
Opened in 1775, this was the first cemetery in BCN to be built outside the city walls. It was destroyed by Napoleon's troops in 1813, and rebuilt in 1849 with its pantheons by renowned architects and *modernista* and *noucentista* sculptors.

RAMBLA DEL POBLENOU
→ **(H1)**
This street, which begins almost right by the Bogatell beach, and is marked out by traditional shops and bars that extend their terraces onto the central passageway, has been the backbone of the cultural, social and commercial life of Poblenou for more than 100 years.

Municipal Sailing Centre → **(F3)**

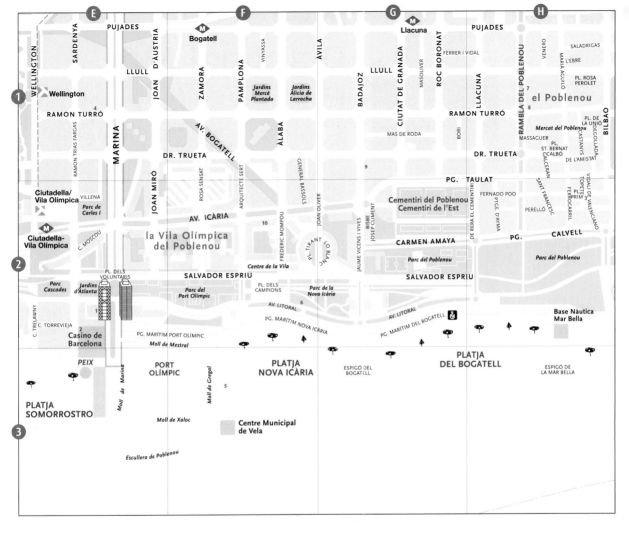

Port Olímpic ➜ (E3, F3)

Nova Icària beach ➜ (F3)

Highlights

PORT OLÍMPIC
→ (E3, F3)
www.pobasa.es
The Olympic Marina, opposite the Olympic Village, occupies a 25-hectare site reclaimed from the sea and is used by sailors and the local community. It is equipped with sailing facilities and schools, and also has a wide variety of restaurants and bars.

Port Olímpic → (E3, F3)

FISH
Avinguda Litoral, 12-14
→ (E3)
The giant fish designed by Frank Gehry, stands at the foot of one of the towers in the Port Olímpic, opposite the sea. A huge structure standing 35 metres high, made from woven strips of copper-coloured steel, which have glimmered in the sunlight since it was built in 1992.
+ INFO: p. 127

Fish, Frank Gehry → (E3)

AVINGUDA D'ICÀRIA
→ (F2)
The Avinguda d'Icària is the main artery in the Olympic Village. It is lined with expressive pergolas: striking tree-like structures of metal and wood, with abstract shapes designed by Enric Miralles.

PARC DEL FÒRUM
BATHING AREA
Plaça del Fòrum, 1
→ (K3, L3)
The Fòrum bathing area is located right on the waterfront. Just like a real beach but without sand, it forms a shallow seawater swimming pool that is ideal for children.

Avinguda d'Icària → (F2)

Fòrum bathing area → (K3, L3)

Sant Martí

Diagonal Mar
Fòrum

The city's hosting of the Forum of Cultures in 2004 led to a series of building developments that transformed the seafront of Sant Martí and completed the renewal of Barcelona's coastline. Following innovative guidelines, the city built a new congress complex (CCIB) on the Forum site, which can host up to 15,000 people, and placed it over a vast water-regulation and treatment facility, heralding a space for a sustainable future.

Parc del Fòrum
One of the latest urban-planning interventions based on the Barcelona "model" (which involves taking advantage of an event in order to improve services and infrastructures). Covering an area of 320,000 m², the precinct is one of the biggest cultural and recreational public spaces on the planet. In addition to the **Forum Building**, the **Barcelona International Convention Centre** and the **Photovoltaic Pergola**, the site also has a marina with 170 mooring berths for boats measuring between 10 and 25 m in length, and 31 berths for large yachts up to 80 m in length. It also has an innovative bathing area and vast plaza (over 100,000 m²) which hosts a wide range of events including the **Primavera Sound Festival** and the **April Flamenco Fair**.

Restaurants
EL COMEDOR
Passeig Garcia Fària, 37-47
→ 1(I2)
T 93 531 60 40
(€30-50) + GROUP MENU
Mediterranean cuisine, right on the seafront, with flavours of home-cooking.

ELS PEIXATERS
DE LA MEDITERRÀNIA
Passeig de Garcia Fària, 33
→ 2(I2)
T 93 266 38 84
(€30-40) + SET LUNCH MENU
Specialises in locally caught fresh fish and seafood.

ESCOLA D'HOSTALERIA
Passeig del Taulat, 243
→ 3(I2)
T 93 453 29 04
(€20-40) + SET LUNCH MENU
Find out what the great chefs of the future are cooking in Barcelona.

INDIGO
Passeig del Taulat, 262
→ 4(J2)
T 93 507 00 90
(€30-50)
International cuisine with fabulous sea views.

LA CANTINA
Pellaires, 30-38 → 5(I2)
T 93 307 09 74
(€20-40) + SET LUNCH MENU
Traditional and fusion cuisine in an old factory.

SAGARDI EUSKAL TABERNA
Avinguda Diagonal, 3
→ 6(K1)
T 93 356 04 76
(€20-40)
Basque cuisine with an endless variety of canapés and grilled meat and fish.

Cafés and bars
At the cutting-edge, seafront hotels: **Pistaccio Lobby Bar** and **Brisa Pool Bar** (Pg. Taulat, 262) → 7(K2); **The Corner Bar** and **The Gym Bar** (Av. Diagonal, 1) → 8(K2). At the Diagonal Mar shopping centre: tapas and beers (**Kurz & Gut**); coffee and ice creams (**Farggi**, **Häagen-Dazs**); fruit juices (**Passion Fruits**, **Smudy**).

Shopping

Shopping centre:
DIAGONAL MAR → (K1)
+ INFO: p. 131

And also
BARCELONA BOSC URBÀ
Pl. del Fòrum → (K2)
www.barcelonaboscurba.com
An urban adventure park with zipwires, suspension bridges, nets, creepers, bungee jumping, and trunks on platforms up to

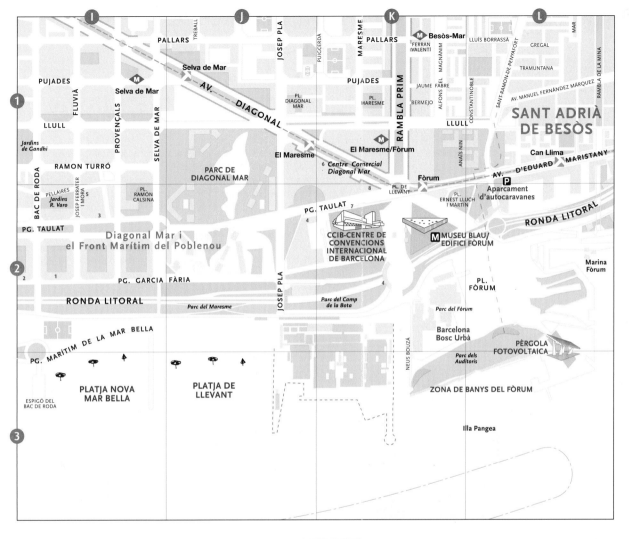

I · J · K · L

1 · 2 · 3

PALLARS — TREBALL
Selva de Mar
AV. DIAGONAL
JOSEP PLA
PUIGCERDÀ
MARESME
PALLARS
Besòs-Mar
LLUÍS BORRASSÀ
FERRAN VALENTÍ
GREGAL
MAR
TRAMUNTANA
PUJADES
FLUVIÀ
Selva de Mar
PUJADES
PL. DIAGONAL MAR
PL. MARESME
RAMBLA PRIM
JAUME FABRE
ALFONS EL MAGNÀNIM
RAFEL
BERMEJO
CONSTANTINOBLE
SANT-RAMON-DE-PENYAFORT
AV. MANUEL FERNÁNDEZ MÁRQUEZ
RAMBLA DE LA MINA
SANT ADRIÀ DE BESÒS
LLULL
Selva de Mar
PROVENÇALS
SELVA DE MAR
El Maresme
El Maresme/Fòrum
LLULL
ANAÍS NIN
Can Llima
Jardins de Gandhi
RAMON TURRÓ
PELLAIRES
Josep Ferrater i Mora
Jardins R. Varo
PL. RAMÓN CALSINA
PARC DE DIAGONAL MAR
6 Centre Comercial Diagonal Mar
8 PL. DE LLEVANT
Fòrum
PL. ERNEST LLUCH I MARTÍN
AV. D'EDUARD MARISTANY
Aparcament d'autocaravanes
RONDA LITORAL
BAC DE RODA
PG. TAULAT
PG. TAULAT 7
4
CCIB-CENTRE DE CONVENCIONS INTERNACIONAL DE BARCELONA
MUSEU BLAU/ EDIFICI FÒRUM
Diagonal Mar i el Front Marítim del Poblenou
Marina Fòrum
PG. GARCIA FÀRIA
JOSEP PLA
Parc del Camp de la Bota
4
PL. FÒRUM
RONDA LITORAL
Parc del Maresme
Parc del Fòrum
Barcelona Bosc Urbà
PÈRGOLA FOTOVOLTAICA
PG. MARÍTIM DE LA MAR BELLA
NEUS BOUZA
Parc dels Auditoris
ESPIGÓ DEL BAC DE RODA
PLATJA NOVA MAR BELLA
PLATJA DE LLEVANT
ZONA DE BANYS DEL FÒRUM
Illa Pangea

6 metres in height. It also has a circuit for children aged between 3 and 8 and the over 8s. Only open at weekends, except in the summer.

PARK & RIDE
Av. Eduard Maristany, s/n
➔ **(L2)**
Parking spaces for mobile homes. €30 per day.
Maximum stay: 72 h.

Parc del Fòrum. Primavera Sound ➔ **(K2, L2)**

Diagonal Mar ➔ **(K1)**

Highlights

CENTRE DE CONVENCIONS INTERNACIONAL DE BARCELONA CCIB
Parc dels Auditoris
→ **(K2)**
The CCIB building, designed by Josep Lluís Mateo, is Barcelona's main convention centre. It has five floors, 45 open-plan rooms, some of them extremely spacious, and can host 15,000 delegates.

PARC DIAGONAL MAR
→ **(J1, J2)**
14 hectares of gently rolling green areas which alternate with lakes; where the land goes in search of the sea, and vice-versa. The park is also known for its metal pergolas, trees and skyscrapers with spectacular views.

MUSEU BLAU EDIFICI FÒRUM
Pl. Leonardo da Vinci, 4-5
→ **(K2)**
T 93 256 60 02
Herzog & De Meuron designed the most eye-catching landmark in the Forum: a triangular building with a rough blue surface, which looks as if it is floating. Here the Museu Blau (Barcelona Museum of Natural Sciences) houses the *Planet Life* permanent exhibition.
+ INFO: p. 128

PHOTOVOLTAIC PERGOLA
Plaça Fòrum
→ **(L2)**
Apart from providing solar energy and being a technological marvel, the imposing photovoltaic cell, measuring 10,500 m² and designed by Torres and Lapeña, provides shade and is a perfect place to walk and look at the sea.

CCIB → **(K2)**

Parc Diagonal Mar → **(J1, J2)**

Museu Blau → **(K2)**

Photovoltaic Pergola → **(L2)**

Sant Martí

El Clot, 22@
and Plaça de les Glòries

El Clot already existed in medieval times when it was known as Clotum Melis (Honey Hollow) due to its fertile farmland. In the 19th centuries, the first flour and textile mills moved here followed by other industries. The former factories have now made way for community spaces, such as the Parc del Clot and La Farinera del Clot. 22@ is Barcelona's new technology district. It runs along the Diagonal, from the **Plaça de les Glòries Catalanes** (a new central area in the city) to the sea and is a must for anyone wanting to discover the future face of the city. The buildings in 22@ have been designed by some of the most famous contemporary architects.

Museums
MUSEU DE LA MÚSICA
Padilla, 155 → **(M2)**
www.museumusica.bcn.cat
The collection is presented through different thematic trails (*Orpheus* for the general public and *Petit Orpheus* for families) that show how music has been a vehicle for expression and communication for humans throughout the ages.

FUNDACIÓ VILA CASAS - MUSEU CAN FRAMIS
Roc Boronat, 116-126
→ **(02)**
www.fundaciovilacasas.com
Houses a collection of Catalan painting in two sections of a former woollen mill dating from the 18th century.

Restaurants

Michelin-starred
DOS CIELOS *
Pere IV, 272-286 → **1(P3)**
T 93 367 20 70
(> €60)
From the 24th floor of the Hotel Me with impressive views, signature haute cuisine by the brothers Javier and Sergio Torres.

CASA PEPE 22 ARROBA
Tànger, 98 → **2(N2)**
T 93 356 96 80 (€20-40)
Renowned delicatessen since 1947, selling cured meats, cheese, smoked produce and tapas.

ELS TRES PORQUETS
Rambla Poblenou, 165
→ **3(02)**
T 93 300 87 50
(€20-40) + SET LUNCH MENU
A new wine bar and restaurant serving top-quality tapas and tasting dishes.

FLORETA
Marià Aguiló, 50 → **4(03)**
T 93 380 47 99
(€20-40)
A great place for tapas and tasting platters with a haute-cuisine twist.

Cafés and bars
CELLER CA LA PAQUI
Sant Joan de Malta, 53
→ **5(02)**
Delightful bodega with a great selection of tapas.

MEGATAVERNA DEL POBLENOU L'OVELLA NEGRA
Zamora, 78 → **6(M3)**
Huge tavern housed in an industrial unit dating from 1908 where you can enjoy a plate of tapas and a beer.

PEPE'S BAR
Pamplona, 91 → **7(M3)**
Barcelona's rock and roll "shrine". The real deal.

Shopping

Shopping centre: BARCELONA-GLÒRIES
→ **(N2, 02)**
+ INFO: p. 148

Also worth visiting are **The Outlet Leather Factory** (Àvila, 105) → **8(N3)** with its affordable leather goods; **Casco Antiguo** (Clot, 131) → **9(01)** for diving equipment; and the **Bodega Sopena** (Clot, 55) → **10(01)** for wines and cavas.

And also
TEATRE NACIONAL DE CATALUNYA
Plaça de les Arts, 1 → **(M2)**
www.tnc.cat
Opened in 1996, in a building designed by Ricardo Bofill inspired by classical architecture. It stages plays from the classic repertoire and works by up-and-coming writers.

CAN FELIPA
Pallars, 277 → **(03)**
Community centre housed

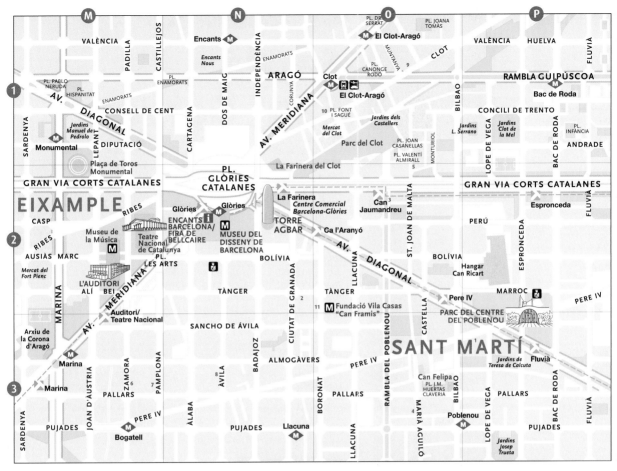

in an old factory which focuses on emerging artists.

PARC DEL CLOT
Escultors Claperós, 55-63 → (O1)
This park stands on land once occupied by factories. Architectural elements play a key role: a section of a façade makes an aqueduct some 25 metres long located inside a lake that culminates in a small waterfall.

LA FARINERA DEL CLOT
Gran Via, 837 → (N2)
Built in the *modernista* style, the former flour mill of San Jaime is now a cultural centre specialis-ing in three core areas: new communication and information technologies, bringing the community together and the recovery of historical memory.

EDIFICIO MEDIA-TIC
Roc Boronat, 117 → 11(O2)
A highly personal design by Enric Ruiz-Geli. It is cubic in shape and has four distinct façades covered in innovative, eco-efficient ethylene tetrafluoroethylene cladding which regulates the light and temperature to ensure maximum energy efficiency and savings are achieved.

Teatre Nacional → (M2)

Encants Barcelona → (N2)

Highlights

L'AUDITORI
Lepant, 150 → (M2)
www.auditori.cat
L'Auditori is the city's state-of-the-art concert venue. Designed by the architect Rafael Moneo it opened in 1999 and has four concert halls seating 2,200, 600, 400 and 152 people.

L'Auditori → (M2)

MUSEU DEL DISSENY DE BARCELONA
Pl. de les Glòries, 37 → (N2)
www.museudeldisseny.cat
Housed in a state-of-the-art building designed by the architect Oriol Bohigas, it brings together, under one roof, the holdings of the former Museu de les Arts Decoratives, the Museu Tèxtil i d'Indumentària, the Museu de Ceràmica and the Gabinet de les Arts Gràfiques. A major collection spanning antiquity to the present day.

Museu del Disseny → (N2)

ENCANTS BARCELONA FIRA DE BELLCAIRE
Pl. de les Glòries, 18 → (N2)
Europe's oldest second-hand market (dating back to the 14th century). A unique atmosphere beneath a spectacular futuristic roof. Monday, Wednesday, Friday and Saturday, 9am-8pm.

PARC DEL CENTRE DEL POBLENOU
→ (P2, P3)
This is Barcelona's newest park. It opened in spring 2008 and was designed by Jean Nouvel, the architect behind the Agbar Tower. The park stands next to the Diagonal and is a shady oasis of calm in the middle of the city offering a new experience to its visitors. Outstanding features include the different pictorial and sculptural elements that line the paths through the park, and the Oliva Artés factory which has been converted into an exhibition space about the city, its history and future.

Encants Barcelona → (N2)

Parc del Centre del Poblenou → (P3)

On the side of Collserola

Sarrià - Sant Gervasi

The district of Sarrià-Sant Gervasi stands on the north side of the Diagonal, at the foot of the Collserola ridge, the city's most important "green lung". It is the result of the annexation of two villages by Barcelona. Its proximity to Collserola and unique natural setting, with springs and green spaces, made it a popular residential area for the moneyed classes in the second half of the 19th century. This is why you'll see *modernista* summer holiday homes alongside the traditional architecture redolent of old villages. The most outstanding examples are the Torre Bellesguard and its viaduct, designed by Gaudí, and the mansions on the Avinguda del Tibidabo, with its famous century-old blue tram, the Tramvia Blau.

Must-sees
✳

COSMOCAIXA
Isaac Newton, 26 | T 93 212 60 50 | www.obrasocial.lacaixa.es → (D1)
CosmoCaixa is the city's science museum and an innovative educational centre which encourages visitors to experience science by observing natural phenomena. Its attractions range from a flooded forest, which recreates the flora and fauna of the Amazonian rainforest, to a planetarium with screenings in 3D.

TORRE BELLESGUARD
Bellesguard, 16-20 | T 93 250 40 93 | www.bellesguardgaudi.com → (C1)
At the beginning of the 20th century, Gaudí built the Torre Bellesguard on the site where King Martí "the Humane" had built his summer residence in the 15th century. The building is in the neo-Gothic style, made of brick, and clad on the exterior with slate quarried near the site, so that it blends in perfectly with its natural surroundings. There is a tower on the left-hand corner of the main façade surmounted by a four-armed cross. Between 1903 and 1905, Gaudí rerouted an old path that went through the property in order to connect Bellesguard with the remains of a medieval tower. He placed the path over a vault underpinned by sloping columns, creating a viaduct that was the precursor of the ones in Park Güell.

PARC D'ATRACCIONS TIBIDABO
Pl. del Tibidabo, 3-4 | T 93 211 79 4 | www.tibidabo.cat → (D1)
The Parc d'Atraccions Tibidabo stands 500 metres above the city. It is a modern amusement park which retains its much-loved character. It opened in 1899, and is part of the sentimental education of generations of Barcelona's boys and girls. The park combines vintage rides from the early days (such as the Talaia, which dates from 1921, and the haunted castle, the Castell Misteriós) and other high-tech attractions which have been added to cater to the most recent trends (such as the head-spinning Hurakan, with its sudden plunges and 360° turns, and the new roller coaster).

CosmoCaixa → (D1)

Torre Bellesguard → (C1)

Parc d'Atraccions Tibidabo → (D1)

Sant Gervasi
+ Gaudí Trail (3)

The former village of Sant Gervasi de Cassoles, which dates back to the middle of the 13th century, was absorbed by Barcelona in 1897. The residential character of the neighbourhood led to the building of many detached houses with gardens, some of them of great architectural value. More than a century ago, they defined the way it looks today and have gradually adapted to the urban layout.

Gaudí Trail (3)

There are two landmarks by this architectural genius in this area. The **Col·legi de les Teresianes**, an austere stone and brick building with a beautiful, light-filled interior, and the **Torre de Bellesguard**, where Gaudí paid his own personal tribute to Catalan Gothic architecture. The interiors are closed to visitors. Download the audioguide Gaudí's Barcelona onto your MP3 player (tickets.visitbarcelona.com) and from the Apple Store (http://apps.barcelona turisme.com).

Restaurants

Michelin-starred

ÀBAC ★★
Avinguda Tibidabo, 1
→ 1(D2)
T 93 319 66 00
(> €60)
Dining rooms in every shade of white provide the backdrop to the creative cuisine of Jordi Cruz.

HISOP ★
Passatge Marimón, 9
→ 2(C4)
T 93 241 32 33
(> €60)
Two young chefs dazzle us with their contemporary Catalan cuisine.

HOFFMANN ★
Granada del Penedès, 14
→ 3(D4)
T 93 218 71 65
(> €60)
Mey Hofmann creates and recreates dishes which retain all the essence, flavour and aroma of the raw ingredients.

VIA VENETO ★
Ganduxer, 10
→ 4(B4)
T 93 200 72 44
(> €60)
Impeccable service. Since 1967, its classic Catalan cuisine has been renowned for its innovative touches and dependability.

CASA FERNÁNDEZ
Santaló, 46
→ 5(C4)
T 93 201 93 08
(€40-50) + GROUP MENU
Home-cooking and cold and hot tapas until 1am. A wide range of beers.

COURE
Passatge Marimon, 20
→ 6(C4)
T 93 200 75 32
(€50-60)
The chef Albert Ventura produces refined, imaginative cuisine based on traditional Catalan dishes.

FLASH-FLASH
Granada del Penedès, 25
→ 7(D4)
T 93 237 09 90
(€20-30)

Specialises in omelettes. Kitchen open from 1pm to 1am. Pop-art interior design.

FREIXA TRADICIÓ
Sant Elies, 22
→ 8(D3)
T 93 209 75 59
(> €60)
Traditional Mediterranean cuisine with the unmistakeable hallmark of the chef Josep M. Freixa.

IL GIARDINETTO
Granada del Penedès, 28
→ 9(D4)
T 93 218 75 36
(€40-50) + SET LUNCH MENU
Decorated like a garden. Serves excellent Italian cuisine.

L'OLIANA
Santaló, 54
→ 10(C4)
T 93 201 06 47
(€45-55) + GROUP MENU
Time-honoured Catalan cuisine in an elegant, light-filled setting.

And also

JARDINS DE LA TAMARITA
Pg. de Sant Gervasi, 47
→ (D1)
These splendid gardens are part of the grounds of an early 20th-century mansion and allow visitors to enjoy the contrast between ordered landscape and spontaneous plant growth.

Sarrià

The origins of Sarrià date back to the 13th century. In 1921, Sarrià was the last village to be absorbed by Barcelona. The old part is located around the main street (Carrer Major de Sarrià). Make sure you take a peaceful stroll through the Plaça del Consell de la Vila, the Plaça de Sarrià, the Plaça de Sant Vicenç and along the Passatge Mallofré to admire the parish church of Sant Vicenç; the old town hall, now the seat of the district council; and soak up the atmosphere of a typical neighbourhood that still feels like a village.

Porta Miralles → (A3)

Vil·la Cecília → (A2)

Parc del Castell de l'Oreneta → (A1)

Restaurants

CASA JOANA
Major de Sarrià, 59
→ 11(A2)
T 93 203 10 36
(€20-30) + SET LUNCH MENU
Retains the style of an old inn with tasty home-cooking.

EL CANALLA
Major de Sarrià, 95
→ 12(A2)
T 93 205 88 06
(€20-30) + SET LUNCH MENU
Restaurant and wine bar with a typical fifties interior. Specialises in tasting platters and small servings.

LA BURG
Pg. St. Sant Joan Bosco, 55
→ 13(A2)
T 93 205 63 48
(€20-30)
Gourmet hamburgers. Includes veggie burgers too.

TRAM-TRAM
Major de Sarrià, 121
→ 14(A1)
T 93 204 85 18
(€45-55) + SET LUNCH MENU
Creative signature cuisine in a typical house with a garden in Sarrià.

VIVANDA
Major de Sarrià, 134
→ 15(B1)
T 93 203 19 18 (€30-45)
The prestigious chef Jordi Vilà presents his superb tapas and tasting platters.

The restaurant has an indoor terrace.

Cafés and bars

BAR TOMÁS
Major de Sarrià, 49
→ 16(A2)
Neighbourhood bar which many consider serves the city's best spicy potatoes.

DOLE
Manuel de Falla, 16-18
→ 17(A3)
Very small bar specializing in omelettes with a loyal local clientele.

Shopping

FUREST
Av. Pau Casals, 3 → 18(C4)
Prestigious family mens-wear brand since 1898.

JOFRÉ
Bori i Fontestà, 2-6
→ 19(B4)
Leading international fashion brands for ladies and children.

ORIOL BALAGUER
Pl. St. Gregori Taumaturg, 2
→ 20(B3)
A world-renowned pastry chef famed for his chocolates and chocolate cakes.

PASTISSERIA FOIX
Plaça de Sarrià, 12
→ 21(B1)
Since 1886. It has made cakes for royal weddings and sends its products around the world.

And also

VIL·LA CECÍLIA AND VIL·LA AMÈLIA
Eduardo Conde, 22
→ (A2)
These gardens, with their centuries-old trees, are located in the spacious grounds of a former private estate and are an oasis of calm.

PARC DEL CASTELL DE L'ORENETA
Montevideo, 45
→ (A1)
A large wooded area that links the city to the Collserola Ridge. It has a picnic area and boasts magnificent views of the city. Visitors can go pony trekking and, on Sundays, from 11am to 2pm, they can ride on one of Europe's best miniature trains.

PORTA MIRALLES
Passeig Manuel Girona, 55
→ (A3)
Designed by Gaudí and built between 1901 and 1902 as the gate to the estate of his friend Miralles. Although it is one of the brilliant architect's minor works, it has an interesting undulating wall top and two entrances: one with lobulate arches for vehicles and one for pedestrians which retains its original iron railings.

Bar Tomás → 16(A2)

Highlights

COL·LEGI DE LES TERESIANES
Ganduxer, 85-105 → (B2)
Austerity is the defining characteristic of the school Gaudí designed for the nuns from the Order of Saint Teresa in 1887. It is mostly built of brick which frames parabolic windows and merlons. One of the most outstanding interior features is the corridor of catenary arches.

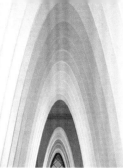
Col·legi de les Teresianes → (B2)

TRAMVIA BLAU
→ (D2)
The Blue Tram, or Tramvia Blau, has been operating for over 100 years. Its vintage cars cover a 1.3 km route on a 93 m gradient, from the Plaça Kennedy to the Plaça del Dr. Andreu, where passengers can transfer to the funicular which runs to the top of Tibidabo.

PLAÇA DE SARRIÀ AND CHURCH OF SANT VICENÇ
Plaça de Sarrià, 1 → (B2)
The church of Sant Vicenç was built in 1781, on the site where a church dedicated to the same saint stood 1,000 years ago. The interior houses a number of 17th-century altarpieces. From time to time, antiques and second-hand book fairs are held in the square in front of the church as well as a farmers' market and open-air exhibitions of paintings by street artists.

Tramvia Blau → (D2)

MERCAT DE SARRIÀ
Pg. de la Reina Elisenda, 8
→ (A1)
www.mercatsarria.com
The market was designed by the architects Marcel·lí Coquillat and Arnau Calvet, and opened in 1911. It was refurbished in 2007. The main façade retains the original *modernista* decorations. Inside there are all kinds of stalls, some of them even prepare dishes and offer product tastings in situ.

Plaça de Sarrià → (B2)

Mercat de Sarrià → (A1)

Collserola

The Parc de Collserola is Barcelona's vast "green lung", an area of forest which winds its way from the Besòs to the Llobregat rivers, and separates the city from the county of the Vallès. Parts of the park have been built on, but it has been a protected area since 1987, allowing it to preserve most of its Mediterranean woodland, comprising pines, ilexes and oaks, and fauna, which ranges from rabbits to wild boars.

Museums

MUSEU D'AUTÒMATES DEL TIBIDABO
Plaça del Tibidabo, 3-4
→ 1(G1)
www.tibidabo.cat
An amazing collection of automata, some of them from the 19th century.

Restaurants

L'ORANGERIE
Ctra. de Vallvidrera al Tibidabo, 83-93 → 2(H1)
T 93 259 30 30
(> €60) + SET LUNCH MENU
Charming restaurant serving creative signature cuisine. Spectacular views.

LA BALSA
Infanta Isabel, 4 → 3(G3)
T 93 211 50 48
(€45-60)
Market-fresh Mediterranean cuisine in a space that won the FAD Architecture Prize.

LA VENTA
Plaça Doctor Andreu, s/n
→ 4(H3)
T 93 212 64 55
(€35-45) + GROUP MENU
A short but mouthwatering menu of Catalan dishes. *Modernista* building.

Cafés and bars

A cluster of BCN classics with stunning city views which are the perfect place for a relaxing drink.

EL REBOST DE COLLSEROLA
Collserola, 31 → 5(H3)
Cafeteria with midday menu and shop selling with Catalan products.

MERBEYÉ
Plaça Doctor Andreu, s/n
→ 6(H3)
With original design by Mariscal, it has altered little since it opened. A cosy place at any time of day.

MIRABLAU
Plaça Doctor Andreu, 2
→ 7(H3)
Bar overlooking the city. Two levels and a terrace with excellent service.

And also

VALLVIDRERA
→ (F1)
Neighbourhood at the top of Collserola which is reached by a funicular railway that opened in 1906 and was refurbished in 1998. Highlights include the church of Santa Maria de Vallvidrera, built between 1570 and 1587 in the late-Gothic style on the site of the original church (987 AD), and the Vallvidrera reservoir.

DINNER UNDER THE STARS
Observatori Fabra
→ (G2)
T 93 431 21 39
From June to September, dinners in the gardens of the Fabra Observatory (1904). Includes a guided tour and the chance to watch the night sky.
www.observatorifabra.com

Off the map:
LES PLANES
Popular with BCN locals for Sunday outings, with its snack bars and barbecues. 20 min. from Pl. Catalunya on Catalan railways (FGC).

CENTRE D'INTERPRETACIÓ DEL PARC DE COLLSEROLA
Ctra. de l'Església, 9 (Ctra. Vallvidrera-Sant Cugat, km 4.7) → (E1)
Exhibition about the flora and fauna in the natural park.

Tibidabo funicular → (G1, H3)

Les Planes

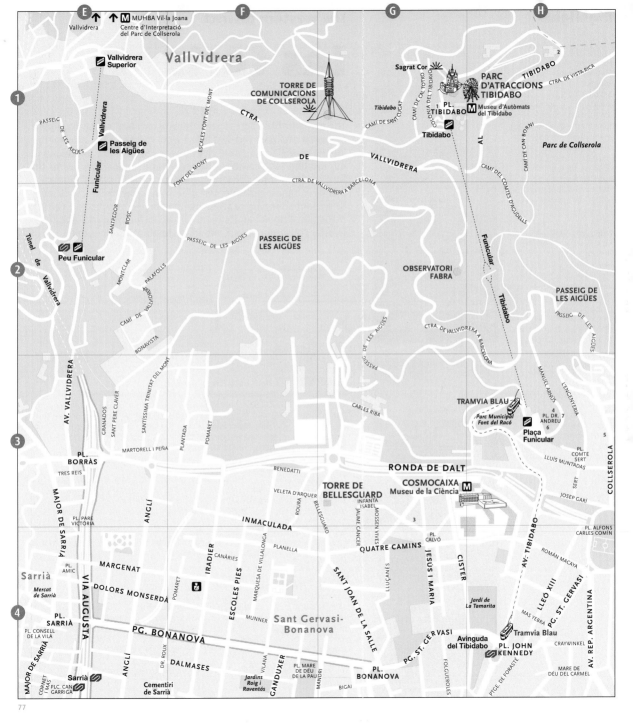

Highlights

COLLSEROLA COMMUNICATIONS TOWER
Ctra. Vallvidrera Tibidabo
➔ **(G1)**
T 93 406 93 54
www.torredecollserola.com
Standing 288 metres high, this is Barcelona's tallest tower. It was designed by Norman Foster and has 13 floors. The observation deck on the tenth floor is open to the public. It stands 560 metres above sea level and has breathtaking views of the city.

FABRA OBSERVATORY
Ctra. Vallvidrera Tibidabo
➔ **(G2)**
www.observatorifabra.com
The Fabra Observatory nestles among the pines on the south-east side of the Collserola Ridge, just below Tibidabo. Since 1904, it has been dedicated to the study of astronomy, meteorology and seismology.

PASSEIG DE LES AIGÜES
➔ **(E2, H2)**
This road winds its way through the Parc de Collserola, and commands impressive, sweeping views of the city and the sea. It is a unique viewing point and a popular place for walkers, joggers and cyclists.

Collserola Tower ➔ **(G1)**

Fabra Observatory ➔ **(G2)**

Passeig de les Aigües ➔ **(E2, H2)**

Les Corts

The district of Les Corts spans the western half of the Avinguda Diagonal, the part furthest away from the sea. It was formerly a village of the same name, which was absorbed by Barcelona during the late 19th century. The area was irrigated by streams that flowed down from Collserola. Once an agricultural settlement, it is now a mainly residential area with some of the city's most important shopping centres, major sporting venues and cultural attractions. However, its green areas, including parks and the nearby Collserola Massif, are its distinguishing features.

Must-sees
✴

CAMP NOU - FC BARCELONA
Avinguda Joan XXIII, s/n | T 902 189 900 | www.fcbarcelona.cat ➔ **(B3)**
The 99,000-seater F.C. Barcelona Stadium is one of the great "cathedrals" of world football. Since it opened in 1957, it has witnessed some of Barça's greatest sporting achievements. Its **Camp Nou Experience** also receives one million visitors a year. It includes a tour of the stadium, museum, the Espai Messi and the multimedia zone, among other iconic areas of the stadium. +INFO: p. 130

PEDRALBES MONASTERY
Baixada del Monestir, 9 | T 93 256 34 34 | www.bcn.cat/monestirpedralbes ➔ **(B1)**
Pedralbes Monastery was built seven centuries ago in uptown Barcelona. Its church and monastic buildings are set out around a beautiful three-tier cloister and are one of the best-preserved examples of Catalan Gothic architecture. The monastery has been home to a community of nuns from the Order of Saint Clare since 1327, and in 1983 opened some of its rooms to the public, which have been converted into museum galleries. The monastery is home to collections of paintings, ceramics, silver and goldware and furniture, as well as the chapel of Sant Miquel, with its murals by Ferrer Bassa. +INFO: p. 128

GÜELL PAVILIONS
Avinguda de Pedralbes, 7 | T 93 204 52 50 ➔ **(B2)**
The gates outside the Güell Estate are one of Gaudí's most richly imaginative works. They depict a fierce winged dragon, which was originally painted in bright colours, its jaws activated by a mechanical device. This wrought-iron gate leads to the caretaker's lodge and the stables that marked the entrance to the estate, which stood just off the Diagonal. Gaudí's patron, Eusebi Güell, had the estate demolished to make way for the Royal Palace, the Palau Reial. For years, the stables were home to the Càtedra Gaudí, a university research centre, which preserves the architect's legacy.

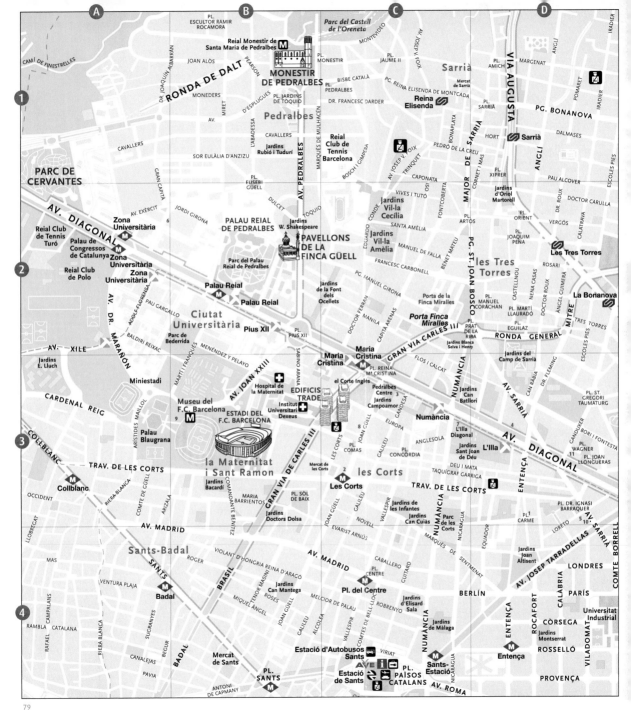

Camp Nou - FC Barcelona ➔(B3)

Pedralbes Monastery ➔(B1)

Güell Pavilions ➔(B2)

Museums
MUSEU DEL
FC BARCELONA
Av. Arístides Maillol,
gates 7 and 9 ➔(B3)
www.fcbarcelona.cat
A pioneering football
museum which attracts
over one million visitors
every year.

Restaurants
LA TERTÚLIA
Morales, 15 ➔1(D3)
T 93 419 58 97
(€20-40) + SET LUNCH MENU
Thought-provoking,
market-fresh cuisine in a
charming building.
LEKU
Joan Güell, 189 ➔2(C3)
T 93 490 38 10
(€40-60) + SET LUNCH MENU
Basque cuisine brought
to you by a young chef
using hand-picked produce
cooked with painstaking
attention to detail.
MUSSOL
PEDRALBES CENTRE
Av. Diagonal, 611 ➔3(C3)
T 93 410 13 17
(€20-30) + GROUP MENU
Typical Catalan specialities
at affordable prices.
NEGRO-ROJO
Av. Diagonal, 640 ➔4(D3)
T 93 405 94 44
(€35-45) + SET LUNCH MENU
Split-level restaurant serving different specialities.
Upstairs, cosmopolitan
dishes. Downstairs, Japa-
nese cuisine.
TOMAX
Loreto, 32 ➔5(D3)
T 93 345 71 48
(€30-45)
Traditional Castilian cuisine made with the finest
produce.
TRITÓN
Alfambra, 16 ➔6(A2)
T 93 203 30 85
(€45-60)
Half a century of market-
fresh cuisine. Specialises in
fish and seafood.

Cafés and bars
SALA BIKINI
Av. Diagonal, 547, ➔7(C3)
With its three different
rooms (the Dry Bikini

lounge, Autanga and the
classic Sala Bikini) which
play different styles of
music and attract different
crowds, Bikini is a Barcelona nightlife classic.

Shopping
Shopping centres:
EL CORTE INGLÉS ➔(C3)
L'ILLA DIAGONAL ➔(C3)
PEDRALBES CENTRE ➔(C3)
+INFO: p. 148

ESPACIO
HARLEY-DAVIDSON BCN
Joan Güell, 207
➔8(C3)
Europe's biggest show-
room for the legendary
motorbike. You'll also
find accessories, techni-
cal clothing and urban
fashions.
LA BOTIGA DEL BARÇA
Av. Arístides Maillol, s/n
➔9(B3)
Official team strips, fashion, pyjamas, baby clothes,
accessories, homeware...
NATCHA
Av. de Sarrià, 45 ➔10(D3)
Patisserie that comes
highly recommended due
to its cakes and chocolates
which range from the tra-
ditional to its own unique
creations.
THE WATCH GALLERY
Avi. Diagonal, 626 ➔11(D3)
A shop dedicated solely to
timepieces. A wide selec-
tion of up to 40 world-
renowned brands.

And also
PLAÇA DE LA CONCÒRDIA
➔(C3)
This square stands in the
heart of the old quarter
of the former village of
Les Corts which became
part of Barcelona in 1897.
It retains a peaceful
atmosphere away from the
hustle and bustle of the
city. Can Deu is the main
landmark in the square. It
is open to visitors and has
modernista elements.

Museu del FC Barcelona ➔(B3)

Güell Pavilions ➔(B2)

Plaça de la Concòrdia ➔(C3)

Pedralbes Monastery ➔(B1)

Highlights

PALAU REIAL DE PEDRALBES
Avinguda Diagonal, 686
→ (B2)
The former Güell Estate was converted into a royal palace in the early 20th century. The palace is surrounded by gardens with tall trees and is close to the university campus.

MATERNITAT
Travessera de les Corts, 159
→ (B3)
The pavilions of the former maternity home, which was begun at the end of the 19th century, form an interesting architectural ensemble combining *modernisme* and *noucentisme*. The gardens are well worth a visit.

TRADE BUILDINGS
Avinguda Carles III, 84-89
→ (B3)
A classic of modern Barcelona architecture at the side of the Avinguda Carles III: four office blocks clad in black glass, dating from 1968 and designed by Coderch de Sentmenat.

PARC DE CERVANTES
Av. Diagonal, 706
→ (A1)
A park with magnificent views of Barcelona and much loved by walkers and sports lovers, particularly cyclists and joggers. It also contains a unique area of 4 hectares: a rose garden with an outstanding collection of more than 10,000 rose bushes from 2,000 different species and varieties.

Palau Reial de Pedralbes → (B2)

Maternitat → (B3)

Trade Buildings → (B3)

Parc de Cervantes → (A1)

Over hills and valleys

Horta-Guinardó

The district of Horta-Guinardó winds its way up the Collserola Ridge, between Gràcia and Nou Barris. It is subdivided into 11 neighbourhoods and forms a border between the urban layout of the city and nature. It has large swathes of green, which include the whole area above the upper ring-road, the Ronda de Dalt, which encroaches on Collserola, part of the Vall d'Hebron and Carmel. Most of the district has uneven landform and sloping terrain, and boasts major healthcare and sporting facilities, as well as places where the pace of life is more relaxed, such as the former village of Horta.

Must-sees

❋
RECINTE MODERNISTA DE SANT PAU
Sant Antoni M. Claret, 167 | www.santpaubarcelona.org
→ (B5)
Domènech i Montaner designed this great hospital complex which covers a surface area equivalent to nine blocks of the Eixample. The project integrates architecture and urban planning and embraces some of the tenets of the utopian garden-city movement. The hospital is divided into 46 pavilions with landscaped areas between them and connected by underground passages which let in natural daylight from above. Most of the pavilions are built with brick and feature a wealth of decorative sculptural elements and mosaics, mainly inspired by Gothic and Mudejar art.
+INFO: p. 130

Recinte Modernista de Sant Pau → (B5)

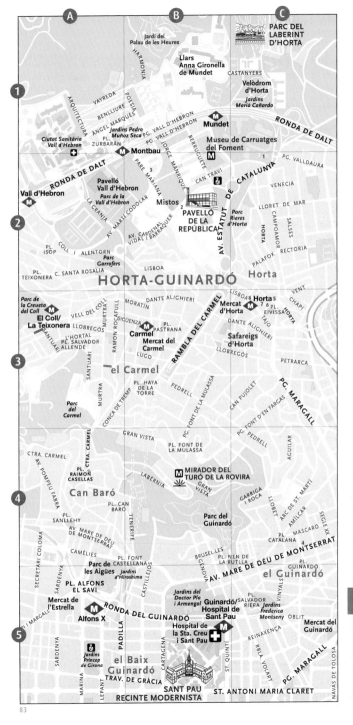

Museums

MUSEU DE CARRUATGES DEL FOMENT

Pl. Josep Pallach, 8 → **(B2)**
Carts, carriages, wagons and clothing and accessories used by coachmen and carters in the 19th and 20th centuries.

Restaurants

CAN CORTADA

Av. Estatut, s/n
→ **1(C2)**
T 93 427 23 15
(€30-40) + GROUP MENU
Mediterranean cuisine and traditional Catalan fare in an 11th-century farmhouse with an attractive garden.

CAN TRAVI NOU

Jorge Manrique, s/n
→ **2(B2)**
T 93 428 04 34
(€40-50) + GROUP MENU
Market-fresh, Catalan cuisine in a setting steeped in the charm of Horta's rural past.

ELS MISTOS

Juan de Mena, 1-3
→ **3(B2)**
T 687 088 832
(€25-40)
Excellent, simple food using the finest Galician products.

LA BÓTA DEL RACÓ

Av. Mare de Déu de Montserrat, 232
→ **4(C4)**
T 93 456 60 01
(€25-40)+ GROUP MENU
Traditional Catalan dishes made using time-honoured methods. Extensive menu.

Cafés and bars

BAR QUIMET

Pl. Eivissa, 10 → **5(C3)**
More than 20 varieties of omelette. Good tapas.

BAR PRATS

Pl. Eivissa, 8
→ **6(C3)**
More than 50 years in the neighbourhood. Tapas, vermouths and beers.

LA BODEGUETA D'HORTA

Pere Pau, 4
→ **7(C3)**
Wines, tapas and a great atmosphere at this old neighbourhood bodega.

Shopping

At **Horta Market** (Tajo, 75) → **8(C3)** and the **Cor d'Horta** shopping area → **(C2, C3)**. More than 270 stalls and shops where you'll receive the friendly, personalised service typical of the neighbourhood.

And also

JARDÍ DEL PALAU DE LES HEURES

→ **(B1)**
Historic garden (1893). It is set out on three south-facing terraces. The first of them features the imposing French-style palace, the Palau de les Heures.

LAUNDRY TROUGHS IN HORTA

Aiguafreda, s/n
→ **(C3)**
A corner of town unknown to many locals. Its houses, with their allotments and laundry troughs, remind us of the rural origins of the area.

MATCH COVER

Av. Cardenal Vidal i Barraquer, s/n
→ **(B2)**
One of the most popular pieces of public art in the city. Its creator, Claes Oldenburg, one of the leading exponents of Pop Art, recreates everyday objects on a giant scale. In this case, a series of humble matches: some still inside the match cover, others scattered on the ground.

PARC DE LES RIERES D'HORTA

→ **(C2)**
Situated below the Pavilion of the Republic, this park provides a link between the biodiversity of the Collserola Ridge and urban green spaces. An easily accessible pathway runs lengthwise through the park which is set out on different levels.

Recinte Modernista de Sant Pau → **(B5)**

Highlights

PARC DEL LABERINT D'HORTA
Germans Desvalls, s/n
→ (C1)

This neo-classical-style garden with its romantic atmosphere has fountains, ponds and water channels. Its architecture and sculptures blend with plant species seldom found in the city. Its centrepiece is the intricate cypress maze. Originally the property of a noble family, the gardens were opened to the public in 1971.

Parc del Laberint d'Horta → (C1)

PAVELLÓ DE LA REPÚBLICA
Av. Cardenal Vidal i Barraquer
→ (B2)

In 1937, at the height of the Civil War, Spain opened its pavilion at the Paris World Fair. The pioneering building, designed by Josep Lluís Sert and Luis Lacasa, was used to present Pablo Picasso's *Guernica*, and works by Joan Miró, Julio González, Alberto Sánchez and Alexander Calder. A faithful replica of the building was built in Horta in 1992, as the headquarters for the study centre, the Centre d'Estudis Històrics Internacionals.

Pavelló de la República → (B2)

MIRADOR
DEL TURÓ DE LA ROVIRA
Marià Labèrnia
→ (B4)

One of the most unique places in Barcelona. This natural lookout point (262 metres above sea level) boasts 360° views of the city. It is also a heritage site containing an anti-aircraft battery that defended the city from the bombing raids by fascist planes during the Spanish Civil War, the remains of a shanty settlement that stood on the site from 1950 to 1990, and a reservoir belonging to the city's water company.

Mirador del Turó de la Rovira → (B4)

The gateway to Barcelona

Sant Andreu

Founded over 1,000 years ago, Sant Andreu is one of the traditional gateways to Barcelona. It has a strong industrial past and is currently immersed in a process of transformation, with the laying of the high-speed train track and the construction of the new station at La Sagrera, which will be the city's second high-speed-train terminal. This major rail project will bring about the redevelopment of Sant Andreu and redefine its centrality.

Restaurants

LA PARADETA
Pacífic, 74 → 1(B3)
T 93 534 65 57
(€20-30)
Fish chosen from the counter at the entrance.

EL LAGAR
Llenguadoc, 6 → 2(B2)
T 93 346 82 70
(€20-30)
Cosy restaurant serving creative Mediterranean cuisine.

MARISQUERIA DOPAZO
Borriana, 90 → 3(B3)
T 93 311 47 51
(€35-50)
Fine Galician seafood for more than 50 years.

RABASSEDA
Pl. Mercedal, 1 → 4(B2)
T 93 345 10 17
(€25-35)
Market-fresh cuisine. Extremely popular with locals. Terrace.

TAVERNA CAN ROCA
Gran de Sant Andreu, 209 → 5(B2)
T 93 346 57 01
(€20-30) + SET LUNCH MENU
Excellent home-made soups and stews.

Cafés and bars

2D2DSPUMA
Manigua, 8 → 6(A2)
Craft beers. More than 200 bottles and five beers on tap.

COLOMBIA
Rambla Fabra i Puig, 1 → 7(B2)
Bar selling fair-trade products.

VERSALLES
Gran de Sant Andreu, 255 → 8(B2)
The social hub of the neighbourhood since 1928. Classic tapas and set lunch menu.

Shops

A vast shopping area stretches from the Plaça del Mercadal along Carrer Gran de Sant Andreu and the Passeig Fabra i Puig → (B2, B3). It includes all kinds of fashion shops, cultural and leisure attractions, food shops...

Shopping centres:
LA MAQUINISTA → (C2)
+INFO: p.148

And also

CHURCH OF SANT PACIÀ
Monges, 27 → (B2)
The young architect Antoni Gaudí worked on the decorative elements inside the neo-Gothic church of Sant Pacià (Joan Torras i Guardiola, 1880). The floor mosaic still survives and was the precursor of the ones he designed for the dining room at the Casa Vicens and inside the Sagrada Família crypt.

PARC DE LA MAQUINISTA
→ (C2)
A park that is home to the locomotive museum, the Museu Històric de la Maquinista.

PLAÇA DEL MERCADAL
→ (B2)
Time seems to have stood still in this beautiful porticoed square situated in the old quarter of the former village of Sant Andreu which was absorbed into Barcelona in 1897.

BAC DE RODA BRIDGE
→ (A3)
The engineer and architect Santiago Calatrava's first foray into the world of bridge design. Built between 1985 and 1987 with curves inspired by the lines of the human body.

Plaça del Mercadal → (B2)

Highlights

CASA BLOC
Almirall Pròixida, 1-5
Pg. de Torras i Bages,
103-105 ➜ **(C2)**
The Casa Bloc is a bold
rationalist landmark: it
was the first example of
social housing for workers
in Spain and combines 200
private duplex apartments
with community gardens.
The block was designed
in 1932 by the architects
from the GATCPAC (Group
of Catalan Architects
and Technicians for the
Progress of Contemporary
Architecture) – Sert, Torres
i Clavé and Subirana – and
it became a benchmark
for progressive architec-
ture. Barcelona's Museu de
Disseny organises guided
tours of Apartment 1/11
which has been restored
to its intended appear-
ance.
Pre-booking is essential
(T 93 256 34 63).

Casa Bloc ➜ **(C2)**

FABRA I COATS
Sant Adrià, 20 ➜ **(B2)**
The Fabra i Coats project
is one of the most ambi-
tious interventions in the
municipal policy of con-
verting disused factories
into cultural facilities.
Over the coming decade,
teaching and creativ-
ity in fields such as art,
music, theatre, dance and
audiovisuals will take the
baton from the manufac-
turing processes carried
out in this factory from
the late 19th to the mid
20th centuries.

Fabra i Coats ➜ **(B2)**

CANÒDROM MERIDIANA
Concepció Arenal, 165
➜ **(B2)**
The former dog track, an
impressive iron structure
that opened in 1964 and
was awarded the FAD
Design prize is now a
public facility: the brand-
new creative-research
park, the Parc de Recerca
Creativa.

Canòdrom Meridiana ➜ **(B2)**

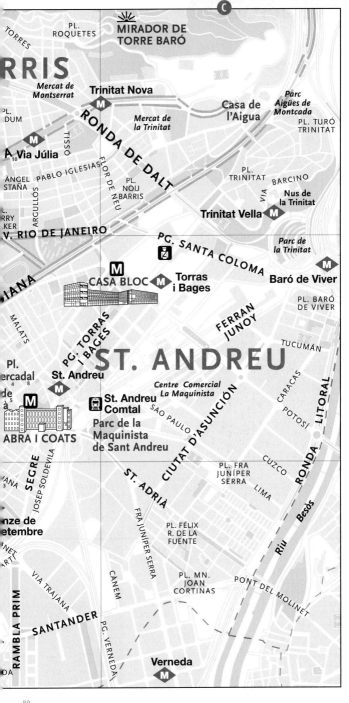

PL.
ROQUETES

TORRES

MIRADOR DE
TORRE BARÓ

RRIS

Mercat de
Montserrat

Trinitat Nova M

Casa de
l'Aigua

Parc
Aigües de
Montcada

PL.
DUM

RONDA DE DALT

Mercat de
la Trinitat

PL. TURÓ
TRINITAT

A Via Júlia M

10

TISSO

FLOR DE NEU

PL.
TRINITAT

BARCINO

ÀNGEL
STAÑA

PABLO IGLESIAS

PL.
NOU
NBARRIS

VIA

Nus de
la Trinitat

ARGULLÓS

RRY
KER

V. RIO DE JANEIRO

Trinitat Vella M

PG. SANTA COLOMA

Parc de
la Trinitat

IANA

CASA BLOC M

Torras
i Bages

M

Baró de Viver M

MALATS

PG. TORRAS
I BAGES

FERRAN
JUNOY

PL. BARÓ
DE VIVER

TUCUMÁN

ST. ANDREU

Pl.
ercadal

St. Andreu M

Centre Comercial
La Maquinista

CARACAS

LITORAL

de
à

4

8

5

St. Andreu
Comtal

SAO PAULO

CIUTAT D'ASUNCIÓN

POTOSÍ

ABRA I COATS

Parc de la
Maquinista
de Sant Andreu

CUZCO

RONDA

SEGRE

JOSEP SOLDEVILA

ST. ADRIÀ

PL. FRA
JUNÍPER
SERRA

LIMA

Besòs

IANA

3

nze de
etembre

FRA JUNÍPER SERRA

PL. FÉLIX
R. DE LA
FUENTE

Riu

VIA TRAJANA

CÀNEM

PL. MN.
JOAN
CORTINAS

PONT DEL MOLINET

NET
RT

RAMBLA PRIM

SANTANDER

PG. VERNEDA

Verneda
M

DA

The newest district

Nou Barris

The district of Nous Barris stands on the other side of the Avinguda Meridiana, which marks the boundary of Sant Andreu, and stretches as far as the foothills of the Collserola Ridge. Attractions include the greenway, the Passeig de les Aigües, and the Parc de Font Magués. This Barcelona district was established relatively recently by successive waves of incomers from the rest of Spain. It also has the most neighbourhoods – there are now 13.

Restaurants

LA BODEGUETA D'EN MIQUEL
Pl. Jardins d'Alfàbia, 3
→ 9 (B1)
T 93 354 45 83 (< €20)
Classic cold tapas and other more original creations made with a skilful combination of gourmet tinned produce.

LA FREIDU
Via Julia, 94
→ 10 (B1)
T 93 353 44 02
(< €20)
Simple bar with a terrace serving delicious tapas.

MESÓN CAN MELI
Arnau d'Oms, 45
→ 11 (A2)
T 93 408 08 16
(€20-30) + SET LUNCH MENU
Specialises in cured meats, sausage and cheese served with great beer and wine.

TXAPELDUN - EGARRI
Pg. Fabra i Puig, 159
→ 12 (A2)
T 93 352 91 01
(€20-30) + SET LUNCH MENU
Basque cuisine. Tapas and great fish.

Cafés and bars

LA ESQUINICA
Pg. Fabra i Puig, 296
→ 13 (A2)
Regional tapas. There's always a queue but service is quick. A classic.

ECHA PAYÁ
Pl. del Virrei Amat, 12
→ 14 (A2)
A great place for a pre-lunch drink, *montaditos* (canapés) and great tinned tapas.

LA BOTIGUETA DEL BON MENJAR
Pg. Verdum, 37 → 15 (B1)
Café where you can also have lunch or dinner. Food to take away.

LOS PINCHITOS
Pi i Molist, 67 → 16 (A1)
Bar with a terrace serving tapas and pintxos (canapés served on cocktail sticks).

Shopping

The Via Júlia → (B1) is one of the neighbourhood's main shopping districts. Better known as the Rambla de Nou Barris, it is home to a plethora of small shops and bars.

Shopping centres:
EL CORTE INGLÉS → (B2)
HERON CITY → (B2)
+ INFO: p. 148

LA TRINIDAD
PANES CREATIVOS
Plaça Garrigó, 5 → 17 (A2)
Master baker Daniel Jordà works with the finest ingredients to make his traditional breads and more innovative creations using squid ink, tomatoes and olives.

VÍA 33 & ARIS
Via Júlia, 33
→ 18 (B1)
Leather goods, belts, bags and travel items.

And also

PARC DEL TURÓ DE LA PEIRA
Pg. Fabra i Puig, 396 → (A1)
Perched high above the city, this park has an almost forest-like atmosphere. In addition to the amazing city views from any of its rest areas, it has children's play areas and picnic tables.

CASA DE L'AIGUA
Garbí, 2 → (C1)
A *modernista* complex dating from 1917 consisting of chlorination pavilions and a water tank. It is now a site of great environmental significance.

HAMLET OF SANTA EULÀLIA DE VILAPICINA
Pere d'Artés → (A2)
A fragment of the city's millennia-old history that preserves the traces of an old rural hamlet including a chapel and two farmhouses.

Parc del Turó de la Peira → (A1)

Highlights

PARC CENTRAL DE NOU BARRIS
Pl. de Karl Marx, s/n
→ (A1)
The 16-hectare Parc Central de Nou Barris is Barcelona's second biggest park, after the Parc de la Ciutadella. It was begun in the late 1990s and is home to the main amenities in the district, including the library. Particularly outstanding are the water features and planting. It has two ponds, one of them with waterfalls.

Parc Central de Nou Barris → (A1)

MIRADOR DE TORRE BARÓ
Carretera Alta de les Roquetes, 328
→ (C1)
This viewing point commands views of Barcelona's working-class districts and the unknown side of the city. It is named Torre Baró after two old towers of the same name, the first dating from the 16th century and the second from the 18th century. The building at the top, known as the Castell de Torre Baró, was built as a hotel in the early 1900s but never completed.

Mirador de Torre Baró → (C1)

PARC DE CAN DRAGÓ
Av. Meridiana, 390
→ (B2)
More than a park, this is a great boulevard with green areas, play areas, sports facilities, swimming pools and places for walking. It was designed by Enric Penyes and its attractions include the replica of Pablo Gargallo's sculpture *Aurigues olímpiques* (Olympic Charioteers) which stands in the centre of the park.

Parc de Can Dragó → (B2)

Barcelona is much more

 Barcelona *is much more*

 Diputació Barcelona

Not far from the city, less than an hour away in most cases, the counties of Barcelona stretch from the Pyrenees to the Mediterranean with a range of leisure activities, art, culture, nature and gastronomy so rich and diverse that it will satisfy all tastes. You'll find an enticing landscape of spectacular mountains dotted with chapels, castles, monasteries and historic relics from different eras; more than 100 km of coastline where you can take part in all kinds of water sports, relax and enjoy the sunshine and beaches, or sample the local cuisine on a beachfront terrace; a land steeped in legends with its unique home-grown art nouveau, or *modernista*, heritage, breathtaking natural landscapes and a deeply rooted tradition of wine tourism. An unbeatable range of attractions which offer something for everyone.

www.barcelonaismuchmore.com

BarcelonaEsMoltMes

@bcnmoltmes

BCNmoltmes

1 Bagà and Pedraforca

The town of Bagà nestles in the foothills of the Catalan Pyrenees in the shadow of one of the most breathtaking, beautiful and iconic massifs in Catalonia, Pedraforca, which stands more than 2,500 m high. The palace of the Barons of Pinós overlooks the old quarter which is protected by the ancient walls and retains the beauty of the medieval ensemble.

2 Natural parks

The network of natural parks around Barcelona contains areas of outstanding natural beauty. There are 12 protected natural areas covering more than 100,000 hectares! A patchwork of Mediterranean and central-European landscapes which is so special that UNESCO has awarded some of them Biosphere Reserve status.

3 Sant Cugat Monastery

This was the most important monastery in the county of Barcelona during the Middle Ages. It consists of a church, cloisters, chapter house and abbot's palace. The original structure was completely fortified and a substantial portion of the walls and many of the towers, which were built in the 14th and 16th centuries, survive today. +INFO: p. 132

4 Granollers

Granollers, the capital of the Vallès Oriental county, stands against the backdrop of Mount Montseny and the Montnegre and Corredor massifs. The most iconic landmark is the old corn exchange, La Porxada, which was built in 1586, but the town museum, the Museu de Granollers, the town hall and the church of Sant Esteve are also well worth a visit.

5 Model villages of the Llobregat

In the late 18th century, many businessmen turned their attention to land with a river running through it, far from the big city, to build their textile mills. Today you can visit this industrial heritage on foot or by bike on signposted trails that pass through villages including Cal Rosal, L'Ametlla de Merola, Casserres and Viladomiu Nou.

6 Rupit, Tavertet and Vall de Sau

The medieval village of Rupit, in the county of Osona, has been named a site of historic and artistic interest. It boasts spectacular views of the Guilleries Massif, Mount Montseny and the crags of Tavertet, Avenc and El Far. The streets and houses in Rupit were built in the 16th and 17th centuries and give the village an ancestral and rustic atmosphere which lends it a special appeal.

Near the city

7 Cardona and the Salt Mountain

Cardona's splendid past stems from salt mining and the salt basin which have been its raison d'être since the 11th century. The monumental ensemble of the castle has been a National Landmark since 1949. The Cardona Salt Mountain is the perfect place to visit with the family to discover spectacular stalactites and stalagmites. +INFO: p. 133

8 Vic

Vic is one vast market: the Saturday market, a market for the senses, a medieval market... Vic has seen the great potential in its range of shops and restaurants. A dynamic and welcoming city where the modern coexists with history and landmarks such as the Museu Episcopal, which houses a splendid collection of paintings and Romanesque and Gothic sculptures. +INFO: p. 134

9 Món Sant Benet

You'll find a unique cultural attraction in the village of Sant Fruitós de Bages: Món Sant Benet. It includes a Romanesque monastery, a *modernista* house and an eco-allotment on the site of the Benedictine monks' vegetable gardens. It also has a hotel and Michelin-starred restaurant.

10 Montserrat

Montserrat is one of the cultural, spiritual and religious symbols of Catalonia. You can see the shrine, the Black Madonna, or "Moreneta", and the boys' choir singing the Virolai. Montserrat is also a natural park with its own unique personality defined by its serried rows of peaks that resemble rounded needles. +INFO: p. 135

11 Terrassa and *modernisme*

Terrassa has a rich cultural and artistic heritage. Its attractions range from its pre-historic and medieval legacy to its industrial architecture which bears the imprint of Catalan art nouveau, or *modernisme*; from the jazz festival and the season of dance, music and theatre, to human tower displays and sports tourism. +INFO: p. 136

12 Circuit de Barcelona-Catalunya

The Circuit de Barcelona-Catalunya opened in 1991 and has become a place of pilgrimage for everyone who loves the smell of petrol and the atmosphere of motor racing. The track hosts the Grands Prix of the Moto GP and Formula 1 World Championships, as well as Rallycross endurance trials and meetings.

13 Beaches on the Costa Barcelona

These beaches are the perfect combination of the Mediterranean, culture and nature. Over 100 km of beaches which have excellent transport links with the city. You can also take part in a wide range of water sports and there are nine marinas and countless sailing clubs where you can enjoy activities associated with the sea.

14 Barcelona wine tourism

The counties of Barcelona are a true haven for lovers of wine tourism. At the different Designations of Origin (DO) you can learn how to distinguish a young wine from a *criança*, take part in the day-to-day tasks at a winery, spend the night at a wine-growing estate, or follow one of the signposted routes through the vineyards.

15 Sitges

The ancient *Blanca Subur* is synonymous with culture. The cradle of Catalan art nouveau – *modernisme* – and a magnet for film buffs, its traditions blend perfectly with its museums and mansions. A town where you can discover incomparable places, walk and relax by the sea, and sample succulent seafood dishes. +INFO: p. 136

16 Gaudí crypt at the Colònia Güell

The crypt at the Colònia Güell (1908-1918) is a must-see landmark if you want to understand Gaudí and the history of architecture. It served as a test bed for a brand-new building process. In 2005, UNESCO named it a World Heritage Site. +INFO: p. 138

17 Llobregat Delta

The delta is considered an area of global significance as it is home to priority species from the Iberian Peninsula in need of protection. This is why it has been declared a Special Protection Area (SPA). You can visit along signposted trails with hides and viewing towers from where you can watch and enjoy the wildlife.

18 Sant Miquel del Fai

A unique landscape with stalactite and stalagmite caves, small ponds and beautiful waterfalls. You can also enjoy the beautiful architectural heritage resulting from the ancient monastery that was built around the church of Sant Miquel (10th century). The monastery dates from the 15th century and is a fine example of the Catalan Gothic style.

Near the city

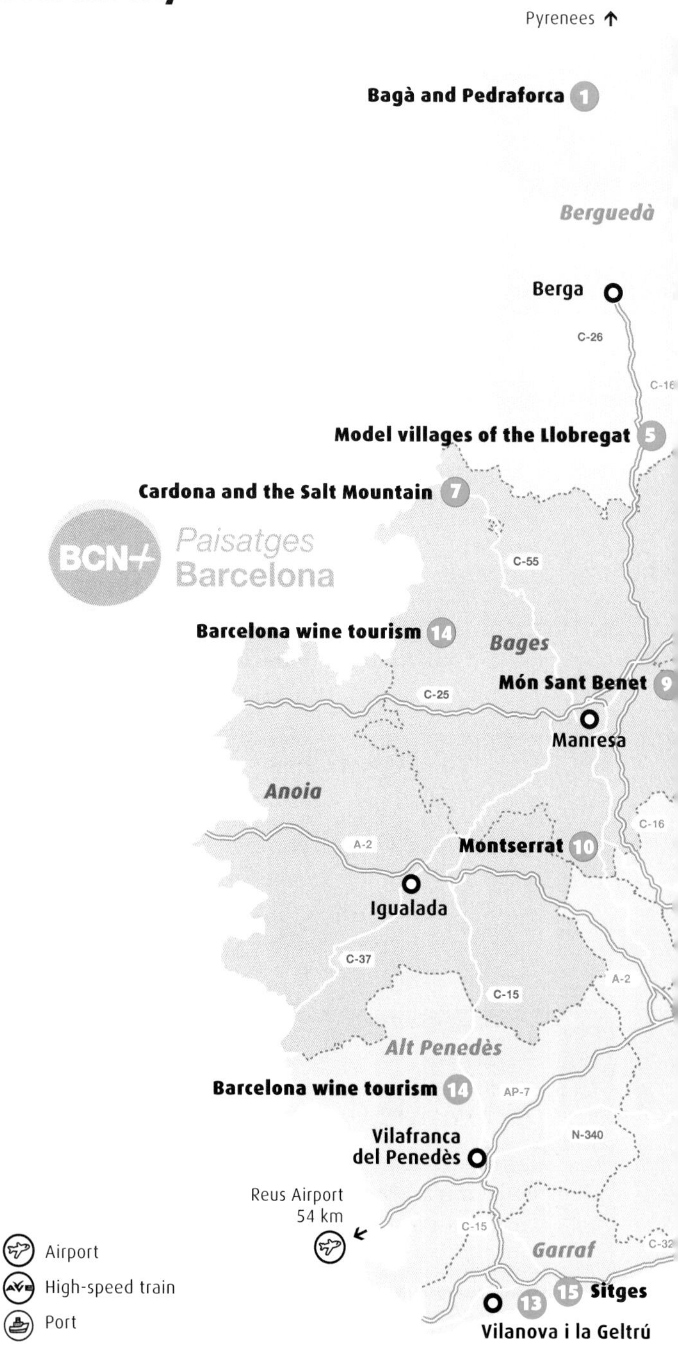

Pyrenees ↑

Bagà and Pedraforca ①

Berguedà

Berga ⊙

C-26

C-16

Model villages of the Llobregat ⑤

Cardona and the Salt Mountain ⑦

BCN+ *Paisatges* Barcelona

Barcelona wine tourism ⑭

Bages

C-55

Món Sant Benet ⑨

Manresa ⊙

C-25

Anoia

C-16

Montserrat ⑩

A-2

Igualada ⊙

C-37

C-15

A-2

Alt Penedès

Barcelona wine tourism ⑭

AP-7

Vilafranca del Penedès ⊙

N-340

Reus Airport 54 km ✈ ←

C-15

Garraf

C-32

⑬ ⑮ Sitges

Vilanova i la Geltrú ⊙

✈ Airport

ⓐᵥₑ High-speed train

⚓ Port

BCN+ *Pirineus* Barcelona

C-37

Osona

6 **Rupit, Tavertet and Vall de Sau**

C-17

8 **Vic**

C-25

C-25

Moià

Girona-Costa Brava
Airport
28 km

Moianès

AP-7

18 **Sant Miquel del Fai**

Vallès Oriental

Vallès Occidental

C-59

4 **Granollers**

C-61

C-32

13

Terrassa and *modernisme*

Maresme

13

11

12 **Circuit de Barcelona-Catalunya**

C-60

Sabadell

C-58

C-33

Mataró

C-16

14 **Barcelona wine tourism**

13 **Beaches on the Costa Barcelona**

3 **Sant Cugat Monastery**

Barcelonès

BCN+ *Costa* Barcelona

Sant Feliu de Llobregat

AP-2

BARCELONA

16

Gaudí crypt at the Colònia Güell

Baix lobregat

17 Barcelona-El Prat Airport

13

Llobregat Delta
Beaches on the Costa Barcelona

Mediterranean sea

Landmarks, museums...

✳

..., iconic buildings and tourist attractions with their history and most important features together with all the practical information you'll need: visiting times and admission prices.

Barcelona icons

Ciutat Vella

Barcelona Cathedral

Opening times: church only (free),
Monday to Friday, 8am-12.45pm and
5.45pm-7.30pm; Saturday and evenings
before public holidays, 8am-12.45pm
and 3.15pm-8pm; Sunday and public
holidays: 8am-1.45pm and 5.15pm-8pm.
Sightseeing tours: Includes a tour
of the church, cloister, choir, roof and
museum (general admission, €7; group
with official guide, €5 per person).
Monday to Saturday and evenings
before public holidays, 1pm-5pm. Sunday and public holidays, 2pm-5pm.

Begun in 1298, the cathedral of the Holy
Cross is one of the most splendid examples of the Catalan Gothic style, which is
characterised by its decorative sobriety
and well-balanced proportions. The
cathedral is a vast building (90 metres
long and 40 metres wide), and was built
next to the city walls, at one end of the
medieval city, on the same site as its
two predecessors: the first cathedral,
an early-Christian basilica dating from
the 4th century, and the second, built

between 1046 and 1058 in the Romanesque style.

The construction process was arduous.
To enable people to continue to worship,
the Romanesque cathedral was gradually dismantled as building work on the
Gothic cathedral progressed, culminating in the middle of the 15th century.
However, the façade remained unfin-
ished without any towers or sculptural
decorations.

Four centuries later, the city hosted the
1888 Universal Exhibition and this triggered the right social and economic conditions that made it possible to complete
the building. The neo-Gothic façade was
inspired by the original project drawn up
by the French master builder Carlí in the
15th century. Its slender lines and abundant decorative elements contrast with
the sober horizontal lines of the rest of
the building. The two towers flanking
either side of the façade were added at
a later date.

The east end of the cathedral consists
of a single apse with nine radiating
chapels that are reached by a wide
deambulatory. The crypt is located
beneath the high altar and is covered
by an almost flat vault consisting of
12 sections. It houses the tomb of Saint
Eulàlia, one of the patron saints of the

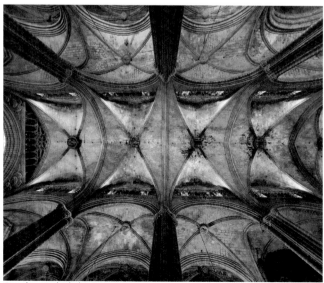

Barcelona Cathedral

Barcelona Cathedral

city, whose remains lie in an alabaster sarcophagus carved by 14th-century sculptors from Pisa.

The naves of the cathedral are separated from the eastern end of the building by a section with no chapels, which serves as the transept. Two octagonal bell towers surmount both ends of this section outside the building. The cathedral is an example of a hall church, meaning that the naves are similar in height. This layout is typical of Catalan Gothic architecture. Made up of four sections, the naves have cross-vaulted ceilings with painstakingly crafted polychrome keystones.

The architects' design was so skilful that, if you look at the ceiling, the building seems to have seven naves instead of three, due to the fact that the ceilings of the side chapels are divided into two small vaults, which are set between buttresses. This intelligent use of space lets in more daylight and gives the interior a highly evocative atmosphere.

The main bell tower with its octagonal base was placed over the section of the central nave closest to the façade: an unusual location in Catalan Gothic buildings. The slender spire at the top, which is the highest point of the building, was built between 1906 and 1913, and was the last major building work carried out on the cathedral.

The lavishly sculpted stone choir, which was created between the late 14th and mid 16th centuries, is located in the centre of the great nave, and spans two sections of the cathedral. The wooden stalls inside the choir are a masterpiece of Gothic sculpture.

The great cloister, which was built between the late 14th and early 15th centuries, adjoins the west wall of the cathedral and is reached from the transept. It is rectangular in shape and has four galleries that appear to have cross-vaulted ceilings underpinned by pointed arches, like the naves inside the building. There is a secluded garden in the centre with a pond where 13 geese swim. The number 13 stands for the age of Saint Eulàlia when she was martyred.

Every year, for Corpus Christi, a hollowed-out egg is placed on the water jet of the Gothic fountain in the cloister, in one of the city's most deeply rooted and popular traditions. It is said that if the egg remains balanced on the stream of water throughout the day, the year will be prosperous.

The Blessed Sacrament Chapel or Chapter House is located next to one of the wings of the cloister. It has an extraordinary star-shaped octagonal vault that was built during the early 15th century.

Museu Picasso

Opening times: Tuesday to Sunday (including public holidays), 9am-7pm (thursday until 9.30pm). Last admissions 30 minutes before closing. Mondays, except public holidays, closed. Annual closing: 1st January, 1st May, 24th June and 25th December.
Prices: €11; visitors aged 18 to 25 and over 65s, €7; under 18s, free.

Carrer Montcada, in the district of La Ribera, is short and narrow, yet

Barcelona icons

Museu Picasso

despite its appearance, it is one of the city's most important streets. Its importance stems from the fact that it was home to Barcelona's nobility for 500 years, from the 13th to the 18th centuries. This explains why the street is a succession of Gothic palazzos of great architectural value.

Five of these palazzos, which stand side by side on the east side of the street, house the Museu Picasso, one of the city's main cultural attractions. The five palazzos – the Palau Aguilar, the Palau del Baró de Castellet, the Palau Meca, the Casa Mauri and the Palau Finestres – were built between the 13th and 14th centuries in the Gothic style and remodelled over the centuries with the addition of Renaissance, baroque and neoclassical elements. They all have the same layout: the rooms are set out around a courtyard with a monumental staircase that leads to the first floor.

Pablo Ruiz Picasso arrived in Barcelona with his family in 1895 when he was barely 14. His father was a schoolteacher. The young Picasso's artistic spirit was forged in the *modernista* ambiance of the Catalan capital, and he lived here for nine years until he left for Paris in 1904.

Picasso retained strong emotional ties with the city throughout the rest of his life and this is why, in 1960, he gave his wholehearted support to the idea mooted by his personal secretary, Jaume Sabartés, to create a museum devoted to his work in Barcelona. The Museu Picasso opened in 1963 and housed Sabartés' personal collection and works by the Malaga-born artist that were on show at the time in different Barcelona galleries. Over the years, the museum's holdings have expanded to include works from other private collections and works donated by Picasso himself.

Highlights include *Motherhood* (1903), *Portrait of Señora Canals* (1905), *Harlequin* (1917) and the series *Las Meninas*, in which the artist dissects Diego de Velázquez's famous painting into 58 oils ranging from a general view to detailed studies.

Palau de la Música Catalana

Guided tours: Length, 55 min. Daily, 10am-3.30pm; Holy Week, 10am-6pm; August, 9am-8pm.
Languages: English, Catalan, Spanish, French and Italian.
Prices: €18 (adults); €11 (students, senior citizens from the EU and groups from 25 people upwards).
Tickets can be purchased at the ticket office, by phone (T 902 475 485) and e-mail (visites@palaumusica.cat).

Built between 1905 and 1908, at the height of the *modernista* building boom in Barcelona, the Palau de la Música Catalana is, together with the Hospital de Sant Pau, the masterpiece of Lluís Domènech i Montaner, one of the key figures of Catalan art nouveau, or *modernisme*.

The Palau is a Unesco World Heritage Site and Barcelona's most popular concert hall. It was built on the site of the former convent in the district of Sant Pere, as an initiative of the Orfeó

Català, the choral society founded in 1891 to carry out important work in disseminating choral music from Catalonia, the rest of Spain and abroad.

Domènech i Montaner's project was paid for by public subscription, including large donations from industrialists who had made their fortunes over the previous decades. It is an ingenious combination of architecture – made from steel and brick – and a bold use of the applied arts, particularly sculpture, stained glass and ceramics. The Palau is a large rationalist structure whose stability made it possible to free up floors and walls in order to gain space that would make it possible to create the perfect acoustics and add a large amount of decorative details that bring colour and vibrancy to the ensemble.

Inside, the building is almost entirely clad in ceramics, with a predominance of floral motifs. Against this colourful backdrop, a series of sculptures protrudes from the walls using an original artistic device that was typical of the fantasy of *modernista* art: the busts of some of the figures are sculpted in relief while the rest of the body is flat and blends into the coloured mosaic.

A German pipe organ dating from 1908 graces the stage, which is flanked by two monumental sculptural ensembles by Pablo Gargallo: one alludes to Catalan folk music and features the bust of one of its key revivalists, the musician Josep Anselm Clavé, and below it an allegory of the Catalan folk song *Les flors de maig* (The Flowers of May), which he wrote. The second sculptural group portrays international composers and includes a bust of Beethoven and scenes depicting Richard Wagner's Valkyries.

To allow natural light into the 2,000-seat auditorium, Domènech i Montaner had it covered by an enormous, rectangular stained-glass skylight. Its centrepiece is an inverted dome that is suspended like a droplet of water about to fall.

Other impressive areas inside the Palau de la Música include the spacious foyer, with its massive pillars and vaulted ceiling, which separates the entrance and the concert hall, and the Lluís Millet hall on the first floor, where concert-goers meet before a performance. The hall is lit by a large stained-glass window.

The exterior of the building is just as sumptuous as the interior. Domènech used brick as the main building material and added coloured ceramics and sculptures as the main decorative elements. The architect chose to round off the

Palau de la Música Catalana

Barcelona icons

corner of the outer walls overlooking the Carrer de Sant Pere and the Carrer de Amadeu Vives and surmounted it with a small dome on the roof. The corner also features a large sculptural ensemble – an allegory to Catalan song by Miquel Blay – at first-floor level.

The base of the façade features robust colonnades that underpin broad and low elliptical arches which lead inside the building. A long balcony runs from the first arch along the main façade forming a complex structure of columns that lends it great depth. Above these columns are busts of Palestrina, Bach, Beethoven and Wagner, who represent different periods in the history of music.

From 1982 until 2008, the centenary year of the Palau, the architect Òscar Tusquets supervised restoration and extension work that opened up new views of the building with the demolition of the church of Sant Francesc de Paula and the addition of a new plaza that gives the building a feeling of space.

Museu d'Història de Barcelona **MUHBA**

Opening times: Tuesday to Saturday, 10am-7pm; Sunday, 10am-8pm (admission free from 3pm).
Closed Monday. Annual closing: 1st January, 1st May, 24th June and 25th December.
Prices: €7; €5 for the under 25s, over 65s and disabled visitors; admission free for under 16s.

Although its collections are distributed among several landmark buildings in the city, the main premises of the Museu d'Història de Barcelona are in the Plaça del Rei, and reached through the Casa Padellàs, a late-15th-century Gothic palace that was moved, stone by stone, from Carrer dels Mercaders when the Via Laietana was being built in 1931. While the Casa Padellàs was being relocated to the site, archaeologists discovered, below the square, the well-preserved streets and foundations of the buildings of Roman and medieval Barcino that span the 1st century BC to the 13th century AD.

The museum opened in 1943 and one of the main attractions is to take a walk underground, along the streets of the Roman and medieval city with its fountains and drainage systems, touch its ancient walls, admire the mosaic fragments of its shops and factories and realise the importance of the Church on society at the time through the magnitude of its religious centre while noticing that different periods in history are buried in layers just a few metres under the city where we walk today.

The visit to the MUHBA is completed by two major architectural landmarks that are part of the Palau Reial Major: the Great Hall, the Saló del Tinell, and the chapel of Santa Àgata. The Palau Reial Major was the official residence of the Counts of Barcelona and subsequently the kings of the Crown of Aragon, and has been remodelled several times since the 11th century.

The Tinell is the biggest hall in the palace and was built between 1359 and 1370, during the reign of Pere the

Museu d'Història de Barcelona

Santa Maria del Mar

Ceremonious. A large number of rooms were demolished to build the hall which covers an area of 33 × 18 metres and has a flat ceiling underpinned by broad, semi-circular arches.

The chapel of Santa Àgata now stands atop the city's medieval walls between the Plaça del Rei and the Plaça de Ramon Berenguer III, on the Via Laietana. It was built on the orders of King Jaume II of Aragon as the oratory of the Palau Reial and was begun in 1302.

With its elegant, airy Gothic forms, the chapel has a single nave covered by a wooden pitched ceiling underpinned by pointed arches and reinforced, like the Tinell, with solid buttresses. The slender octagonal tower is its most eye-catching feature from the outside and one of the main landmarks on Barcelona's medieval skyline.

Santa Maria del Mar

Opening times: Monday to Saturday, 9am-1pm and 5pm-8.30pm; Sunday and public holidays, 10am-2pm and 5pm-8pm.

From the late 10th century onwards, Barcelona's growing population began to spread beyond the narrow confines of the walled Roman city. The merchants, shipwrights and stevedores, and other trades associated with commerce and harbour life, moved to the east of the city, between the city walls and the sea. Before the new millennium, these guilds had built the church of Santa Maria de les Arenes near the beach, to meet the religious needs of the new town known as Vila Nova del Mar, which was later absorbed by Barcelona as the district of La Ribera.

La Ribera enjoyed a period of great splendour as a result of the large-scale economic development of Barcelona and the Crown of Aragon during the 13th and 14th centuries. The building of Carrer Montcada provided ample proof of

Barcelona icons

this. Crammed with palaces, the street became the home of the new merchant classes who were vying with the Italian states to gain control of Mediterranean commerce. Further proof of this prosperity was the building of a new church on the site of Santa Maria de les Arenes. It was to be called Santa Maria del Mar, and was built in the Gothic style that was so widespread throughout Europe during the late Middle Ages. The church competed in size with Barcelona Cathedral and showed the strength of the new bourgeois class that was funding it.

So great was their economic power that Santa Maria del Mar, or the *cathedral of the sea* as it soon came to be known, was completed in little more than 50 years. This was an extremely short period in which to build a great Gothic church as projects of this kind usually took centuries to complete. Santa Maria del Mar was begun in 1329, the year of the conquest of the island of Sardinia, which completed the dominance of the western Mediterranean by the Catalan-Aragonese Crown. It was finished in 1383, with only the two bell towers that stand on either side of the main façade remaining unbuilt. One of these was completed in 1496 and the other in 1902.

The fact that Santa Maria del Mar was built over such a short period of time lends it a great stylistic unity, which is the result of the involvement of relatively few master builders. This explains why the church is taken as a paradigmatic example of Catalan Gothic art, characterised by sober decorative elements which make it easier to distinguish the purely architectural features from the decorative ones; by the profusion of horizontal lines as opposed to the radical vertical lines of the International Gothic style; by the predominance of solid panels over empty spaces in the walls and the choice of the hall-style layout in which the side naves and central nave are of equal or similar height, creating flat roofs, a radically different model to the French Gothic and European styles. At Santa Maria del Mar, the buttresses that help support these powerful walls create 12 small chapels in each of the side naves.

Another unusual characteristic of the church is the 13-metre span between the columns: the broadest in a Gothic building. The nave is more than 50 metres wide and is divided into just four sections, highlighting the slenderness of the sparsely decorated octagonal columns which stand 18 metres high. The side naves are half as wide as the central nave, and this accentuates the balance and harmony of the church interior.

In the east end of the church, however, the distance between the columns is drastically reduced in order to separate the deambulatory from the altar, creating an evocative forest of columns that contrasts with the feeling of space in the rest of the church.

Images of Saint Peter and Saint Paul occupy niches on either side of the west door on the main façade. At the top, our attention is drawn to the magnificent rose window which allows light to flood into the church from mid-day to dusk. The original stained glass in the rose window fell out as a result of the earthquake in 1428 which killed 22 people. The window was replaced at the end of the 15th century by glass-makers working in the Flamboyant style and it is the one we can see today.

Most of the decorative elements inside the church (including the Gothic choir stalls, the baroque high altar and the huge 18th-century pipe organ) were completely destroyed by a fire in 1936 during the days just after the outbreak of the Spanish Civil War.

Santa Maria del Mar

El Born Centre de Cultura i Memòria

El Born
Centre de Cultura i Memòria

Opening times: Tuesday to Sunday, 10am-8pm.
Prices: free admission to the building; visits to the archaeological site, €5.50; under 8s, free.

This cultural centre is situated in the Mercat del Born building, Barcelona's former central food market built between 1874 and 1878 under the supervision of the architect Josep Fontseré and considered the most successful example of wrought-iron architecture in Catalonia. It has a rectangular floor plan and two main sections joined by a series of domes and four smaller sections. The market was

El Born Centre de Cultura i Memòria

open for a century and when restoration work was being carried out in 2002 to convert it into the Biblioteca Provincial de Barcelona, the builders found major archaeological remains which completely changed its destiny.

The centre houses the best-preserved remains of a medieval and modern city. The site showcases an area of the city that was demolished following the conquest of Barcelona by the Bourbon troops in 1714. During the War of the Spanish Succession, the city had been under siege for more than a year. However, following the victory of Felipe V, Barcelona was considered a rebellious city and forced to demolish 1,262 houses in the Ribera district to build the largest military citadel in Europe. The complex had a radial layout and was designed to prevent any further attempts by the city to rise up against the Bourbon monarchy.

The Born showcases the archaeological site and features a permanent exhibition about Barcelona as it was in 1700, as well as a series of temporary exhibitions. It also hosts a programme of events based on a variety of cultural disciplines: language, literature, music, film, dance, puppet theatre, etc. It also houses the bookshop Bestiari which specializes in books about the history of the city, and a restaurant and bar run by the Moritz brewery. The Born is a unique and exceptional landmark. It is unlike other similar spaces in the world as it is accessible and open to anyone who wants to visit or simply walk through as if it were just another city street.

Barcelona icons

Mercat de la Boqueria

Opening times:
Monday to Saturday, 8am-8.30pm.
Closed: Sunday.

Barcelona's extensive network of well-tended fresh food markets, which can ably compete with modern hypermarkets, set the city apart from most major cities in the west. The market of Sant Josep, better known as the Boqueria, is the jewel in the crown of the 39 markets in the network. Covering an area of 6,000 square metres, it is Spain's biggest fresh-food market and one of the main ingredients of the great culinary prestige Barcelona enjoys today.

Its origins can be traced back to the itinerant open-air market that established itself outside the city walls, on La Rambla, in front of the gate of Santa Eulàlia, or La Boqueria, from the end of the 13th century. However, permanent premises weren't built until the middle of the 19th century to cater to the hundreds of stalls selling meat, fish, fruit, vegetables, flowers and a wide array of fresh produce and foodstuffs for the people of Barcelona. Space for a market was lacking inside the city walls due to the narrowness of the streets and squares. The first permanent market in the area was designed in 1840. It was built on land that had been freed up with the demolition of the former convent of Sant Josep – hence its official name.

The wrought-iron structure that still covers the market went up in 1914. It is made from five identical sections, without walls or metal enclosures around its perimeter. The *modernista* arch that presides over the main entrance dates from the same period. It is also made of wrought iron and is surmounted by stained-glass panels set into cement columns covered in *trencadís*, a mosaic technique using broken tile shards that had been invented a few years earlier by Antoni Gaudí.

Palau Güell

Opening times: Tuesday to Sunday, 10am-8pm (April to October) and 10am-5.30pm (November to March). Closed: Monday, 1st and 6th January, 25th and 26th December.
Prices: General, €12; reduced (students over 18 and over 65s from the EU), €9; children aged 10 to 17, €17.50; under 10s, free.

Born in 1846, Eusebi Güell is one of the leading exemplars of the entrepreneurs who gave impetus to Catalan industry during the second half of the 19th century, fostering a trend that had a notable influence on the culture, politics and society of the region.

Impressed by the designs of the young Antoni Gaudí, Güell soon signed up the brilliant architect to refurbish his summer residence in the district of Les Corts de Sarrià and in 1885 he had no hesitation in entrusting him with the design of his new town house, just off La Rambla, in the centre of Barcelona old town.

Mercat de la Boqueria

Palau Güell

At the time, all the eminent Barcelona families were moving to the new Eixample district that had been laid out just 30 years earlier by Ildefons Cerdà and was equipped with all the modern conveniences that were lacking in the narrow streets of the old town. However, Güell remained committed to La Rambla and El Raval, a neighbourhood whose social and sanitary conditions had notably declined due to the overcrowding caused by the massive influx of people from the rest of Spain who had come here in search of work.

This is why the businessman and patron of the arts suggested Gaudí design a townhouse that would face inwards, with an austere façade and a luxurious interior, set out around a central lobby with vertical proportions that ran from the ground floor to the top of the building, surmounted by a parabolic dome pierced by a large central lantern surrounded by small perforations resembling stars.

The inward-facing architecture of the building enabled Güell to isolate himself from the bustling atmosphere of Carrer Nou de Rambla and to organise concerts, literary gatherings and cultural encounters in the rooms of his residence while, outside, the working classes sought entertainment in much more mundane pursuits.

The façade of the Palau Güell is extremely restrained in comparison with most of Gaudí's works. Güell is said to have made predominant use of grey calcareous stone on the façade, arranged in rectilinear forms and almost devoid of decorative elements, in order to convey the values of Christianity, with deliberate austerity, to the decadent Barcelona of the end of the 19th century.

Inside, the building looks like a sumptuous townhouse, with marble the main material used as a wall and floor covering. The ground floor was designed to allow carriages to enter and leave the building – the coach house in the basement is one of Gaudí's most thought-provoking spaces; the first floor was for entertaining guests; the Güell family lived on the mezzanine floor; and the servants lived on the top floor which was covered by a flat roof where Gaudí eschewed the overall sobriety of the project and designed 20 chimneys that are clad in the widest variety of colours and textures.

Barcelona icons

Museu d'Art Contemporani de Barcelona MACBA

Opening times: Monday, Wednesday, Thursday and Friday, 11am-7.30pm; Saturday, 10am-9pm; Sunday and public holidays, 10am-3pm.
Tuesday, except public holidays: closed.
Prices: €10; students and groups of 15 people upwards: €8; over 65s, unemployed and under 14s, free.

Since the 1950s, Barcelona had aspired to having its own museum of contemporary art that would showcase works by the most prestigious Catalan artists of the post-Civil War period. In 1995, after years of effort and changes in fortune, this wish became a reality with the opening of the Museu d'Art Contemporani de Barcelona (MACBA), a major cultural facility built on the site of the old poorhouse, the Casa de la Caritat.

The prestigious American architect Richard Meier secured the brief to create this elongated building, with a main façade that is 120 metres long. The predominant straight lines contrast with a circular volume that covers four floors and connects the different galleries.

The winner of the Pritzker Prize (which is often referred to as the Nobel Prize for Architecture) in 1984, Meier is a rationalist architect who is strongly influenced by Le Corbusier whose main concern is to ensure natural light floods into every corner of the building he is designing. With its huge windows and skylights, the MACBA is no exception. Even the galleries on the ground floor let in natural light from above as a result of the system devised by Meier. The architect asked for some of the ironwork to be removed from the line of the façade to allow light to filter into this space.

The MACBA shares another of the essential traits of Meier's buildings: its white cladding. White is the architect's favourite colour due to its purity, reflective properties and changing tonalities throughout the day.

The collection on show inside the museum's galleries gives us a clear idea of the artistic trends that emerged during the 20th century, particularly over recent decades, although it tends to avoid exhibiting works in purely chronological order.

As you would expect, Catalan art is widely represented, with works by Joan Brossa, Antoni Clavé, Antoni Tàpies, Modest Cuixart, Josep Guinovart, Josep Maria de Sucre, Antoni Vila Arrufat, Albert Ràfols Casamada, Joan Miró, and many more besides. Contemporary Spanish artists featured include Miquel Barceló, Eduardo Chillida and Jorge Oteiza, and the international art scene is represented by artists as diverse as Alexander Calder, Marcel Duchamp, Brassaï, Jean-Michel Basquiat and John Cage.

Museu d'Art Contemporani de Barcelona

Museu d'Història de Catalunya

Museu d'Història de Catalunya [MHC]

Opening times: Tuesday to Saturday, 10am-7pm; Wednesday, 10am-8pm; Sunday and public holidays, 10am-2.30pm; Mondays, except public holidays, closed.
Prices: €4.50; over 65s and under 25s, €3.50; under 8s, free.

The Palau de Mar is a huge building, larger than a football pitch (it covers a surface area of 1 hectare). Built in 1881, it was initially used as the General Trade Warehouses to store the goods that were unloaded at Barcelona harbour. Since 1996, it has been home to the Museu d'Història de Catalunya, a cultural complex designed to disseminate historic events in Catalonia.

The warehouses are one of the few surviving buildings from Barcelona's old port and are among the most highly prized architectural ensembles from Catalonia's rich industrial heritage. They were built to store the goods that were not intended for domestic consumption and were loaded back onto other ships to continue their journey to their final destination. With this aim in mind, the engineer Maurici Garrán designed a spacious, innovative building with outer walls made of brick and a flat roof – the best insulation to protect goods from the bad weather and fire – and an inner framework of laminated steel, which was extremely effective when an open-plan space that could withstand heavy loads was required.

In Barcelona at the time, the harbour area was known as the docks and the General Trade Warehouses were inspired by the English dockland architecture of the period. However, as they had been built some distance away from the harbour mouth, they were seldom used for their intended purpose. The building was put to a number of uses, and was eventually restored for the Olympic Games and converted into the headquarters of the Museu d'Història de Catalunya. The museum's permanent exhibition tells of the historic events and everyday life in Catalonia at different periods, from the Lower Palaeolithic to the present day: its roots, the birth of the nation, the conquest of the Mediterranean, its location on the edge of the Spanish Empire, industrialisation, the recovery of national identity, Franco's repression and subsequent reinstatement of devolved government bodies.

L'Aquàrium Barcelona

Opening times: 10am. Closes: Monday to Friday, 8pm; weekends, 8.30pm; throughout July and August, 9.30pm.
Prices: €20; children aged 5 to 10, €15; aged 3 to 4, €7; over 65s, €18.

Located in the Port of Barcelona, the Aquarium is one of the biggest sea life centres in the world, with a total of around 11,000 examples of 450 distinct species. While it faithfully reproduces all the ocean environments on the planet, including spectacular coral reefs, the

L'Aquàrium Barcelona

Barcelona icons

Aquarium specialises in Mediterranean ecosystems, which occupy 21 of the 35 marine exhibits which are housed there. The largest of all is the monumental Oceanarium, with the main attraction being the numerous sharks which can be seen from the glass underwater tunnel, 80 metres long. Also of note is the exhibition with small aquariums, called *Planeta Aqua*. This is where you can find many of the small creatures that have adapted to the very diverse and extreme aquatic conditions which exist: glacial temperatures, the darkness of the deep sea abyss, warm tropical waters... And you can also discover the importance of the Earth's seas in the development of our planet over more than 3,500 million years. A very important area for families with children is *¡Explora! (Explore!)*, an interactive space, both educational and enjoyable in character. Designed so that children can find out more about the marine world, it has more than 50 interactive games to touch, look at, listen to, investigate and discover nature.

Reials Drassanes Museu Marítim

Opening times: Monday to Sunday, 10am-8pm. Annual closing 25th and 26th December and 1st and 6th January.
Prices: €7; visitors over 65s, students under 25, €3.50; Sunday from 3pm and under 17s, free.

The Reials Drassanes, the best-preserved medieval shipyards in the world, stand at the point where La Rambla meets the harbour waters. They were begun in the 13th century and constructed in several phases using a highly functional and rational building method.

In 1255, Pere the Great, the King of Catalonia-Aragon, warned that Barcelona's original shipyards were becoming obsolete and ordered the building of a new shipbuilding complex in the south of the city, outside the city walls. Initially, the building was a simple courtyard surrounded by porticoed walls and with turrets at each corner. However, a century later, in 1378, the entire surface area of the shipyards was covered over by eight parallel vaulted naves underpinned by broad square arches and clad in wood.

Reials Drassanes - Museu Marítim

This functional, understated and spacious layout made it possible to build up to 30 galleys simultaneously. This capacity was pivotal in making the Crown of Aragon one of the Mediterranean's main military and trading powers, as most of the ships in the Catalan-Aragon fleet were built here.

At the beginning of the 17th century, the Catalan government decided to add three new naves to the wing closest to La Rambla and adhered strictly to the design of the medieval building. In the 18th century, the two central naves were joined together to form a higher single nave. This structure survives today.

During this period, the Drassanes came under the ownership of the Spanish army and a defensive wall was built around them. The shipyards were used for another purpose: first as a barracks and then as a weapons arsenal. By the mid 19th century the army had left and the Drassanes were restored. Since 1941, they have been home to the Museu Marítim, a cultural facility with a permanent exhibition that hosts temporary exhibitions to disseminate every aspect of seafaring life and show the close historic relationship between the city and the marine environment.

L'Eixample

Basilica of the Sagrada Família

Opening times: November to February, 9am-6pm; October and March, 9am-7pm; April to September, 9am-8pm.
Prices: basilica, €18 (seniors and students, €16); audioguided tour, €26 (seniors and students, €24); audioguided tour + towers, €35 (seniors and students, €33); under 10s and disabled visitors, admission free.

The Sagrada Família is one of the iconic symbols of Barcelona and one of the most famous churches in the world. This is partly because of its unique architecture, created by the genius Antoni Gaudí, and partly because its construction process has mirrored the age of the great cathedrals, when it took two centuries to build a great Gothic church. The first stone of the church was laid in 1882 and Gaudí, its originator, died in 1926, but the Sagrada Família is still under construction more than a decade into the 21st century.

The genius of *modernista* architecture devoted 43 years of his professional life to supervising work on the church, from the age of 31 to a few days before his death. He put all his technical and artistic know-how into the building. This prompted him to say that nature was the greatest inspiration for his work and that by observing it he drew the necessary elements to create the structures and decorative features that make his buildings so unique.

Curiously enough, Gaudí wasn't the first architect to work on the Sagrada Família. The church, which was an initiative of a devout Barcelona bookseller, was originally designed in the neo-Gothic style by Francesc de Paula del Villar, who was the official architect of the bishopric at the time. Nevertheless, the differences in criteria between Villar and the developer made it possible for the young Gaudí – a very promising artist who had barely completed two projects – to take over the venture a year after it had begun, when only part of the crypt and apse had been built.

To avoid wasting the money that had already been invested, Gaudí didn't discard what had been built, but he had no hesitation in changing the project completely, making it much more ambitious. Technically, the architect developed a revolutionary structure, that is robust yet light and could scale extraordinary heights without the inclusion of buttresses. The highest point of the central nave is 45 metres, the existing towers stand 125 metres high and, when it is built, the dome will stand 170 metres high.

Basilica of the Sagrada Família

Barcelona icons

Basilica of the Sagrada Família

Symbolically, Gaudí became a true expert in the Catholic liturgy, so that he could adapt the church to all the requirements of worship. Throughout the years, the huge vertical and horizontal spaces inside the building that occupies an entire block in the Eixample were transformed into a true Bible in stone, with sculptural references to countless Biblical passages and characters.

The north-east-facing Nativity façade may be Gaudí's greatest legacy. During the last few years of his life, the great architect focused all his energy on ensuring the project for the symbolic elements on this façade was well under way, to provide his successors with clear pointers to his decorative ideas for the entire church. The façade depicts the main events in the birth, childhood and adolescence of Christ with sculptural groups replete with dynamism and warmth that depict well-known scenes from the New Testament, such as the Annunciation, the Adoration of the Magi, the flight into Egypt, the Massacre of the Innocents and the Presentation at the Temple.

At the time of Gaudí's death, only the crypt, apse, part of the cloister and the Nativity façade had been completed, and the four remaining towers were nearing completion. However, the architect's death, the financial problems encountered by the developers, and the outbreak of the Spanish Civil War ten years later, brought work to a standstill. Building recommenced in 1954 with the Passion façade.

Gaudí's original plans and sketches were destroyed in an arson attack during the Civil War, but they showed a church with five naves and a transept, a unique cloister in the style of a deambulatory that encompasses almost the entire building, three monumental facades with porticos and 18 towers: 12 bell towers dedicated to the apostles, four towers dedicated to the evangelists, one dedicated to the Virgin Mary, and the tallest, dedicated to Christ, that will eventually surmount the dome, making the Sagrada Família the city's tallest building.

Only eight of the 18 towers have been completed: those on the Nativity and Passion façades. The symbolic elements on the latter, by the sculptor Josep Maria Subirachs, contrast sharply with the vitality and innocence of the opposite façade, as they depict the suffering and death of Jesus Christ using angular, hieratic figures, in a tableau devoid of ornamentation, as Gaudí had intended in his original sketches.

The interior of the church once again proves Gaudí's creative genius. In order to cover over a space for 14,000 worshippers and a choir of 1,200 singers, the Catalan architect once again drew inspiration from nature to create the tree-like column that branches out to a great height to underpin a series of curious vaults in the shape of palm leaves with lanterns that allow natural light into the building. Gaudí envisaged four types of columns designed according to the weight they had to bear: the lightest – 1.05 metres in diameter – are made from sandstone; the ones measuring 1.40 are granite; and the ones measuring 1.75, are basalt, while the four columns that bear the most weight, located at the intersection of the central nave and transept, are 2.10 metres in diameter and made of porphyry, an extremely resistant igneous rock.

Just a few metres away from this grand and sumptuous décor, next to the Passion façade, a simple, single-storey brick building attracts the attention of visitors. It is the Sagrada Família school which was designed by Gaudí to educate the children of the neighbourhood – at the time, a working-class district – and the children of the masons who were working on the church. At first sight, the building looks simple, although the undulating shape of its roof and its walls conceal a boldness that amazed the father of rationalism, the Swiss architect Le Corbusier, when he visited Barcelona in 1928.

Casa Milà "La Pedrera"

Opening times: Monday to Sunday, 9am-8.30pm (27th February to 2nd November and 26th December to 3rd January) and 9am-6.30pm (3rd November to 24th December).
Admission: 22.50€; students, 19.50€; children aged 7 to 12, 10.25€; under 7s, free. The audioguide is included with the admission price.

In 1906, Antoni Gaudí had already gained great popularity in Barcelona as the architect of the Sagrada Família and the designer of the homes of some of the most powerful industrialists of the time. One of these, the Casa Calvet, on Barcelona's Carrer Casp, had won a prize from the city council as the best building of 1900. Five years later, another of Gaudí's works, the full-scale refurbishment of the Casa Batlló, won the admiration of experts and laypeople because of its boldness and creativity.

One of the new admirers of Gaudí's style was the property developer Pere Milà, whose father was one of Batlló's business partners. Milà was recently married and he decided to commission Gaudí to build his new home on the corner of Passeig de Gràcia and Carrer de Provença. As was customary at the time, the developer was to live on the first floor and the upper floors would be put up for sale or rent.

Gaudí was at the height of his creative powers when he designed his most personal residential building, which was met with incredulity by its owners – who he eventually fell out with – and Barcelona society as a whole, who nicknamed the building *pedrera* (the Catalan for quarry) due to the naturalistic forms of its façade, a true architectural sculpture in undulating stone that contrasts with the audacious tangle of wrought iron that makes up the railings of the balconies and terraces.

Today, opinions have changed and La Pedrera is considered one of Gaudí's major landmarks. When the architect began working on the design for the Casa Milà he was so sure of his structural and aesthetic approach that he allowed himself to relinquish traditional building methods and to investigate as-yet-unexplored technical and artistic paths. The result of this journey, La Pedrera, is a building of a boldness that was deemed inappropriate at the time.

On a vast corner site, Gaudí was courageous enough to design a large, six-storey building with a basement and attic space based on a revolutionary structure of pillars and cast-iron girders which allowed him to dispense with load-bearing walls. This enabled him to tailor the interior layout of every flat to the needs of their occupants, and made him the forerunner of the concept of the open-plan floor adopted by the rationalists two decades later.

In order to reinforce this ideal combination of resistance and lightness, the architect designed a free-standing façade which is a self-supporting

Casa Milà "La Pedrera"

Barcelona icons

Casa Milà "La Pedrera"

structure, separate from the rest of the building, to which it is attached by small girders set into the blocks of stone.

Another innovation that Gaudí had saved for the Casa Milà was the inclusion of one of the first car parks in Spain in the basement. This meant he had to design a spacious lobby that would be big enough to allow vehicles to manoeuvre freely. Gaudí finally created a double lobby with one entrance from the corner and another from Carrer de Provença, to make it easier for cars to circulate.

This double lobby utilised the open space left by the two interior courtyards, which were designed to let the maximum natural light into the inner areas of the building, some of which were some distance away from the façade. Light was so important to Gaudí that he decided to dispense with the monumental staircase leading to the upper floors to avoid blocking out light in the courtyards, which were transformed into interior façades. The architect had two lifts fitted instead. These were seen as a great novelty at the time. Gaudí designed three stairwells in less visible areas which were connected to the service areas on each floor.

The first floor, which was reserved in its entirety for the Milà family, covers a surface area of 1,300 square metres, the equivalent of ten large apartments in the neighbourhood. It has 35 rooms, including living rooms, bathrooms, kitchens and servants' quarters, and is the only floor that is accessible from the lobbies by two flights of steps designed for the sole use of the Milà family. On the upper storeys, every floor is divided into three or four dwellings, all of them with their main façade, rear façade and inner courtyard.

This large amount of available space enabled Gaudí to devise an extensive decorative programme. The Catalan architect put his great creativity and the professional skills of his associates to the test in order to endow the building with countless ornamental details that involved painters, sculptors, plasterers, ceramicists, cabinetmakers, metalworkers and glassworkers. Among all these contributions from artists and artisans, the hexagonal tile with its marine motifs that Gaudí designed for the games room on the first floor is particularly memorable. It was later transformed into the paving stones on Passeig de Gràcia and has since become a symbol of Barcelona.

In contrast with this ornamental richness, the attic space is pure architecture. Gaudí designed it to house the heating and cooling systems to protect the rest of the building from the rigours of winter and summer, and the laundry, where clothes were washed and dried. The attic is an open-plan space with 270 catenary arches – the parabolic construction Gaudí introduced to the world of building – made entirely of brick.

Unadorned and evocative, this structure underpins the rooftop, an area that cannot be seen from the street and is seldom considered by architects, which Gaudí transformed into a dreamlike landscape, bursting with a variety of forms, textures and lustres.

Casa Batlló

Opening times: Every day of the year, 9am–9pm.
Prices: general, €22.50; students and senior citizens, €19.50; children aged 7 and under, free (audioguide included).

With the development of the Eixample district, the wide, central Passeig de Gràcia became the avenue of choice for wealthy Barcelona families. The industrialists who had made their fortunes during decades of feverish economic activity competed with one another to commission the top architects of the day and build the most luxurious, comfortable houses along this boulevard.

The finest example of this rivalry is the so-called "block of discord", on the western side of Passeig de Gràcia between Carrer Consell de Cent and Carrer Aragó. Stretching for just over 100 metres, it is the site of the Casa Lleó Morera, designed by Lluís Domènech i Montaner, the creator of the Palau de la Música; the Casa Mulleras, by Enric Sagnier Villavecchia, who designed the church at the top of Tibidabo; the Casa Amatller, by Josep Puig i Cadafalch, who designed the Casa de les Punxes; and the Casa Batlló, by Antoni Gaudí, which was begun in 1904.

The commission was particularly unusual for the mastermind behind the Sagrada Família, as a building with sober architectural lines that had been built 29 years earlier already stood on the site purchased by the industrialist Josep Batlló. Batlló suggested demolishing

Casa Batlló

the house, but the architect persuaded him to preserve and refurbish it, adding an extra storey and attic, and radically altering its exterior and interior.

In spite of having to adhere to a pre-existing structure, at the time Gaudí was at the height of his creative powers and imbued the building with all his artistic personality, to the extent that the Casa Batlló and Park Güell are considered to be the buildings which saw him completely dispense with the influences of historic styles – Gothic, Moorish, baroque... – and begin to apply his own artistic convictions, in all their purity, based on the shapes he observed in nature.

In his endeavours to make the building taller, Gaudí came up against the restrictions of municipal guidelines. In order to safeguard his project and comply with

Casa Batlló

Barcelona icons

the law, the architect designed a curved roof with rhomboid tiles that resemble the scales of a dragon, and created a terrace on the corner with the neighbouring Casa Amatller, so that passers-by would be able to see the continuity between the two buildings from Passeig de Gràcia.

Although Gaudí preserved the original layout and size of the windows, he clad the original walls in stone, ceramic and glass, making the façade of the Casa Batlló one of the main attractions of Passeig de Gràcia, capturing the attention of passers-by, in spite of the spectacular neighbouring buildings.

The first-floor gallery and balconies, carved in stone with curious organic shapes that look like bones, dominate the lower half of the façade, while on the upper half, small glazed ceramic shards gleam in the sunlight on a slightly undulating surface, creating a similar effect to viewing an impressionist painting.

Gaudí saved the most important structural renovations for the light well, by widening it considerably in order to allow in more light and improve ventilation, without sacrificing space for the staircase used by the other residents in the block. Moreover, in order to make the most of overhead light, the architect had the entire light well clad in highly reflective tiles and covered the small indoor terraces of the ground-floor flats in glass tiles.

Inside the building, the two most unusual spaces are the first-floor flat, designed as the owner's residence, and the attic. Both are fine examples of the naturalism that imbued Gaudí's work at the peak of his career. On the mezzanine floor, this trend is seen particularly on a decorative level, due to the cladding on the walls, whereas in the attic, Gaudí's preference for organic forms is shown in the structure of the space, as the succession of catenary arches gives visitors the impression that they are inside the thoracic cavity of a large animal.

Casa Lleó i Morera

Visits: Monday to Saturday (always with a guide). Tickets only available on line (www.casalleomorera.com).
Prices: general, €15; over 65s and under 25s, €13.50; under 12s, free.

This residential block was designed by Lluís Domènech i Montaner and built between 1902 and 1906. It is featured on the Art Nouveau European Route and is one of the iconic landmarks of Catalonia's home-grown art nouveau, *modernisme*, as well as one of the architect's key works.

With its façade surmounted by a decorative pinnacle, the building is a harmonious combination of different elements that reveal classical and medieval influences. The architect surrounded himself with artists and craftsmen who were renowned for their creative abilities. Worth special mention are the sculptures by Eusebi Arnau in the lobby of the first floor which depict a popular folk song, *La Dida de l'infant-rei* (The nurse of the child king); the sculptures by Antoni Juyol on the façade (at first-floor height four female figures show the technological breakthroughs of the age: the phonograph, electricity, the telephone and photography, respectively); Antoni Rigalt's stained-glass in the monumental window at the rear of the house; the mosaics and ceramics on the staircase and first floor by Lluís Bru, Antoni Serra and Mario Maragliano; and the work by the cabinetmaker Gaspar Homar.

The Casa Lleó Morera stands on the corner of the block known as the "manzana de la discordia", or block of discord. The local residents gave it this name in the early 20th century as it competed in style with two other *modernista* buildings on the block: the Casa Amatller, by Puig i Cadafalch, and the Casa Batlló, by Antoni Gaudí.

Casa Lleó i Morera

Fundació Antoni Tàpies

Fundació Antoni Tàpies

Opening times: Tuesday to Sunday, 10am-7pm; Monday, closed.
Prices: €7; students and senior citizens, €5.60.

In 1984, during his search for permanent premises to house a museum for his works, the Catalan painter and sculptor Antoni Tàpies visited the building that had once been home to the publishing house Montaner i Simon, in the heart of the Eixample district. Although in a state of neglect, following its closure, Tàpies realised that the building was the ideal site for his foundation.

Montaner i Simon was one of Spain's leading publishers during the late 19th and early 20th centuries. In 1882 they moved to a building in the Eixample with a basement, ground floor and three storeys that had been designed by the young architect Lluís Domènech i Montaner, the nephew of one of the owners who, years later, was to design the Palau de la Música and Hospital de Sant Pau.

The Montaner i Simon building was a pioneer in many aspects: along with Gaudí's Casa Vicens it was Barcelona's first *modernista* building, and it was the first city-centre building to have an exposed brick façade and a wrought-iron structure. The use of these materials, closely associated with the industrialisation process, reflect the use of the building for manufacturing, although Domènech i Montaner imbued it with a number of structural and ornamental features characteristic of a town house.

The façade combines classical-style decorative elements with Moorish-inspired details and is surmounted by Tàpies' sculpture *Cloud and Chair* which was made to tie in with the opening of the museum, in 1990. Made from anodised aluminium tubing and stainless-steel mesh, it enhances the height of the building that stands between two taller blocks, and highlights its new function as a museum.

The museum hosts temporary exhibitions and is also a showcase for more than 300 works by Tàpies, the standard-bearer of informalism and one of the most renowned exponents of contemporary Spanish art. In the basement – which once housed the publishing house presses – you can see the artist's private collection, with works by Goya, Zurbarán, Picasso, Miró, Georges Braque, Hans Arp, Paul Klee and Wassily Kandinsky, among others.

Barcelona icons

Gràcia

Park Güell

Opening times: 27th March to 1st May and 29th August to 29th October, 8am-8.30pm; 2nd May to 28th August, 8am-9.30pm; 30th October to 26th March, 8.30am-6.15pm.
Prices: general, €8 (€7 online); children aged 7 to 12 and over 65s, €5.60 (€4.90 online); children aged 6 and under, free.

In the years spanning the end of the 19th to the beginning of the 20th centuries, Barcelona was in the throes of a building boom. The development of the Eixample on the broad unpopulated plain multiplied the surface area of the city which spread to the boundaries of the small neighbouring towns and villages and eventually absorbed them.

Some businessmen saw the great business potential of this property boom. Among them was the industrialist Eusebi Güell, the friend and patron of Antoni Gaudí, who had discovered the concept of the garden city on his trips to England. This urban-planning movement sought to bring together the best of rural and city life in a single area.

In 1900, Güell sought Gaudí's help in designing a garden city on land in the north of Barcelona. The development was called Park Güell, and the industrialist wanted to give it a symbolic value that would hark back to Christian values and Catalan traditions as a way of combating the alienation of the new industrial society.

Gaudí took charge of the design of the communal areas of the park, from the gatehouses to the Calvary at the highest point of the park, as well as the marketplace, the monumental staircase, the plaza and network of paths. Completely enclosed by a security wall, the park originally had 60 triangular plots where each property owner could build their house according to basic building standards.

Gaudí was faced with a huge amount of building work so he chose to design prefabricated-concrete modules in different shapes and for different uses. By covering them in *trencadís* – ceramic shards – in a variety of colours and textures, the architect managed to keep building moving along at an efficient pace, without giving onlookers the impression that Park Güell was a "mass-produced" project.

The administrative offices and the caretaker's lodge stand on either side of the main gate, their dreamlike forms marking the boundary between the sombre city and a development bursting with happiness and colour.

In his application of the symbolic elements suggested by Güell, Gaudí approached the ascent from the gatehouses to the summit of the park as a path of Christian purification. The flight of steps that connects the entrance with the marketplace is the first section of this path. Here you will find the park's best-known feature: the dragon clad in colourful *trencadís* mosaic.

Park Güell

The marketplace was designed so that the residents wouldn't have to leave the estate to look for provisions, and is inspired by the temples of Ancient Greece. Its vaulted ceiling features one of the jewels of the park: the ceramic soffits depicting the sun and moon designed by the architect and artist Josep Maria Jujol, who was a follower and associate of Gaudí's.

The Doric columns in the marketplace underpin the vast plaza, a sandy esplanade designed as a meeting place for the residents. A curving cement bench encloses the entire plaza providing a place to sit as well as a balcony and viewing point over the city. The bench is more than 100 metres long and is entirely covered in *trencadís* mosaic; it was designed – like the soffits in the marketplace – by Jujol, and can be considered one of the first abstract artworks.

For Gaudí, one of the greatest challenges of the park was the design of its network of paths as it went beyond the parameters of architecture to embrace the field of town planning. The steeply sloping terrain of the hillside where the park was built made it necessary for the architect to design a series of viaducts supported by sloping columns. To give a natural appearance to the ensemble, Gaudí had these structures clad in unhewn limestone quarried on the site.

In spite of the undisputed brilliance of these structural and decorative solutions, the Park Güell development project was a failure. In 1914, with all the communal areas completed, only 60 of the plots had been sold. This led Güell to bring building work to a halt. In 1922, the city council purchased the complex and turned it into a public park, which in recent decades has become one of Barcelona's main tourist attractions, a status consolidated in 1984 when it was declared a Unesco World Heritage Site.

Casa Vicens

The interior of the building isn't open to the public.

Considered Gaudí's first major building. This summer villa was built between 1883 and 1888 and commissioned by the tile manufacturer, Manuel Vicens Montaner. The building solutions are extremely simple with straight lines predominating over the curve and Arab-inspired features such as the plaster muqarnas inside and brick muqarnas outside. Gaudí placed balconies on the corners of the façade but they weren't to the master builder's liking. After they were completed, he waited up all night outside the building expecting them to fall off.

The outstanding exterior decorative elements include the colourful ceramic cladding on the façades with motifs inspired by the flora found on the estate which became a constant feature of the architect's work. The tiles on the façade are based on the French marigold (*Tagetes patula*) which grew on the site, and the wrought-iron railings, made by a master ironsmith, depict the fan palm

Park Güell

Barcelona icons

Casa Vicens

(*Chamaerops humilis*), which was also an abundant species on the estate. The interior of the house is like a fairy tale, with multicoloured wooden beams decorated with floral motifs, sgraffiti walls depicting reeds, rose bushes and other plants that were found by the neighbouring Cassoles stream, and a smoking room with a flat ceiling of muqarnas which triggers thoughts of the Alhambra in Granada.

Sants-Montjuïc

Museu Nacional d'Art de Catalunya

Opening times: Tuesday to Saturday, 10am-6pm (October to April) and 10am-8pm (May to September); Sunday and bank holidays, 10am-3pm; Monday except public holidays, 1st January, 1st May and 25th December, closed.
Prices: general, €12 (valid for two days during 1 month from date of purchase); under 16s and over 65s, €0; free entry, every first Sunday of the month and every Saturday from 3pm.

In 1919, an American art dealer and antiquarian set out on an expedition to the Pyrenees to buy Romanesque murals with a view to selling them on to museums in the United States. He hired the services of the Stefanoni family, a dynasty of restorers who were masters of the *strappo* technique, which made it possible to detach frescoes from the wall and move them without any damage.

The photographer on the expedition alerted the Museum Trust, which supervised art exhibitions in Catalonia, and they purchased all the frescoes and commissioned the Stefanonis to remove them. The Stefanonis visited all the counties in the Pyrenees in search of the murals which had been recorded years earlier by a number of experts, including the *modernista* architect Lluís Domènech i Montaner.

The frescoes were placed under the protection of the Museum Trust until the Museu Nacional d'Art de Catalunya opened on Montjuïc in 1934, with this collection of outstanding Romanesque paintings as its key attraction. Over the decades, the MNAC has acquired holdings from other periods, from the late Middle Ages to the 20th century, and currently houses the most important collection of Catalan art across the ages.

The museum is housed in the Palau Nacional de Montjuïc, a landmark building which was the headquarters of the 1929 Barcelona International Exhibition. Designed in the historicist eclectic style that was in fashion at the time, the Palau Nacional combines classical Renaissance elements with others inspired by baroque art and styles that were strongly rooted in Catalonia, the rest of Spain and Europe. The central dome is reminiscent of the domes of Saint Peter's in Rome and Saint Paul's cathedral in London, while the towers at the sides are inspired by the Giralda in Seville.

The museum's holdings are exhibited in chronological order. The visit begins with the murals from the Pyrenees, which make up the world's most important collection of Romanesque painting, and continues with a substantial selection of Gothic, Renaissance, baroque and modern paintings and sculptures, with works by Spanish and other world-renowned artists, including Fra Angelico, Tiepolo, El Greco, Velázquez, Zurbarán, Rubens, Goya Rodin, Sorolla and Picasso, and a broad sample of 19th-century Catalan art, spanning *modernisme* to the avant-garde, with works by Marià Fortuny, Ramon Casas, Joaquim Vayreda, Isidre Nonell, Santiago Rusiñol, Antoni Gaudí, Josep Llimona, Pablo Gargallo, Salvador Dalí and Julio González.

Other works on display include the important bequest of the Catalan politician Francesc Cambó and part of the Thyssen-Bornemisza collection.

Museu Nacional d'Art de Catalunya

Fundació Joan Miró

Opening times: Tuesday to Saturday, 10am-6pm (November to March) and 10am-8pm (April to October); Thursday 10am-9pm; Sunday and public holidays 10am-2.30pm; Closed Mondays, except holidays.
Price: general, €12; students, €7; under 15s, free.

In 1968, the galleries of the Hospital de la Santa Creu hosted the first major exhibition of works by the Barcelona-born painter and sculptor, Joan Miró, one of the greatest exponents of surrealism. The success of the exhibition led Miró and the organisers to consider the possibility of creating a permanent museum devoted to his work in the city.

Miró entrusted his friend Josep Lluís Sert with the project for the building. Sert was the co-founder of the influential GATCPAC, a group of architects whose aim was to promote rationalist architecture and the work of its key representatives: the Swiss architect Le Corbusier and the Germans Walter Gropius – the founder of the Bauhaus – and Mies van der Rohe.

In order to fill the galleries of the building designed by Sert, the Fundació Joan Miró was set up in 1975, with works donated by the artist, as well as from the collections of Joan Prats – one of the prime movers behind the foundation –, Miró's wife, Pilar Juncosa, whose collection mainly comprised his early works, and other collectors.

The museum opened that same year on a site on Montjuïc provided by the city council. In accordance with his aesthetic ideas, Sert's building is an example of rationalist architecture. The exhibition space is set out around a central courtyard, a device inspired by the most ancient Mediterranean traditions, while an octagonal tower ties in with medieval Catalan architecture.

Fundació Joan Miró

Barcelona icons

All the rooms and galleries inside the museum – which was extended in 1987 and 2001 according to Sert's original criteria – are filled with natural light as the result of the inclusion of huge overhead lanterns in a quarter-cylinder shape and wide panoramic windows that afford views of the city. In order to give all the spaces inside the museum a human scale, Sert used a *modulor*, a set of measurements devised by Le Corbusier for this purpose.

The wonderful environment created by Sert provides the setting for more than 200 paintings, some 180 sculptures and 8,000 drawings by Miró, as well as other textiles and ceramics by the artist. This broad retrospective of Miró's work is completed by creations by contemporary artists of the calibre of Marcel Duchamp, Max Ernst, Julio González, Fernand Léger, Henry Moore, Antoni Tàpies and Eduardo Chillida.

Mies van der Rohe Pavilion

Opening times: Monday to Sunday, 10am to 8pm.
Price: general, €5; students, €2.60; under 16s, free; Bus Turístic and Barcelona Card, 20% discount.

Following the success of the 1888 Universal Exhibition, which brought about a large-scale transformation of the area of the city occupied by the military citadel, Barcelona soon embarked on another event that would once again bring it to worldwide attention. The instigator of the idea was the architect and politician Josep Puig i Cadafalch, the co-designer of the project along with his *modernista* colleagues, including Lluís Domènech i Montaner and Enric Sagnier i Villavecchia. On this occasion, the area under development was Montjuïc Hill, where the Palau Nacional, Magic Fountain, Olympic Stadium, Poble Espanyol, Teatre Grec and the different palaces and halls that later became the permanent headquarters of the trade fair were built.

Curiously enough, none of the buildings became the greatest architectural landmark of the 1929 Exhibition. That accolade went to the German Pavilion, a temporary structure that was demolished just a few weeks after the exhibition closed. This unique building was designed by the rationalist architect Ludwig Mies van der Rohe. Although relatively small in size and built on a site on the edge of the exhibition ground, it nonetheless became one of the most influential buildings of 20th-century architecture.

Despite its importance, the German Pavilion was dismantled in 1930 and the reusable materials sold. Fifty years later, in 1980, the Catalan architect Oriol Bohigas had the idea of rebuilding an exact replica of the pavilion on its original site. Completed in 1986, it stands to the west of the Magic Fountain, across the road from the Casaramona Factory, where its ground-breaking design continues to delight visitors and passers-by.

Built from steel, glass and four types of marble, the German Pavilion marked the beginning of the Modern Movement: a pioneering architectural trend that advocated simple forms, a lack of ornamentation and the use of steel and reinforced concrete as the main building materials. Mies van der Rohe was one of the pioneers of the movement, which came about as a reaction against art nouveau. It represented a break with classic styles and aimed to take architecture back to its original function – to create spaces for living – and to distance it from its simple aesthetic postulates.

A symbol of the democratic ethos of the Weimar Republic – the regime that came to power following the First World War – the pavilion designed by Mies van der Rohe is quite a simple structure, created from a succession of orthogonal planes. It rests on a plinth of travertine marble and has two reflecting pools

Mies van der Rohe Pavilion

and a flat roof underpinned by eight cruciform steel columns. The non-load-bearing marble walls are combined with large expanses of glass that foster interaction between the interior and exterior of the building. To complement this essential piece of architecture, Mies van der Rohe designed the Barcelona Chair, which has become a true design icon, and placed the sculpture *Morning*, by the German Georg Kolbe, in the centre of one of the pools.

CaixaForum
Casaramona Factory

Opening times: Monday to Sunday, 10am-8pm. Wednesday in July and August, 10am-11pm. Closed: 25th December and 1st and 6th January.
Price: €4.

The Catalan art-nouveau movement, *modernisme*, reached the pinnacle of its splendour while the region was experiencing a major industrial boom. It was only natural that both activities would come together in interesting industrial *modernista* architecture, of which the Casaramona Factory is one of the finest examples.

After a fire at his yarn and cloth mill on Montjuïc, the textile entrepreneur Casimir Casaramona, who was a pioneer in the introduction of electricity to industrial manufacturing, commissioned the architect Josep Puig i Cadafalch, the designer of the Casa Amatller and the Casa de les Punxes, to plan a new, more modern, safer facility.

In 1911, Puig i Cadafalch designed a major industrial complex on a square floor plan that is a harmonious combination of functionality and aesthetics. Taking inspiration from medieval castles, the complex comprises 11 buildings of different heights and surface areas, built from brick and iron. The units are rectangular, with a flat roof and Catalan vaulting underpinned by cast-iron columns. The arches rest on buttresses that protrude from the outer walls and are surmounted by pinnacles that detract from the horizontal layout of the ensemble. Two towers that were used as water tanks flank the perimeters of the complex.

In spite of the painstaking design and construction, the new factory was only operational for a short period of time. Casaramona died the same year it opened (1913) and the premises were abandoned for good in 1919. Following the Spanish Civil War, the complex was used as a police barracks. In 1963, the bank, La Caixa, purchased the building and decided to restore it and convert it into the headquarters of Caixaforum (2002), a major exhibition centre that stages temporary exhibitions of works from the extensive art collection of "La Caixa" Foundation.

CaixaForum - Casaramona Factory

Barcelona icons

Palau Sant Jordi

Palau Sant Jordi

For 150 years, the organisation of major international events has been one of the engines of urban growth in Barcelona: from the 1888 Universal Exhibition to the 1929 International Exhibition, and more recently, the 1992 Olympic Games and the 2004 Forum of Cultures.

Of these four events, the Olympics played the most decisive role in raising the profile of Barcelona around the world as a dynamic, cutting-edge city and brought about the redevelopment of the Poblenou district – where the Olympic Village was located – and Montjuïc, where most of the competitions were held. The most widely admired building on the Olympic hill is certainly the Palau Sant Jordi, the greatest architectural legacy of the great sporting event.

The multipurpose, indoor sporting arena was designed by the Japanese architect Arata Isozaki, and can host a wide variety of sporting events as well as concerts and other entertainments. The Sant Jordi can seat 17,000 and this capacity can easily be expanded to 24,000 as the result of the modular layout of the stands.

This structural flexibility is one of the main assets of the Sant Jordi, and since it opened in 1990, it has hosted clay-tennis tournaments, indoor motorcycle competitions and been a venue for the 2003 World Swimming Championships, when a 50×25 metres swimming pool was constructed inside the complex.

However, the most eye-catching feature of Isozaki's landmark is the giant roof which has a span of 128×106 metres, making it bigger that a football pitch. Made from glazed ceramic tiles and underpinned by a lightweight yet durable web of articulated steel tubing, it was built on the ground and raised into position using a powerful hydraulic system, a process that took ten days to complete. The exterior of the building is organic in shape and has become one of the iconic landmarks in the Montjuïc Olympic Ring. The centre of the roof is studded with semi-spherical skylights and the undulating shape of the skirt section around the perimeter is inspired by the Mediterranean.

Sant Martí

Agbar Tower

The French architect Jean Nouvel, the winner of the prestigious Pritzker Prize in 2008, was commissioned to design the Agbar Tower, the office building that has become the brand image of the technology district 22@: a vast industrial site covering a surface area equivalent to 200 football pitches.

In the year 2000, the area began to be transformed into a hub for businesses with large R+D departments, as well as universities, research centres, housing and green areas.

The Agbar Tower stands on a plot adjacent to the Plaça de les Glòries – one of the key areas already featured on Ildefons Cerdà's city plan – and is named after its owners, the Barcelona water company, Aigües de Barcelona. The 34-storey tower has four floors below ground level. At 144 metres high, it is the city's third tallest building. According to the designer, the unusual elliptical shape of the building is a tribute to the *modernista* architect Antoni Gaudí, who used a very similar shape for his New York hotel project which never came to fruition.

The tower comprises two oval cylinders surmounted by a glass and steel dome. The inner cylinder houses the lifts, stairs and offices, and the outer one, clad in glass and aluminium, includes one of the key features of the skyscraper: more than 4,500 LED devices that generate thought-provoking luminous images on the façade, a spectacular night-time display that is seen to its full potential on public holidays and special occasions.

Frank Gehry's *Fish*

During building work on the Olympic Village for the 1992 Games, the American Frank Gehry, one of the world's most in-demand architects, was commissioned to design a sculptural structure that was to be placed at the foot of the skyscrapers in the Olympic Marina. The designer of the prestigious Guggenheim Museum in Bilbao, Gehry is the standard bearer of deconstructivism and introduces organic forms drawn from nature into his architecture, so that many of the buildings he designs, modelled on eye-catching curves, end up resembling vast sculptures.

This is why it is only natural that the design of sculptural figures is one of his passions. Indeed, the evocative, tapering form of the fish, with its glimmering scales, had captured his imagination as an art object since childhood. It therefore comes as no surprise that fish are a main feature in Gehry's work, such as the Fishdance Restaurant in Kobe (Japan) and the goldfish in the Olympic Marina, a vast structure made from interwoven steel strips that reflect the copper and golden tones of the sun.

Agbar Tower

Fish

Barcelona icons

Museu Blau

Museu Blau MCNB

Opening times: Tuesday to Friday, 10am-6pm; Saturday, 10am-7pm; Sunday and public holidays, 10am-8pm.
Prices: €6; over 65s and under 29s, €2.70; under 16s, free.

The Museu Blau is the resplendent centre for Barcelona's natural science museum. It opened in 2011, in the Forum Building, the main site for the 2004 Forum of Cultures in Barcelona. The Museu Blau or "Blue Museum" was a project by the prestigious studio of Swiss architects, Herzog & de Meuron, who also designed the Beijing National Stadium, the Allianz Arena football stadium in Munich and the extension of the Tate Modern in London, and adapted the Forum Building for its final use for exhibitions.

With an immense floor area in the form of an equilateral triangle 180 metres on each side and 25 metres high, the Forum Building has a surface area of 9,000 square metres with vast potential as a museum. *Planeta Vida* (*Planet Life*) is the name of the permanent exhibition at the Museu Blau. It uses the best contemporary criteria to exhibit the 4,500 most representative pieces from the more than three million which were in the collections of the former city museums of geology, zoology and botany. These museums opened in the 19th century to give people the opportunity to discover the natural heritage of Catalonia, the Mediterranean and other regions of the world. The other noteworthy displays are: *La biografia de la Terra* – a journey through the history of life on Earth; *Els laboratoris de la vida* – a series of small exhibitions on specific themes related to biology; temporary exhibitions and *Niu de Ciència*, a zone created to awaken scientific curiosity in children, suitable for the under 6s.

Les Corts

Pedralbes Monastery

Opening times: April to October, Tuesday to Friday, 10am-5pm; Saturday, 10am-7pm; Sunday, 10am-8pm. November to April, Tuesday to Saturday, 10am-2pm; Sunday, 10am-5pm. Closed: Monday.
Price: general, €5; under-30s and over-65s, €3.50; under-16s, free.

Located to the west of the former village of Sarrià, the purity and consistency of the Royal Monastery of Pedralbes make it one of the finest surviving examples of the Catalan Gothic style. These virtues are the result of the speed at which it was built – the main building work took scarcely 13 months –, the few alterations it has undergone throughout its seven centuries in existence and, because, during most of its long history, it has been home to a community of nuns from the Order of Saint Clare, who have zealously guarded it and ensured its conservation.

The monastery is a showcase for many works of art and religious furniture. It was founded in 1327 by Queen Elisenda of Montcada, the fourth wife of King Jaume II of Aragon. Following the king's death, Elisenda moved into a palace adjoining the monastery. Her remains lie in a double-sided tomb located between the church and the cloister which is covered by a reclining statue of the queen. On the side viewed from the church by worshippers, the queen is carved in marble and wears a crown and her royal robes. On the side viewed from the cloister – which can only be seen by the nuns – the monastery's founder is sculpted in terracotta and wears a plain Franciscan habit.

The monastery is set out around a monumental three-tier cloister, each side 40 metres long. The first two

Pedralbes Monastery

tiers were built in the 14th century and are underpinned by pointed arches, while the third, which was added in 1412, is a simple structure of architraves, with octagonal columns and a sloping roof.

The main rooms inside the monastery – the chapter house, the abbey, the refectory and many of the nuns' cells – open onto this large cloister. One of the highlights is the chapel of Sant Miquel, which is totally covered in frescoes painted in 1346 by Ferrer Bassa in a style inspired by the brushwork of the Tuscan genius of the *Trecento*, Giotto di Bondone.

The church, which occupies an entire wing of the cloister, features the understated decoration and predominant horizontal lines of the Catalan Gothic style.

It has a single nave, with seven sections with ogival vaults and side chapels placed between the buttresses.

Outside the monastery building, opposite the square leading into it, stands the *Conventet*, or little convent, which was built in the 14th century to house the friars who provided spiritual guidance for the nuns. The building was restored in 1920 by the *modernista* and *noucentista* architect Enric Sagnier i Villavecchia, who added a tower from the ancient wall that once surrounded the monastery and decorated it with Romanesque elements from the church of Santa Maria in Besalú which had been demolished.

Pedralbes Monastery

Barcelona icons

Camp Nou
FC Barcelona

Opening times: (Museum visit and Camp Nou tour) 7th January to 27th March and 13th October to 19th December, Monday to Saturday, 10am-6.30pm; Sunday, 10am-2.30pm. 28th March to 12th October, Monday to Sunday, 9.30am-7.30pm. Closed: 25th December and 1st January.
Prices: general, €23; children aged 6 to 13, €18; under 6s, free.

FC Barcelona, one of Barcelona and Catalonia's main sources of pride, lived through a golden age in the 1940s and 50s, due, in part, to the leadership of the extraordinary Hungarian striker Ladislao Kubala, whose amazing skill was the main reason why the old stadium in Les Corts couldn't cope with the demand for seats. In 1954, building work on a new stadium began in the same district, less than a kilometre away from the old one.

It opened in 1957 and soon came to be known as the Camp Nou (New Stadium) because nobody could agree on an official name. With a 93,000-spectator capacity, it became Europe's largest all-seater stadium, a position that was reinforced following an extension in 1981 which saw its capacity increase to 120,000. It didn't lose this status, despite a subsequent reduction to the current capacity of 99,000 carried out to comply with safety standards stipulating that all spectators must have a seat.

Originally designed by the architect Francesc Mitjans, Camp Nou has hosted matches from the 1964 European Nations Cup, the 1982 World Cup (the third grandstand was built for the event), the 1992 Olympic Games and the 1989 and 1999 European Cup finals, as well as huge concerts by such famous names as Michael Jackson, Bruce Springsteen and U2.

However, Camp Nou is best known as the home ground of FC Barcelona, one of the world's most prestigious clubs which has won European titles in football, basketball, handball and ice hockey. That's why the stadium and its adjoining museum – which takes a thorough look at the history of the club and showcases all its trophies – have become Barcelona's second most visited tourist attraction, only surpassed by the Sagrada Família.

Horta-Guinardó

Recinte Modernista de Sant Pau

Opening times: Monday to Saturday, 10am-4.30pm (November to March) and 10am-6.30pm (April to October); Sunday and public holidays, 10am-2.30pm.
Prices: €10; visitors aged 16 to 29 and over 65s, €7; under 16s, free.

The Hospital de la Santa Creu was founded in 1401 in the Raval district and was the city's main hospital for

Camp Nou - F.C. Barcelona

more than 400 years. The breakthroughs made in healthcare and hygiene during the 19th century led the medical and municipal authorities to warn that the Gothic-style building was no longer suitable for treating the sick.

After several decades fraught with controversy, work on a new hospital to replace the old one in the Raval began in 1902. The project was made possible due to donations from Pau Gil i Serra, a Catalan banker living in Paris who gave half of his inheritance to ensure the project came to fruition. The people in charge of the new hospital appended the Saint's name of the patron to the hospital as a tribute to his generous donation. In just a few years time, it came to be known as the Hospital de Sant Pau.

The project was awarded to the great *modernista* architect Lluís Domènech i Montaner, who was commissioned to design the Palau de la Música a few years later. A large plot of land on the northern edge of the Eixample was purchased to house the hospital covering a surface area equivalent to nine blocks: a vast area that made it possible to build the largest civil ensemble of the *modernista* era in Catalonia, with 27 pavilions as well as the administrative buildings and other services.

However, by 1911, Gil i Serra's donation had been used up, bringing building work to a halt. The main building and nine medical pavilions had been completed. Building work recommenced three years later under the supervision of Domènech i Montaner's son Pere Domènech i Roura. He oversaw the building of four more pavilions, adhering faithfully to the *modernista* canons stipulated by his father, in spite of the fact that the aesthetic movement was considered somewhat dated. Domènech i Roura designed the last buildings in the complex in a baroque-influenced monumentalist style in the late 1920s. The notable differences in style compared with those of his predecessor can be seen in the hospital church and the convalescent home.

In his original design, Domènech i Montaner presented an integrated project that brought together architecture and town planning and took on board some of the key ideas behind the utopian theory of garden cities. Indeed, the hospital consists of a series of individual pavilions, separated by broad landscaped areas and connected by underground passageways that let in light from above. Strangely enough, the complex is set out on diagonal lines, in contrast with the grid system of the Eixample, breaking the discipline stipulated by the town planner Ildefons Cerdà, whose postulates were never to the liking of Domènech i Montaner.

Most of the buildings are made from exposed brick and feature a whole host of sculptural decorative elements in ceramic and mosaic, largely inspired by Gothic and Moorish art. The administrative block, at the northern end of the Avinguda de Gaudí, gives passers-by wonderful and unique views as a result of the diagonal arrangement and the pointed spire of the clock tower which is inspired by Nordic architecture.

The pavilions are set out in a regular pattern at a distance from one another and consist of a large open-plan room without any architectural divisions and roofs underpinned by eight pointed arches. There are additional rooms on either side of the open-plan room. Outside the building, Domènech i Montaner chose to break up the square lines of the pavilions by placing circular turrets at the corners.

Recinte Modernista de Sant Pau

Barcelona icons

Barcelona is much more

Sant Cugat Monastery

How to get there: Ferrocarrils de la Generalitat Catalunya (FGC): lines S1, S2, S5 and S55; Plaça Catalunya-Sant Cugat (journey time 25 min) + 10 min on foot.
Opening times: (cloisters) Tuesday to Saturday, 10am-1.30pm and 3pm-7pm; Sunday and public holidays, 10am-2.30pm; (church) 9.30am-12.30pm and 6pm-8pm.
Admission: free.

The monastery is Sant Cugat del Vallès's architectural jewel. It was the most important monastic ensemble in the county of Barcelona in medieval times. Today it consists of a church and cloisters which are home to the main galleries of the town museum, the Museu de Sant Cugat. You can visit them on a free guided tour on the first Sunday every month.

The chapter house and monks' cells are placed around the cloisters and the abbot's palace stands on the west side. The monastery complex was totally fortified and a substantial portion of the walls and many of the towers, which were built in the 14th and 16th centuries, survive.

The monastery dates back to the 9th century when the decision was taken to link the church, which contained the remains of Sant Cugat, to an adjacent fortification. Although a community of monks is believed to have been living there as early as the 5th century, the first documents supporting this theory date from 878 AD. Building work on the new monastery began in the middle of the 12th century. The existing church was extended and, in 1350, work was carried out to fortify the monastery. An aqueduct was built in the 14th century to improve the water supply. A section of the aqueduct, the Can Vernet bridge, survives today.

The Romanesque cloisters (12th century) are the most outstanding feature due to the structure and quality of the carvings on the capitals. A second storey was added in the 16th century and the atrium at the entrance built. The cloisters are more than 30 m long and were designed by the artist Arnau Cadell. The floor plan is almost square and has semi-circular arches underpinned by twin columns. Each column is decorated with capitals painstakingly carved with a variety of motifs, from animals to advice on good manners for the monks (for instance, how to help the brothers get rid of lice). The Gothic basilica is another key element. The building is 52 m long and 23 m wide and has three naves with vaults underpinned by columns. The rose window is 8.2 m in diameter and bears a close resemblance to the ones in Barcelona and Tarragona cathedrals. The church houses the *Altarpiece of All the Saints* (1375), by Pere Serra, which is one of the finest examples of the Catalan Gothic school.

Sant Cugat Monastery

Cardona and the Salt Mountain

How to get there: Bus; Estació del Nord - Cardona (journey time 1 h 50 min).
Opening times: Parc Cultural la Muntanya Sal (guided tours only), Sunday, 10.30am-4.30pm; Saturdays, 10.30am-1.30pm ; Tuesday to Friday, 11.30am-1.30pm. Cardona Castle, Tuesday to Friday, pre-booking essential; Saturday and Sunday, 10.30am-2.30pm and 4pm-7pm.
Admission: Parc Cultural la Muntanya Sal, general, €11; 5 to 11 year olds, €6; senior citizens, €8.50. Cardona Castle, general, €6; 7 to 16 year olds and senior citizens, €4; under 6s, free.

Inside the Salt Mountain

Cardona's splendid past stems from salt mining and the salt basin which have been its raison d'être since the 11th century. It has one of the oldest town charters in Europe which stipulates that the townsfolk have the right to extract salt forever. Cardona Castle was never defeated and was the home of the powerful dynasty of the Count-Dukes of Cardona. A medieval town sprang up due to the abundance of salt and it became a strategic crossroads governed by merchants and muleteers who built the historic centre of Cardona.

Cardona Castle enjoys privileged views of the valleys of the Cardener river. Its location was dictated by the need to defend access to the salt basin. From the 11th to the 15th centuries, it was the home of the lords of Cardona: the "wealthy lords of the salt", who were related to the main royal houses of Europe and were so influential that the Duke of Cardona was known as "the king without a crown".

The monumental ensemble of the castle has been a national landmark since 1949. Highlights include the Minyona Tower, the Courtyard of the Dukes, the ramparts, the views over the salt basin and, in particular, the collegiate church of Sant Vicenç, an example of Catalan-Lombard-style architecture. The church was consecrated between 1029 and 1040 and is one of the major jewels of Romanesque architecture in Catalonia. It has a floor plan in the form of a basilica consisting of three naves with a transept at the end which has three semi-circular apses attached to it. The central nave has a wide chancel with a crypt beneath

Cardona Castle

Barcelona icons

it. A round barrel vault covers the nave. Other highlights include the pantheons of Duke Ferran I (c. 1539) and Count Joan Ramon Folc I (1668). Outside, there are the remains of a Gothic cloisters and courtyard (14th and 15th centuries) and around them are the rooms that were part of the abbey and the counts' palace, which now house the hotel, the Parador Duques de Cardona.

The old town of Cardona was declared a Cultural Asset of National Interest, in the historic ensemble category, in 1992. Its origins date back to the first half of the 11th century, when a small borough or suburb developed around the market that was held at the foot of the castle mount. In addition to the small porticoed squares of the market and Santa Eulàlia, other noteworthy landmarks include the Romanesque church of Sant Miquel, the chapel of Santa Eulàlia and the Graells palace and gate.

The Salt Mountain is one of Cardona's main attractions. This unique geological phenomenon has been mined since Neolithic times and was documented as long ago as Roman times as "a great mountain of pure salt that grows as the salt is extracted" (Aulus Gellius, quoting Cato the Elder, 2nd century AD). The Parc Cultural de la Muntanya de la Sal opened in 2003 to bring the Salt Mountain to a wider audience and highlight its importance.

The Cardona salt basin is a depression shaped like an elongated ellipse covering an area of 110 ha that is 1,800 m long and 600 m wide. Its natural features have earned it a place in the Plan of Areas of Natural Interest of Catalonia. The salt outcrops are located inside this depression and this is why it was formerly known as *El Salí* (the saline place) and is currently known as the salt basin.

It is the perfect place to visit with all the family: a special vehicle takes you down 86m underground and there you'll visit 500m of galleries on foot to discover spectacular stalactites and stalagmites and the different salt seams: sodium, potassium and magnesium.

Vic

How to get there: Rodalies Catalunya (suburban rail - RENFE), line R3: Plaça Catalunya - Vic (journey time 1 h 25 min).

When you walk through the old town in Vic you'll be transported back to the past and history of Catalonia. The streets in the old town, with their medieval layout, are a compendium of every architectural style, from the Roman era to Catalan art nouveau, *modernisme*. There is a signposted trail featuring 32 buildings, all of them of historic, architectural and artistic interest. Highlights include the 2nd-century Roman temple; the cathedral with its mix of architectural styles, from the Romanesque crypt and belfry to the Gothic cloisters and baroque and neoclassical elements; the 14th-century city walls; a number of baroque and *modernista* buildings, and the town hall comprising the original Gothic-style building and the subsequent

Vic

baroque-era extension. The trail begins and ends in the Plaça del Mercadal, the heart of the city. It is reminiscent of the squares of the Italian Renaissance and is transformed into a sea of colour during the weekly market that has been held here every Tuesday and Thursday since medieval times. You can buy the finest local produce, from fruit and vegetables to excellent cured meats, especially the thin, cured sausage, *fuet*.

The Museu Episcopal is another must-see attraction. Founded in 1891, the current building, which was designed by the architects Federico Correa and Alfonso Milà, dates from 2002. Highlights include the collection of painting and Romanesque and Gothic sculptures which is one of the best in Europe.

Montserrat

How to get there: Ferrocarrils de la Generalitat (FGC), line R5: Plaça d'Espanya - Monistrol Montserrat (journey time 1 h 5 min) + rack railway (20 min).

Montserrat is one of the cultural, spiritual and religious symbols of Catalonia. Just half an hour away from Barcelona, the Parc Natural de Montserrat allows you to discover the quirky natural rock formations. The country's climbers are well acquainted with them. In fact, it could be said that, while Montseny is Catalonia's climbing school, Montserrat attains university level in this discipline. The great difficulties associated with the rocks on

Montserrat

Barcelona icons

the serrated ridges and the height of the needles make "the mountain of a thousand peaks", as the poet Joan Maragall described it, a mythical place for lovers of climbing, via ferratas and gorges.

Montserrat is particularly renowned as the site of the basilica of the Virgin of Montserrat, the patron saint of Catalonia, and has been home to a Benedictine community for nearly 1,000 years. The image of the virgin inside the basilica is a 12th-century Romanesque wooden carving. Its characteristic dark colour has led her to be nicknamed the "Moreneta", or black madonna.

The Benedictine monastery was founded in 1205 by Abbot Oliva. It is not only a place of retreat but has always been an important and active cultural centre in Catalonia: its library houses the oldest written text in Catalan (12th century) and extensive holdings of documents. Its museum showcases works by Caravaggio, Berruguete, Miró, Dalí, Picasso and El Greco. The basilica is also home to the oldest boys' choir in Europe: the Escolania de Montserrat.

Terrassa and *modernisme*

How to get there: Ferrocarrils de la Generalitat (FGC), line S1: Plaça Catalunya - Terrassa Rambla (42 min).

The city of Terrassa is the joint capital of the Vallès Occidental county, together with Sabadell. It awaits its visitors with open arms. Its rich cultural and artistic heritage is the perfect complement to a modern city eager to offer its services. Its attractions range from its medieval legacy, which you can admire as you walk through the gardens of the monumental ensemble of the Romanesque churches of Sant Pere, Sant Miquel and Santa Maria, to the imprint of Catalan art nouveau – *modernisme* – in the city's architecture; from the international jazz festival and the season of dance, music and theatre, to human tower displays and sports tourism

In the late 19th century, the textile sector was instrumental in the construction of unique *modernista* buildings. These included industrial facilities such as the Vapor Aymerich, Amat i Jover, which is currently home to the science and technology museum, the Museu de la Ciència i la Tècnica de Catalunya, houses, such as the Masia Freixa and the Casa Alegre de Sagrera, and public buildings, including the food market, the Mercat de la Independència, City Hall, the Escola Industrial, the Teatre Principal, the Gran Casino and the Parc de Desinfecció. *Modernisme* embodied a period of splendour which is remembered every May when the city plays host to the Fira Modernista, with markets, dances and costumes that take you back to Terrassa as it was in 1900.

Sitges

How to get there: Rodalies Catalunya (suburban rail - RENFE), line R2: Barcelona-Sants - Sitges (journey time 42 min).

Terrassa. Masia Freixa

The painter and writer Santiago Rusiñol fell in love with this fishing and farming town, its light and beaches, and set up his home and studio here in 1891. Known as Cau Ferrat, it later became a museum and refuge for many art-nouveau and avant-garde artists from all over Europe. This made the small town into a highly bohemian destination. Cau Ferrat still has paintings on display by Rusiñol himself, Casas, Picasso, Nonell and even El Greco. The house is located in the old town, on a narrow street in the Baluard hill quarter, in an area known as the "Racó de la Calma" (corner of calm).

In addition to Cau Ferrat, you can also visit a number of *modernista* mansions and museums that remind us of their late 19th-century heyday, such as the Palau Maricel and Museu Maricel.

Sitges is located 37 km south of Barcelona. With its pretty streets and beaches, it still retains all the charm that provided inspiration for these artists. The town offers a whole host of sandy beaches, beachfront cafés and nightspots.

Every year the town hosts two major festivals: the Festival Internacional de Cinema Fantàstic de Catalunya (the world's number one fantasy film festival which has established a solid reputation and become a must for film buffs and filmgoers who want to keep up with the latest trends and new technologies in cinema and audiovisual production) and Carnaval (one of the oldest, most famous and lively carnivals in Catalonia).

Sitges. Palau de Maricel

Sitges. Racó de la Calma

Barcelona icons

Gaudí crypt at the Colònia Güell

How to get there: Ferrocarrils de la Generalitat (FGC), lines S4, S8 and S33: Plaça d'Espanya - Colònia Güell (23 min).
Opening times: Monday to Friday, 10am-5pm (1st November to 30th April) and 10am-7pm (1st May to 31st October); Saturday, Sunday and public holidays, 10am-3pm.
Admission: general, €7 (with audioguide, €9); senior citizens and under 16s, €5.50 (with audioguide, €7.50).

In 1890, the industrialist Eusebi Güell moved his textile mill from Barcelona to Santa Coloma de Cervelló, 23 km outside the city. The move involved the design and creation of a new model village to house the workers and their families. He built semi-detached houses, an athenaeum, a theatre, a school, shops, gardens and a church. Antoni Gaudí was commissioned to design the church in 1898 but the official laying of the foundation stone did not take place until 1908. Work came to a standstill in 1918 when Güell died and Gaudí was only able to complete the crypt.

The church at Santa Coloma became one of Gaudí's most cherished projects and was a test bed for the technical trials he would later apply to the Sagrada Família.

Gaudí didn't just restrict himself to drawing and sketching his projects; he tried out a completely new procedure. First, he drew the ideal form of a church. He then used this initial sketch to design an extremely simple but ingenious structure. He calculated the loads that the arches and columns would bear and made a series of small canvas bags filled with lead shot which were 10,000 times lighter than the original calculated load. He hung these bags on interconnected

Gaudí crypt at the Colònia Güell

strings to create the actual shape of the arches on a scale of 1:10. In this way, Gaudí harnessed the geometrical properties of this type of curve which he transformed into the catenary arch. He took a photograph which, when placed upside down, created the correct functional shape of the arches. In other words, he built the arch with the exact shape of the pressure curve.

The crypt at the Colònia Güell shows Gaudí at the height of his artistic powers. A porch with parabolic arches marks the entrance to the church and there is another on the lower level, in the form of a grotto, a leitmotiv of Gaudí's architecture. Inside he alternated circular brick pillars with sloping columns made with basalt quarried at Castellfollit de la Roca (Garrotxa) which was rough hewn giving an impressive expressionistic effect. Gaudí said that in the Book of Exodus, God said to Moses from the burning bush: "If you make an altar of stones for me, do not build it with dressed stones, for you will defile it if you use a tool on it". This explains why the builders worked on the stone with wooden mallets.

The crypt at the Colònia Güell is a must-see landmark if you want to understand Gaudí and the history of architecture.

Restoration work on the crypt began in 2002, and in 2005 UNESCO placed it on its World Heritage List.

Catalonia, a diverse region

Catalonia and its capital, Barcelona, make up a Mediterranean destination with a millennia-old history, its own culture and language, a rich monumental heritage and natural landscapes: from the peaks of the Pyrenees, which stand over 3,000 m high, more than 250 km of ski slopes, cultural attractions, including the Romanesque churches in the Vall de Boí, which are World Heritage Sites, the *falles* in the Pyrenees, which have been inscribed on the Intangible World Heritage List, to the Ebre Delta, the largest wetland area in Catalonia. You'll also find the Costa Brava, Figueres and Girona, with the surrealist heritage of Salvador Dalí, Tarragona, with the legacy of the Roman Empire, and Lleida, with its 13th-century Romanesque cathedral and the rock art sites of the Mediterranean Basin, which have also been awarded World Heritage status.

Figueres
Roses

● **Girona**
Girona - Costa Brava
Palamós

Lleida - Alguaire
● **Lleida**

Barcelona is much more
→ p. 92

● **BARCELONA**
Barcelona - El Prat

Camp de Tarragona
Reus
Tarragona

Mediterranean sea

Airport
Port
High-speed train

Barcelona, capital of Catalonia

Calella de Palafrugell

Girona

Surreal experiences, exceptional witnesses to Greek and Roman civilisations, more than 100 km of ski slopes, enchanted lakes, medieval villages, havens for scuba divers, volcanoes among legendary beech woods, Benedictine monasteries, seaside villages and 200 km of beaches and coves that have bewitched a plethora of European avant-garde artists await you in the counties of Girona. Make sure you don't miss out!

Do you like the Mediterranean? On the Costa Brava you'll find the essence of the Mediterranean character: dreamlike beaches and coves, fishing villages, such as Calella and Cadaqués; places for scuba diving, like the Illes Medes; wetlands – the Aiguamolls de l'Empordà – with their magnificent biodiversity; wild, breathtaking coastlines such as Cap de

Creus; the archaeological ensemble of Empúries (6th century BC - 6th century AD) which was the gateway to the Iberian Peninsula for the Greek and Roman civilisations; the finest cuisine the Mediterranean diet can offer.

Do you prefer the mountains? In addition to the volcanic area of the Garrotxa with its magnificent beech wood – the Fageda d'en Jordà –, you have kilometres and kilometres of ski slopes. In addition to La Molina, Masella and Vallter 2000, you can visit Vall de Núria, a ski resort with a shrine that has been a place of worship for eight centuries. It is far away from traffic and can only be reached by the rack railway. In summer, the resorts become centres for leisure and mountain activities, including hiking, climbing, MTB trails and riding, among others.

For lovers of art and culture, Figueres and Girona are simply unmissable. In Figueres, you'll find Salvador Dalí's Theatre-Museum, a temple to surrealism. In addition to the museum, you can also visit the Gala Dalí Castle in Púbol, and the Salvador Dalí House in Portlligat, which make up the Daliesque

Dalí Theatre-Museum in Figueres

Triangle. In the city of Girona, you'll find the cathedral, which has the widest Gothic nave in the world, and be able to wander through the Call, one of the world's best-preserved medieval Jewish quarters, or across Eiffel's iron bridge that spans the river Onyar and offers delightful views of the brightly painted 19th-century houses.

Girona

Seu Vella in Lleida

Lleida

The counties in Lleida province offer a wide diversity of culture and landscapes. They are home to the largest ski area in Catalonia; excellent rivers for adventure sports such as rafting; two extraordinary UNESCO World Heritage Sites: the ensemble of Romanesque churches in the Vall de Boí and prehistoric rock paintings; a national park; Romanesque and baroque cathedrals; one of Europe's best performing arts festivals and a wide range of gastronomy. Enjoy yourself, have fun and savour them all!

If you like high-mountain landscapes, such as the Lleida Pyrenees, you'll find the biggest ski area in Catalonia in the Vall d'Aran. In the Vall de Boí, in addition to the ski resorts, you'll be able to enjoy some of the purest examples of European Romanesque architecture: nine churches that have been awarded UNESCO World Heritage status. If you prefer adventure sports, the Parc Olímpic del Segre, which was one of the sites for the 1992 Olympics, is the perfect

Barcelona, capital of Catalonia

Sant Climent de Taüll

Parc Nacional d'Aigüestortes

place for rafting, hydrospeeding, open-kayaking, etc. And at the Parc Nacional d'Aigüestortes i Estany de Sant Maurici, which has nearly 200 high-mountain lakes, you'll come into contact with the majestic Pyrenean landscape.

In the counties on the plain, in addition to the rock art sites of the Mediterranean Basin – which have also been awarded World Heritage status – you'll be able to visit towns such as Agramunt, where the nougat, known as *torró*, was first made in Spain; Tàrrega, with its Fira de Teatre al Carrer, one of Europe's most dynamic performing arts festivals; Balaguer which has the largest porticoed square (14th century) in Catalonia; and Les Borges Blanques, the county capital

where one of the finest olive oils in the world is produced: DO Garrigues. If you like star-gazing you can't afford to miss the Parc Astronòmic del Montsec-Centre d'Observació de l'Univers.

In the city of Lleida, the capital of the region, you can visit the imposing Seu Vella, the 13th-century Romanesque former cathedral on top of the walled hill, the current baroque-style cathedral, the Muslim fortress and City Hall (Palau de la Paeria) which is medieval in origin. Don't miss the city's most popular festival, the *Aplec del Cargol*, where you'll be able to sample some of the tastiest snail dishes in Catalonia.

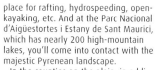

Tarragona

Adventures for the family and an adrenaline rush for thrill-seekers at the biggest theme park in the south of Europe; the city where Emperor Augustus lived for two years and made the capital of Hispania; the birthplace of *castells*, the human towers that have been awarded UNESCO Intangible Heritage status; the Cistercian trail featuring three medieval monasteries, one of them a World Heritage site; kilometres of beaches with fine golden sands that are perfect for families because of their shallow waters; and some of the world's most renowned wine-producing regions. Can you afford to miss it?

PortAventura Park is the biggest theme park in the south of Europe, with the highest roller coaster on the continent (Shambhala), a water park (Costa Caribe Aquatic Park), an area for families

(SésamoAventura), more than 30 rides and attractions and 15 performances every day. The park is on the Costa Daurada, or Golden Coast, so named because of the colour of its sands,

Roman amphitheatre in Tarragona

with its renowned coastal resorts, such as Salou.

If you prefer the peace and quiet of inland areas, you can go on the Cistercian Trail which includes the monasteries of Santa Maria de Vallbona, Santes Creus and Santa Maria de Poblet. The latter is a UNESCO World Heritage Site. You can also explore the walled town of Montblanc (14th century), where, according to legend, Saint George confronted the dragon, or visit the wineries in Montsant or Priorat which have been awarded Protected Designation of Origin status and produce some of the most highly prized wines in the world. And if you like traditional folklore, make sure you don't miss Valls, the birthplace of *castells*, the human towers that have been awarded Intangible Heritage status.

And, of course, you can't miss the city of Tarragona, with its important Roman legacy. Emperor Augustus lived here and made it the capital of Hispania Citerior. The city, which retains the walls, circus, praetorium and amphitheatre overlooking the sea, has been declared a UNESCO World Heritage Site. You'll also be able to enjoy the medieval quarter, with its Gothic cathedral, and the Serrallo, the fishermen's quarter where you'll be able to sample typical fish and seafood dishes.

PortAventura Park

Tamarit

Music, culture, traditions, shopping...

... and lots more activities you can enjoy in Barcelona and the surrounding area, including major international sporting events, entertainments and nightlife, etc.

Practical guide

Barcelona Shopping Line

The city is home to the famous **Barcelona Shopping Line**, the 5 km retail area with 35,000 shops where you'll find every item imaginable. It begins in the old town, Ciutat Vella, goes through the Plaça de Catalunya, up Passeig de Gràcia and along the Diagonal. Most of the area is pedestrianised so it's a pleasant experience to go from shop to shop without worrying about the traffic and to enjoy some of the city's most attractive and iconic landmarks. The Barcelona Shopping Line features a wide variety of shops, and includes leading brands such as Cartier, Clarks, Mango, Desigual, Diesel, Guess, Lacoste, Custo, Max Mara, Kiehl's, Montblanc and Rabat, to name just some (www. barcelona shoppingline.com).

Shopping centres
The most characterful shops are highlighted in each area in the guide. The next page features a list of the major shopping centres which have cafés and restaurants, entertainment complexes, shops selling clothes, accessories, shoes, decorative goods, jewellery, sporting goods, toys, perfumes, computers, phones, souvenirs, etc.

1. El Corte Inglés
Pl. de Catalunya, 23
Pl. de Catalunya, 14
Av. Portal de l'Àngel, 19
Av. Diagonal, 617
Av. Diagonal, 471-473
Passeig d'Andreu Nin, 51
www.elcorteingles.es
Since 1935. Spain's department store par excellence.

2. Pedralbes Centre
Av. Diagonal, 609-615
www.pedralbescentre.com

3. L'Illa Diagonal
Av. Diagonal, 545- 565
www.lilla.com

4. Bulevard Rosa
Passeig de Gràcia, 53
www.bulevardrosa.com

5. El Triangle
Plaça de Catalunya, 1-4
www.eltriangle.es

6. Maremagnum
Moll d'Espanya, 5
www.maremagnum.es

7. Arenas de Barcelona
Gran Via, 373-385
www.arenasdebarcelona.com

8. Barcelona Glòries
Av. Diagonal, 208
www.lesglories.com

9. Diagonal Mar
www.diagonalmarcentre.es

10. Heron City
Av. Río de Janeiro, 42
www.heroncitybarcelona.com

11. La Maquinista
Passeig de Potosí, 2
www.lamaquinista.com

Shopping areas
You'll find shopping areas all over the city where modern and time-honoured shops co-exist. When you visit them you'll experience friendly, professional personalised service that epitomises the Mediterranean style.

Near Barcelona
La Roca Village
Santa Agnès de Malanyanes
La Roca del Vallès
www.larocavillage.com
Shopping village where you'll find top designer labels from Spain and abroad reduced by up to 60%.

Eight shopping towns
There could be nothing more pleasant than doing some shopping in parts of the old town that are full of history, landmark buildings and charming streets. In Granollers, Igualada, Mataró, Terrassa, Sitges, Vic, Vilafranca del Penedès and Vilanova i la Geltrú you'll find the world's leading brands and time-honoured shops.

Tax-free
Travellers residing outside the EU are entitled to a refund on the VAT paid on purchases in the city (excluding hotels and restaurants). Ask the shop assistant for your tax-free cheque (if the cost of your purchase exceeds €90.16) and present it at customs along with the goods purchased when leaving the EU. You can cash your cheque in a number of ways, according to the options provided by the participating outlet: at the airport or at the EU borders. You can also cash it in advance at the Turisme de Barcelona information offices in Plaça de Catalunya and at 7, Passatge de la Concepció. For further information, visit www.barcelonashoppingline.com and www.globalblue.com, www.premiertaxfree.com, www.traveltaxfree.com

Shopping

Shop window display

Festivals and traditions

In addition to Christmas, New Year and Epiphany, Barcelona celebrates other festivals which are bursting with typical Mediterranean vitality. Winter is Carnival time, with a big parade in the city. In spring, Sant Jordi (Saint George's Day) is a unique celebration focusing on a passion for books and roses. In summer, Sant Joan (Saint John) has bonfires and fireworks as its centrepiece. The 11th September is the Diada (Catalan National Day) and after that, it's time for La Mercè, Barcelona's main festival, packed with cultural events, traditional folklore and festivities. Many neighbourhoods in the city (Gràcia, Sants, Ciutat Vella...) hold their own festivals (http://cultura popular.bcn.cat).

Popular culture

Make sure you don't miss the displays of traditional folk culture: the *sardana* (www.fed.sardanista.cat), the Catalan dance par excellence, is performed in groups with the participants forming a large circle and joining hands. The circle moves sideways as the dancers mark time. There are several styles of sardana but the music is always performed by the *cobla* band, comprising 11 musicians who play traditional wind instruments. In Barcelona, people dance the *sardana* in front of the cathedral every Sunday at 12 noon. *Diables* (www.diables.cat) are another typical manifestation of popular Catalan folklore. They take centre stage during the city's festivals and dance through the streets to the rhythm of drums alongside dragons and other figures from the city's bestiary, spewing out sparks and flames. And you mustn't forget the human towers, or *castells* (www.castellers debarcelona.cat and www.cccc.cat), which can stand up to 10 tiers high. In 2010, UNESCO awarded them Intangible Cultural Heritage status because they are so distinctive and unique.

Near Barcelona
Carnaval

Dating back 300 years, the **Vilanova i la Geltrú** carnival is one of the festivals that is richest in symbols and rituals. Two of the highlights are the sticky food fights held on the Thursday before Lent – **Dijous Gras** – where everyone ends up covered in meringue, and the procession of Les Comparses,

Castells

Diables

held on the Sunday morning, when hundreds of people take part in the famous battle of the sweets. The most irreverent processions take place in **Sitges**: during the Rua de la Disbauxa and the Rua de l'Extermini, thousands of people parade through the streets wearing outrageous fancy dress costumes, proving that the traditional can go hand in hand with the modern. **Torelló** is another town where people pull out all the stops for carnival. Its own peculiar events that set it aside from the rest, include the Guita Tita, a figure in the shape of a huge phallus that parades through the streets during the Pullassu parade, and the night of the Senyoretes i Homenots, a boisterous procession of cross-dressers.

La Patum
During Corpus Christi, the town of **Berga** hosts La Patum, a festival dating back to medieval times where fire, music, devils and traditional parades of mythical beasts play a central role. The event is so spectacular and awe-inspiring that it was named a UNESCO Masterpiece of the Oral and Intangible Heritage in 2005.

Diada de Sant Fèlix
In **Vilafranca del Penedès**, 30th August is a special day for human towers, or *castells*, another magnificent example of Intangible World Heritage. Four of the leading associations of *castellers* create thrilling towers up to ten tiers high.

La Passió
In the weeks around Easter, a number of towns, such as **Olesa de Montserrat**, **Esparreguera** and **Mataró**, stage traditional Passion plays re-enacting

the life, death and resurrection of Christ. In some cases the tradition dates back more than 500 years. All the local residents take part and the performances, featuring 300 actors, an orchestra and choir, last more than five hours.

Corpus Christi
The towns of **Sitges** and **La Garriga** are transformed into a blaze of colour during Corpus Christi. Flowers take centre stage and their heady perfume fills the air as the locals decorate the streets with traditional floral carpets.

Fira de l'Avet
In early December, the town of **Espinelves** hosts one of the most distinctive Christmas markets in Catalonia, the Fira de l'Avet, where you can buy fir trees, hand-crafted goods and typical foods.

Pessebre vivent
Around Christmas time, the town of **Corbera de Llobregat** hosts one of the oldest live Nativity scenes in Catalonia on a 700 m route beneath the spectacular rocky formations of the Penya del Corb. More than 200 actors take part in the re-enactment of the main Biblical scenes

from the birth of Christ.

La Fia-Faia
As night falls on Christmas Eve, in **Bagà** and **Sant Julià de Cerdanyola**, hundreds of people bearing torches (*faies*) come down the mountain in a spectacular procession ending at the church. The tradition dates back to the 14th century.

Sardana

Practical guide

Sport

Barcelona's passion for sport dates back to the end of the 19th century when it spearheaded the introduction of a whole host of sporting specialities to Spain. This tradition has left the city a legacy of many sporting clubs, some of them founded over one hundred years ago. It has also been chosen to host the Olympic Games and as the site of the first sports theme park, **Open Camp** (www.opencamp.com), situated in the Montjuïc Olympic Ring (p. 63).

Turisme de Barcelona's **Barcelona Sports** programme publishes a guide featuring the main international sporting events. Barcelona is in great shape. Experience our city through sport!

Football
Champions League
FC Barcelona will be taking part in top-level European competitions, as it does nearly every year. For matches, visit www.uefa.com
First Division
Two century-old clubs, FC Barcelona and RCD Espanyol, play on alternate weekends in one of the world's top football leagues. To buy tickets, hire a box or VIP seat: www.fcbarcelona.cat; www.rcdespanyol.com and visitbarcelona.com
Tournaments
During the summer break, the city hosts the **Joan Gamper Trophy** (www.fcbarcelona.cat) and the **Ciutat de Barcelona Trophy** (www.rcdespanyol.com).

Motor sports
The **Spanish Formula 1 Grand Prix** (www.circuitcat.com) is held from 8th to 10th May. June: the **Cinzano Catalan Grand Prix**, which is part of the **World Motorcycle Championship** for Moto 3, Moto 2 and MotoGP classes (www.circuitcat.com). February: the **Barcelona Indoor Trial & Enduro**, the first in this speciality. www.rpmracing.es
Practice
Circuit de Catalunya www.circuitcat.com T 93 571 97 00
The public can hire cars and motorcycles for 30-minute practice sessions all year round. See website for times and prices.

Tennis
At the end of April, the Real Club de Tenis Barcelona hosts the **Barcelona Open Banc Sabadell - Conde de Godó Trophy** (www.rctb1899.es), Spain's oldest tennis tournament. ATP World Tour 500. The club was founded in 1899.
Practice
Club de Tennis Vall Parc (www.vallparc.com; T 93 212 67 89); **Nova Icària Esports** (Av. Icària, 167; T 93 221 25 80); **Tennis Pompeia** (Foixarda, s/n, Montjuïc; T 93 325 13 48); **Club Bonasport** (Vista Bella, 11; T 93 254 15 00).

Equestrian sports
In February, the city hosts the **International Showjumping Competition** (www.csiobarcelona.com), which is part of the Samsung SuperLeague (the top eight competitions on the world showjumping calendar). It is organised by the Real Club de Polo de Barcelona, founded in 1897. www.rcpb.com
Practice
Escola Municipal d'Hípica (Av. Muntanyans, 1; T 93 426 10 66); **Hípica Sant Pau d'Ordal** (www.hipicasantpau.com; T 938 99 30 29).

Classic regatta

Golf

Practice

On Montjuïc, includes equipment hire. On Sunday, Green Fee Pitch&Putt. Times and prices: www.golfmontjuic.com

Yachting

In May the city hosts the **Trofeo Conde de Godó** sailing tournament and in July, the **Regata Puig Vela Clásica**. They are both organised by the Real Club Náutico de Barcelona which has a history dating back more than 130 years (www.rcnb.com).

Practice

Centre Municipal de Vela (Moll de Gregal, s/n; T 93 225 79 40); **Base Nàutica** (Av. Litoral, s/n; T 93 221 04 32).

Cycling

In March the city hosts the **Volta Ciclista a Catalunya** (www.voltacatalunya.cat). In June, the city centre is the setting for the bike and skating festival, the **Festa de la Bici i els Patins**, which attracts more than 15,000 participants (www.bcn.cat/festadelabici).

Practice

The section "Getting around the city" on the **visit barcelona.com** website features more than 30 options for hiring bikes or signing up for guided tours to suit all tastes.

Athletics

The half-marathon, the **Mitja Marató de Barcelona**, takes place in February. (www.edreams mitjabarcelona.com). The **Barcelona Marathon** is in March (www.maratobarcelona.com), and attracts more than 20,000 participants. And Barcelona's oldest and most prestigious race, the **Jean Bouin**, is in November. (www.jeanbouin.mundo deportivo.es).

Barcelona also plays host to some of the world's most massively attended community races. In April, the city hosts the **Cursa del Corte Inglés** (www.cursaelcorteingles.net), which set a Guinness World Record in 1994 that remains unbeaten today, with over 109,457 participants. In April, the city hosts the firefighters' race, the **Cursa Bombers** (www.cursabombers.com)

and, in September, as part of the city's main festival, the **Cursa de la Mercè** (www.bcn.cat/cursamerce).

Practice

There are also many areas for jogging (Passeig de les Aigües, Montjuïc, Park Güell, Parc de la Ciutadella, the waterfront, Parc de l'Oreneta...). The city has four athletics stadiums: **Estadi Municipal Joan Serrahima** (Camí del Polvorí, 5-7; T 93 423 80 35); **Estadi Municipal Can Dragó** (Roselló i Porcel, 7-11; T 93 276 04 80); **Complex Esportiu Municipal Mar Bella** (Av. Litoral, 86-96; T 93 221 06 76); **Estadi de la Universitat de Barcelona** (Av. Diagonal, 695-701; T 93 403 93 70).

Swimming

In addition to its magnificent beaches, the city also has a wide range of swimming pools: **Aiguajoc, Centre de Fitness** (Comte Borrell, 21-33; T 93 443 03 35); **Club Natació Atlètic Barceloneta** (Pl. Del Mar, s/n; T 93 221 00 10); **Club Natació Catalunya** (Ramiro de Maeztu, 27;

Camp Nou, FC Barcelona Stadium

Practical guide

T 93 213 43 44); **Club Natació Montjuïc** (Segura, s/n; T 93 331 82 88); **Poliesportiu Marítim - Centre Talassoteràpia** (Pg. Marítim, 33; T 93 224 04 40); **Piscines Bernat Picornell** (Av. de l'Estadi, 30-40; T 93 423 40 41); **Piscina Municipal Perill** (Perill, 16-22; T 93 459 44 30); **Dir Diagonal** (Ganduxer, 25-27; T 93 202 22 02).

Skating

In June, you can skate through the city's streets and see the halfpipe displays by world champions at the **Festa de la Bici i els Patins** (www.bcn.cat/ festadelabici).
All year round, the seafront is the ideal place to skate in safety (www. patinar-bcn.org).
For **ice-skating**: Skating (Roger de Flor, 168; T 93 245 28 00).

Near Barcelona
Golf

You'll find a superb selection of world-class golf courses less than one hour away from the centre of Barcelona. The most prestigious clubs on the coast are Sant Andreu de Llavaneres, Sant Vicenç de Montalt and Sitges, three courses that provide the perfect conditions to play 365 days a year, aided by the mild Mediterranean climate. Further inland you'll find golf clubs at Sant Esteve Sesrovires, El Brull, Terrassa, Rubí, La Roca del Vallès, Vallromanes and Sant Cugat del Vallès, with courses designed by renowned experts.

Athletics

Barcelona Provincial Council organises the **Challenge de Mitges Maratons** (www.diba.cat/ web/esports), a series of 13 half-marathons held in the counties of Barcelona. In September, in Sabadell; in October, in Sant Cugat, Roda de Ter and Igualada; in December, in Mataró, Vilanova i la Geltrú and Vilafranca del Penedès; in January, in Sitges and Terrassa; in February, in Granollers, Barcelona and Gavà-Castelldefels; and in April, in Montornès-Montmeló-Vilanova-La Roca.

Sailing

The Costa Barcelona, with its long coastline and mild Mediterranean climate, has a range of resources and services in keeping with its prime location. Its marine resorts are the true jewels in the crown because they make the sea accessible to anyone who wants to enjoy the water, not just professional and amateur sailors. The two marine resorts in the counties of Barcelona are close to the city. One is south of the Catalan capital, right on the seafront at **Vilanova i la Geltrú** (www. estacionauticavilanova. com), and the other, to the north, on Dunes beach in **Santa Susanna** (www. stasusanna-online.com/ es/esport794). There is a water sports centre in **Pineda de Mar** (www. nauticapinedademar.com). Sailing and windsurfing are the two water sports par excellence. You can learn the rudiments or hone your skills at any of these sailing centres. Kayaking, scuba diving, water-skiing and sailboarding are just some of the other thrilling activities on offer. If you prefer canoeing, the Canal Olímpic de Catalunya, in **Castelldefels**, which was built for the 1992 Barcelona Olympics, offers state-of-the-art facilities.

Club de Golf Llavaneras

Beaches

Barcelona has more than 4.5 km of Blue Flag beaches (which comply with EU standards regarding water quality, environmental management and education, safety and services), that can be used all year round because of the mild climate, although the official bathing season (when all services are provided, including disabled access, the loan of newspapers, books, sporting equipment and children's toys) is from 15th March to 12th October. There is a bathing area for nudists (www.bcn.cat/platges).

Costa Barcelona

In addition to 4.5 km of city beaches, the Costa Barcelona, which stretches for more than 100 km, also offers all kinds of beaches and coves (see p. 95).

Beaches

Nightlife and entertainment

Theatre

Barcelona is a city with a long-standing theatrical tradition, particularly where independent and avant-garde performances are concerned. Some of its companies (**La Fura dels Baus**, **Comediants** and **Tricicle**) are known throughout the world. Others, such as the **Teatre Lliure**, **La Cubana** and **Dagoll Dagom**, have earned great prestige in Europe. The city has 27 theatres (ranging from 3,000-seater venues for musicals to smaller pocket-theatre venues seating under 100), which include two major publicly funded complexes: the **Teatre Nacional de Catalunya** (Pl. de les Arts, 1; T 93 306 57 00; www.tnc cat) opened in 1996. It has three theatre spaces seating 870, 450 and 400 people respectively;

and the **Ciutat del Teatre**, located in 19th-century-style buildings constructed for the 1929 International Exhibition. It is home the **Mercat de les Flors-Centre de les Arts de Moviment** (Lleida, 59; T 93 426 18 75; www.mercatflors.cat) which opened in 1985 as a theatre and is now a dance venue. It has two theatre spaces seating 664 and 80 people; and the **Teatre Lliure Montjuïc** (Pl. de Santa Madrona, 40-46; T 93 228 97 47; www.teatrelliure.cat) which opened in 2001 and has two venues seating 800 and 200 people.

Musicals

A few years ago, the city revived the genre and now hosts musicals by international companies as well as home-grown productions which can be seen at **Barcelona Teatre Musical**, the **Tivoli**, the **Victòria** and **BARTS**.

El Paral·lel

The avenue with a theatrical flavour.

(See p. 61)

Film

In 1897, just two years after the Lumière brothers screened their films in Paris, Fructuós Gelabert shot a film with a screenplay in Barcelona, *Brawl in a Café*. In 1904, Antoni Gaudí designed the interior of a cinema on La Rambla – the Sala Mercè – which sadly no longer exists. Franco's dictatorship imposed a law whereby all foreign films had to be dubbed. However, the original versions can be seen today at the **Filmoteca de Catalunya** (Pl. Salvador Seguí, s/n); **Maldà** (Pi, 5); **Balmes** (Balmes, 422); **Méliès** (Villarroel, 102); **Renoir Flori-**

Teatre Nacional de Catalunya

Gran Teatre del Liceu

World music concert

dablanca (Floridablanca, 135); **Texas** (Bailèn, 205); **Verdi** (Verdi, 32); **Verdi Park** (Torrijos, 49); **Yelmo Icària** (Salvador Espriu, 61) and **Zumzeig** (Béjar, 53).

Music
Classical

Barcelona has three major venues. Two of them are historic landmarks known by music-lovers from around the world. They are the **Gran Teatre del Liceu**, (Rambla, 51-59; T 93 485 99 00; www.liceubarcelona.cat), which has been one of the main opera houses since the 19th century, and the **Palau de la Música Catalana** (Palau de la Música, 4-6; T 902 442 882; www.palaumusica.cat), a *modernista* masterpiece which is considered the world's most beautiful concert hall. The third, **L'Auditori** (Lepant, 150; T 93 247 93 00; www.auditori.org) is a modern building designed by the architect Rafael Moneo and the home of the Orquestra Simfònica de Barcelona i Nacional de Catalunya. The three concert venues have launched the initiative **Barcelona**

Obertura (www.barcelonaobertura.org) to bring the city's programme of classical music and opera to worldwide attention.

Jazz

The city has a thriving jazz community (local talents and musicians from other cities such as NY and London). Make sure you visit **Jamboree** (Pl. Reial, 17); **Harlem Jazz Club** (Comtessa de Sobradiel, 8; **Jazz Sí** (Requesens, 2); **Milano Cocktail Bar** (Ronda Universitat, 35).

Flamenco

Barcelona has one of the most dynamic flamenco scenes in the country and is always receptive to up-and-coming artists whether they perform classic or new-style flamenco. **Tablao Cordobés** (La Rambla, 35); **Tarantos** (Plaça Reial, 17); **El Tablao de Carmen** (Av. Francesc Ferrer i Guàrdia, 13).

Clubs

Barcelona is a cosmopolitan city with a groundbreaking, vibrant club scene. Many of its venues are known throughout Europe. They host live concerts and DJ sets. Some have restaurants and sev-

eral dance floors playing different styles of music until 4am. **Razzmatazz/ The Loft** (Pamplona, 88; www.salarazzmatazz.com); **Otto Zutz** (Lincoln, 15; www.ottozutz.es); **Sala Apolo** (Nou de la Rambla, 111-113; www.sala-apolo.com); **BARTS** (Av. Paral·lel, 62; www.barts.cat); **Pacha** (Dr. Marañón, 17; www.clubpachabcn.com); **Moog** (Arc del Teatre, 3; www.masimas.com); **Shôko Lounge Club** (P. Marítim, 36, www.shoko.biz); **Duvet** (Còrsega, 327; www.duvet.es); **Luz de Gas** (Muntaner, 246; www.luzdegas.com); **Arena Classic** (Diputació, 233; gay friendly; www.arena disco.com); **Arena Vip** (Gran Via, 593); **Bikini** (Av. Diagonal, 547; www.bikinibcn.com); **Zac Club** (Diagonal, 477; www.zac-club.com); **Elephant** (Passeig dels Til·lers, 1; www.elephantbcn.com); **Sidecar** (Pl. Reial, 7; www.sidecarfactory.com); **Dietrich** (Consell de Cent, 255; gay friendly); **Metro** (Sepúlveda, 185; www.metrodiscobcn.com; gay friendly); **Magic Club** (Passeig Picasso, 40; www.magic-club.net).

Palau de la Música Catalana

Flamenco

Club

Practical guide
Festivals

Grec
Festival de BCN
This festival, which runs throughout July, presents ground-breaking performances from the world of theatre, dance, music and circus (www.barcelona.cat/grec).

Music
Primavera Sound
In May, the best and most innovative music from the indie, folk, pop and rock scene (www.primavera sound.com).
Sónar
In early June, the world's most important Festival of Advanced Music and Multimedia Art (www.sonar.es).
Jardins del Palau Reial de Pedralbes
At the end of June, this music festival showcases some of the world's leading performers (www.festivalpedralbes.com).
BAM
In September, during Barcelona's main festival, you can enjoy free concerts by performers from Spain and around the world (www.bcn.cat/bam).
Other festivals
Festival de Guitarra de Barcelona
www.theproject.es
Festival Internacional de Jazz de Barcelona
www.theproject.es
Ciutat Flamenco
www.ciutatflamenco.com
Hipnotik Festival
www.hipnotikfestival.com
Mas i Mas Festival
www.masimas.com/festival
Festival Mil·lenni
www. festival-millenni.com
Fira Mediterània
Manresa (www.fira mediterrania.cat)
Festival Internacional de Música Popular i Tradicional
Vilanova i la Geltrú (www.vilanova.cat/fimpt)
Mercat de Música Viva
Vic (www.mmvv.cat)
Altaveu
Sant Boi de Llobregat (www.festivalaltaveu.cat)
Festival Internacional de Jazz de Terrassa
(www.jazzterrassa.org)
Mostra de Jazz
Sant Boi de Llobregat (www.santboi.cat/mostrajazz)
Festival Internacional de Música Francesc Viñas
Moià (www.joventuts musicals.cat/moia)
Festival Internacional de Música de Cantonigrós
Cantonigrós (www.fimc.es)
Festival de Música Clàssica
Castell de Santa Florentina
Canet de Mar (www.santaflorentina.com)
Blues Cerdanyola
Cerdanyola del Vallès (www.bluesdecerdanyola.com)

Film
Festival Internacional de Cinema Fantàstic de Catalunya
In early October, **Sitges** plays host to one of the world's foremost horror and science fiction festivals (www.sitgesfilm festival.com).
Other festivals
Festival In-Edit
www.in-edit.org
Filmets Festival Internacional de Curtmetratges
Badalona (www.festival filmets.cat)
Festival Internacional de Cinema de Muntanya i Aventura
Torelló (www.torello mountainfilm.cat)

Circus
Festival Circ Cric
Sant Esteve de Palautordera (www.circcric.com)
Festival Internacional de Pallasos de Cornellà
Cornellà de Llobregat (www.cornella.cat/ca/Pallassos.asp)

Primavera Sound

Trade fairs and congresses

Barcelona's geographical location, economic and cultural vibrancy and the quality of its services and infrastructures have made it the leading international congress city in the south of Europe. The Barcelona International Convention Centre is one of the main venues (auditorium: 3,155 seats) www.ccib.es Other venues include the Catalonia Congress Centre (auditorium: 2,000 seats) www.pcongresos.com and the Barcelona Congress Centre (auditorium: 1,650 seats) www.fira barcelona.com.

Fira de Barcelona is the biggest trade fair site in Spain and one of Europe's leading exhibition facilities. It holds 70 trade shows with 35,000 businesses participating, and attracting three million visitors. It hosts 15 of Europe's benchmark trade fairs. These include **Construmat** (the third most important in Europe); **Alimentaria** (ranks second in the world); **Mobile World Congress** (the biggest mobile technology fair); **EIBTM** (the global meetings and incentive exhibition); and **Denim by**

Première Vision and **080 Barcelona Fashion** (creative streetwear) www.firabarcelona.com

Gran Via trade fair site

080 Barcelona Fashion

◆◆◆ Barcelona Turisme

visitbarcelona.com

Information offices

They provide **tourist and cultural information** (maps, guides and publications about Barcelona), a **hotel booking service** (more than 300 hotels) and **sell tourism products** (Barcelona Bus Turístic, Barcelona Card, Barcelona Walking Tours, Metro Walks, Teleentradas, Tiquet 3, Catalunya Bus Turístic, city travel cards, etc.).

Plaça de Catalunya
Address: Plaça de Catalunya, 17-S. Opening times: daily 8.30am-9pm. This office also has: BCN Original gift shop and Global Blue VAT refund service.

Plaça de Sant Jaume
Address: Ciutat, 2 (Barcelona City Hall). Opening times: Monday to Friday, 8.30am-8.30pm, Saturday, 9am-7pm, Sunday and public holidays, 9am-2pm. This office also has: BCN Original gift shop.

Sants Station
Address: Plaça dels Països Catalans. Opening times: daily 8am-8.30pm. This office also has: BCN Original gift shop.

Airport Terminals 1 and 2
Address: Airport Terminals 1 and 2. Opening times: daily 8.30am-8.30pm.

Cathedral
Address: Plaça Nova, 5 (Col·legi d'Arquitectes). Opening times: Monday to Saturday, 9am-7pm, Sunday and public holidays, 9am-3pm.

Columbus Monument
Address: Plaça Portal de la Pau. Opening times: daily 8.30am-8.30pm. This office also has: BCN Original gift shop and the Wine Tourism and Wine Information Point.

Triangle
Address: Plaça de Catalunya, 1-4 (El Triangle shopping centre). Opening times: Monday to Saturday, 9am-8pm.

Glòries
Address: Plaça de les Glòries Catalanes. Opening times: daily, 10am-5pm.

Rambla-Liceu
Address: La Rambla, 51-59. Opening times: daily 9am-6.30pm.

Rambla-Amadeu Bagués
Address: La Rambla, 88. Opening times: daily 9am-9pm.

Information booths

They provide tourist and cultural information and are located in the city's main sightseeing areas.

Colom (Plaça Portal de la Pau)
Estació del Nord (Alí Bei, 80)
Plaça Catalunya Nord
Plaça Catalunya Sud
Plaça Catalunya-Bergara
Plaça Espanya
Sagrada Família
Sagrada Família 2
Sants (Plaça de Joan Peiró)
World Trade Center

Publications of interest

Barcelona Restaurants Map
Barcelona Shopping Map
Barcelona Metro Walks guide
Barcelona Official Map
You can read the BCNGuide and other publications at the visitbarcelona.com newsstand.

Tourist information
visitbarcelona.com
Tel. [34] 93 285 38 34
info@barcelonaturisme.com

Emergency phone number: 112

Barcelona is the first city in the world to be given **Biosphere World Class Destination** certification, a distinction awarded by the Institute of Responsible Tourism (ITR), an organisation closely linked to UNESCO. The award recognises the city as a sustainable tourism destination in the economic, socio-cultural and environmental spheres.